by Wendy Piersall
Founder of Woo! Jr. Kids Activities Blog Network

Foreword by Heather B. Armstrong
Founder of dooce.com

Mom Blogging For Dummies®

Published by
Wiley Publishing, Inc.
111 River Street
Hoboken, NJ 07030-5774

www.wiley.com

For general information on our other products and services, please contact our Customer Care Department within the U.S. at 877-762-2974, outside the U.S. at 317-572-3993, or fax 317-572-4002.

For technical support, please visit www.wiley.com/techsupport.

Wiley also publishes its books in a variety of electronic formats and by print-on-demand. Not all content that is available in standard print versions of this book may appear or be packaged in all book formats. If you have purchased a version of this book that did not include media that is referenced by or accompanies a standard print version, you may request this media by visiting http://booksupport.wiley.com. For more information about Wiley products, visit us www.wiley.com.

Library of Congress Control Number: 2011930316

ISBN: 978-1-118-03843-7 (pbk); 978-1-118-12824-4 (ebk); 978-1-118-12825-1 (ebk); 978-1-118-12826-8 (ebk)

Manufactured in the United States of America

10 9 8 7 6 5 4 3 2 1

WILEY

About the Author

Wendy Piersall started blogging in early 2006, thinking *quite literally* that "Maybe one or two other moms might be interested in hearing about my past experience as an entrepreneur." Little did she realize what she was getting into as her blog quickly snowballed into a now five-year long career. Thanks to blogging, Wendy has written for Entrepreneur.com, been featured on the *Today Show,* ABC News, and WGN-TV, and has traveled all over the country to speak on Web 2.0 business topics. She currently earns a living from her Woo! Jr. Kids Activities Blog Network, making more money than she ever was able to in a regular job.

Wendy's experience as a marketing professional and blogger has allowed her to view the industry from a number of very diverse perspectives. She has worked with ad agencies and corporations and understands the brand and business side of mom blogging. She has also written on a wide variety of blog topics and established over 25 blogs, allowing her to understand the needs of bloggers in many different industries. She has earned a living from blogging in many different ways, so she has direct experience with all the topics covered in this book, knowing firsthand what works and what doesn't work. *Mom Blogging For Dummies* is a book she has wanted to write since 2007, and hopes it can serve as a guide for any mom who wants to turn a blog into a career.

Dedication

This book is dedicated to my husband Dave and my three children, who always inspire me to be a better woman and mom both personally and professionally. They also put up with a lot of frozen-pizza dinners and dirty laundry while I was writing this book. Additionally, it's dedicated to my parents, who have always supported me through the really horrible *and* best times of my life. This book might never been written if it weren't for my father and his love of technology; he taught me how to crudely code games on our TRS-80 Radio Shack computer before I was 10 years old. He gets all the credit for my geeky ways.

It is also dedicated to the mom-blogging community as a whole, especially to the amazing women who absolutely deserved to be mentioned in this book and weren't. I couldn't squeeze all that talent into a *ten-thousand*-page book, let alone a 384-page book. None of us would be where we are today without the help and support we have given each other over the years. I'm so happy to be able to share all this knowledge with you, and hope we can continue to pay it forward as we welcome more women bloggers into the momosphere.

Author's Acknowledgments

This book would not have been possible if it weren't for some truly amazing people that I am proud to call colleagues and friends. Thanks so much to Ellen Gerstein, whom I met at BlogHer many years ago, and has gently (finally!) coaxed this book out of me with much patience and skill. Thanks also to Amy Fandrei, Jean Nelson, and the rest of the Wiley team for helping me to turn my thoughts and knowledge into a book that turned out better than I thought possible. And hugs to *WordPress For Dummies* writer Lisa Sabin-Wilson for helping to show this new book author the ropes in the publishing world.

There are far too many bloggers and social media professionals who have taught me so much over the years, and I wish I had the room to thank all of them. But there are a few who can take some real credit for where I am today, and those people are Darren Rowse, Liz Strauss, Rick Calvert, Kelly McCausey, Marla Tabaka, Ted Murphy, and Char Polanosky. There were a few professionals who made themselves more available than necessary to help with the research for this book, especially lawyers Evan Brown and Christopher Borders from Hinshaw & Culbertson LLP, whose combination of legal smarts and web savvy made their help indispensable.

I absolutely must give a shout out to the team at my West Chicago Starbucks, who provided me with unbelievable support and encouragement while I spent many, many hours in their café. Thank you Brandi, Nick, Josh, Whitney, and Judd, for making me feel so at home — and for the lattes that literally helped make this book possible.

Lastly, I want to thank all of the true pioneers of the mom-blogging industry, especially the BlogHer team and Heather Armstrong. These women opened doors that had never been opened before, and paved the way for so many of us to build this thriving mom-blogging community that is far larger and more influential than the sum of its parts. You ladies rock my world.

Publisher's Acknowledgments

We're proud of this book; please send us your comments at http://dummies.custhelp.com. For other comments, please contact our Customer Care Department within the U.S. at 877-762-2974, outside the U.S. at 317-572-3993, or fax 317-572-4002.

Some of the people who helped bring this book to market include the following:

Acquisitions, Editorial, and Media Development

Project Editor: Jean Nelson

Acquisitions Editor: Amy Fandrei

Senior Copy Editor: Barry Childs-Helton

Technical Editor: Melanie Nelson

Editorial Manager: Kevin Kirschner

Media Development Project Manager: Laura Moss-Hollister

Media Development Assistant Project Manager: Jenny Swisher

Media Development Associate Producers: Josh Frank, Marilyn Hummel, Douglas Kuhn, Shawn Patrick

Editorial Assistant: Amanda Graham

Sr. Editorial Assistant: Cherie Case

Cartoons: Rich Tennant (www.the5thwave.com)

Composition Services

Project Coordinator: Katherine Crocker

Layout and Graphics: Nikki Gately, Corrie Socolovitch

Proofreader: Penny L. Stuart

Indexer: Valerie Haynes Perry

Publishing and Editorial for Technology Dummies

Richard Swadley, Vice President and Executive Group Publisher

Andy Cummings, Vice President and Publisher

Mary Bednarek, Executive Acquisitions Director

Mary C. Corder, Editorial Director

Publishing for Consumer Dummies

Kathleen Nebenhaus, Vice President and Executive Publisher

Composition Services

Debbie Stailey, Director of Composition Services

Contents at a Glance

Table of Contents

Foreword

1n the early months of 2001 while I was working as a web designer in Los Angeles, I bought a domain name, signed up to pay $13 a month to a hosting provider, and published a poem about milk on the Internet. You could say that my life was dazzling.

I coded that website by hand, uploaded files to a server in Michigan, and continued to write about life as a single woman living in California, all because I wanted a way to keep a dozen or so of my friends around the country up to date on my life. I never thought that anyone other than those dozen people would read it.

That website now supports my family (a husband and two daughters) and two full-time employees. I still write about my life, but now I'm a wife, a mother, and a dog owner. I no longer detail the many live concerts I've attended or apple martinis I've drunk in a single week. My content is now determined primarily by my toddler's sleep schedule and whether or not she has bitten a dead animal.

I'm what many refer to as a *mommy blogger*. It's a bit of a mouthful, that word, and depending on who you speak to, it's also pretty loaded. Some women who do what I do reject this label altogether because they consider the term *mommy* to be belittling. I understand this complaint, but I'm quite proud to be a member of this movement, this revolution of women determining their own destinies. That sounds dramatic because, well, it is.

If you ask me what I do I will gladly tell you that I am a mommy blogger. I write about life as a mother and wife, what it's like to live in suburban middle America, how I sometimes wish I could get in the car, drive to Montana, and assume a new identity because I can't take one more episode of *Barney*.

I've also written candidly about the postpartum depression I experienced after the birth of my first child, and in doing so I discovered a community of women who had survived that kind of pain. Their support during that time saved my life. That's dramatic.

A giant group of women have started their own websites to chronicle their experiences as mothers, and yes, this often includes entire pages about our children. That practice receives a lot of criticism, and I myself have been the target of some of the most vitriolic judgment capable in a human being. Our children will surely resent us one day, and if it's not about our writing then it will be because we're still in our pajamas when their dates show up (HAVE WE NO DECENCY?!).

But I believe (and I know most of us believe) that one day our children will look at the thousands upon thousands of pages we have written to them, the love letters, the detailed descriptions of what it felt like to watch them walk into their first classroom, and they are going to be so proud that we were brave enough to do this. Because we've declared that this is important work, hard and sometimes frustrating work, and we didn't wait around for permission from someone else to say so.

We've also rebuilt our village. We've helped each other feel less alone. And many of us have turned this into a way to help support our families. Many of us make money off of our writing to help pay for food, for utilities, for the preschool that will eventually end up as a casual mention in a blog post.

I'm one of the very lucky ones who makes enough money to support my family. But I've been in this space for over a decade and have honed my voice to a very distinctive note. My husband also works as my business manager and handles the relationship we have with our ad partners. And despite what the perception may be, we rarely sit around in our pajamas feeding each other popcorn.

I work harder at this job than I have at any other in my life. The hours are long, and I don't get to go on vacation. I always pack a laptop when I travel, and I travel for several days at a time at least every other month. As a business, I have to keep up with a never-ending flow of e-mail, Twitter responses, Facebook requests, and whether or not a pitch from an advertiser works with my brand.

We mommy bloggers are constantly asking ourselves if what we're doing feels right. Is this post written well enough to publish? Should we work with a certain advertiser? How do we handle bad press? What is off limits concerning our children? And where do we go from here?

Sometimes I like to refer to myself as *The Cautionary Tale* because a lot of the mistakes one should avoid when deciding to start a blog were all made by me at some point. I alienated myself from my family. I lost my job. I angered a whole political party. But I've learned a lot and have redrawn my boundaries over and over again along the way.

This book is going to show you how to do what we do, whether you want to go big or are aiming for something a little less intense. You'll find everything from the basics, like how to get started and how to find your voice, to more complicated issues like ethics and ad networks. This book also mentions those pesky little mistakes you should avoid, like, say, DON'T WRITE ABOUT YOUR BOSS.

Jump in and get started. We can't wait for you to join our conversation.

— Heather B. Armstrong, founder of dooce.com

Introduction

Back in 2007, when I first met Ellen Gerstein (who has written many books for Wiley) at a BlogHer conference, I started to think about ideas for when I might want to write a book someday. The first idea that came to me was a *Mom Blogging For Dummies* book. Back then, I'm not sure that either I or the rest of the world would have been ready for that book to be published. People were barely getting to know what a blog was; I was still struggling to find a winning combination of content and revenue as a blogger myself. Mom bloggers had a few amazing success stories in 2007, but they were few and far between.

By the end of 2010, only three short years later, mom bloggers not only numbered in the millions, but we had become a force to be reckoned with. Every week I was seeing a colleague on the news or national television shows. Heather Armstrong of Dooce.com landed a gig with HGTV. Ree Drummond of ThePioneerWoman.com had an instant bestselling book called *The Pioneer Woman Cooks* and had sold the movie rights to her next book before it was even finished. Wiley and I agreed that the time had come to put out a book just for us mom bloggers.

This isn't just a repackaged book of regular blogging advice with a different title and cover. Moms and mom bloggers have a unique position in the blogosphere. Many mom bloggers, even now, set out just to have fun — never thinking that their blogs will become businesses. Hey, fun is fine — and it can be very challenging to turn a personal blog into a revenue-generating business. Additionally, mom bloggers are 21 percent more likely than the general blogging population to be approached by a brand. That's true *even though* only 13 percent of moms who blog write about family or parenting topics. Most mom bloggers aren't stereotypical "mommy bloggers" writing only about their kids; instead, they write about everything from home renovation to religion and politics.

This book is the handbook I wish I'd had five years ago when I started a hobby blog that accidentally turned into a blogging business. Throughout the book, I cover all the mom-specific issues I just mentioned — plus give you the soundest blogging advice I can share, based on five years' worth of big failures and even bigger successes. I cover a lot of the basics regarding blog setup, topic choices, and the written and unwritten blogging rules. But for those of you who may have a few months' or years' experience under your belt, I cover some very advanced marketing and business topics too. Things like selling your own advertising, getting media coverage, expanding your blog into a larger Web magazine, and how to use your blog to open the doors to amazing career opportunities.

About This Book

If you're very new to blogging, you may want to read this book from front to back. But you don't have to. Each chapter can also stand on its own and act as a reference guide. So feel free to jump into the book anywhere and read about whatever topic is most interesting to you. If I need to reference information in another chapter, I let you know where to find that information in another section or chapter in this book.

The *For Dummies* format makes it easy to find the information you need at any time. If I ever have to get geeky or technical on you, I make sure I explain it all in plain language so you don't have to wade through a bunch of jargon. This is good, because in real life, I use way too much jargon and I think it ticks people off sometimes.

Conventions Used in This Book

I am not the kind of person who deals with repetition or structure very well, but sometimes consistency can be a good thing. For openers, it makes stuff easier to understand. In this book, those consistent elements are *conventions*. I always use italics to identify and define new terms. Kind of the way I just did.

Whenever you have to type something, I put the stuff you need to type in **bold** type so it's easy to see.

When I type URLs (Web addresses) within a paragraph, they look like this: www.dummies.com.

What You Don't Have to Read

I use sidebars to contain helpful information, but they aren't really necessary to read to understand the chapter. I'm a big-picture kind of gal, so for those of you who also like the big picture, these sidebars may be helpful to you.

Foolish Assumptions

Because it's not very practical to include every single bit of information that was ever published on blogging in this book, I had to make a few assumptions about things you already know:

- You already know what a blog is, have read blogs, and may have even started a blog yourself.

- You know enough about blogs and blogging to know that some people make a living at it — and that running a business comes with the added responsibilities of keeping track of expenses, claiming your income on your tax returns, and handling potential legal liability (as is the case with any business).

- You're familiar with surfing the Internet and are comfortable communicating online, including using social networking sites such as Facebook and Twitter.

- You have an interest in learning at least a little bit about the technical side of Web publishing, including basic HTML and search engine optimization.

- You have a love of the written word, because blogging entails a *lot* of writing. (Technically, that could also be a love of the spoken word, in case you're more interested in videoblogging or podcasting. But you'll still have to do a lot of writing.)

How This Book Is Organized

I divided this book into parts, which I organized from beginner to more advanced topics. You can skim the table of contents or index and simply jump in wherever you want to know more about a specific topic.

By design, this book enables you to get as much (or as little) information as you need at any particular moment. You can look up quick info as you work, or sit down with a cup of joe and read chunks at a time.

That said, there are two chapters I really hope you'll read:

- **Chapter 4** talks about five specific blogging business models, and explains what it takes to succeed with each one. If you aren't sure what you really need to know and what doesn't apply to you, this chapter shows you exactly what your particular blog or idea needs if it's going to succeed.

✔ **Chapter 9** covers some pretty important industry-specific information —
and some of the legal matters you need to know about blogging. These
include the FTC guidelines and contest and sweepstakes laws.

Part I: Discovering the Fun and Advantages of Mom Blogging

This part covers the real blogging basics; I talk about the bare-essentials
information needed to get a blog up and running. I even cover a few technical
tips for getting set up on WordPress or Blogger. I also talk about the special
circumstances that many mom blogs need to take into consideration — especially family privacy issues.

Part II: Building Your Blogging Empire

Here I talk about what you need to know about when you've moved past blogging as a hobby and want to begin blogging for profit. Turning a blog into a
business requires that you approach blogging in a much different way.

This part is where I give you all the tips of the trade so you can get started
on the right foot and don't have to make a lot of course corrections later.
Specifically, I help you understand how blogs make money and get traffic,
how to promote yourself, how to measure your success, and how to really
know what your readers want from you.

Part III: Working with Advertisers and Brands

This part is the real meat of the book, and is where I get to show you the
money. Even some really successful bloggers have privately taken me aside
and asked me about some of the information in this part. Advertisers and
brands live in a very different online world from the one bloggers inhabit.
They speak an almost entirely different language. In these chapters, I show
you how to take what you know and what you've accomplished as a blogger
and translate it into brand-speak so you can really show off all you have to
offer. I also explain why advertisers are so hung up on such details as how
many readers or Facebook friends you have.

Part IV: Expanding Your Blogging Empire

In this part, I talk about the "Now What?" phase of blogging, as in, "I've had some success, *now what* do I do next to take it to the next level?" This part is where I get to show you how to use your blog to open doors to opportunities and create real, lifelong careers. Topics include how to hire writers and develop an online magazine, create a thriving Internet community, land a book deal, get a dream job, or even sell your blog someday. This part is where I get to show you how to think like a real entrepreneur and turn your blog into a business that creates reliable, long-term income for you and your family.

Part V: The Part of Tens

The Part of Tens is where I get to share with you some of the best mom blogging success stories around. I chose ten financially successful mom bloggers, each of whom makes a living in a different way. Some sell a lot of advertising, some write books, others work with Fortune 500 brands, and some are freelancers, artisans, and consultants. A couple of them have used their blogs simply as steppingstones to get where they wanted to go — and created amazing careers for themselves along the way.

I also get to share with you some of the biggest blogging blunders — some of mine, and some from fellow bloggers. These gaffes aren't just annoying — they could actually put you out of business. Don't worry; I show you what we did wrong *and* what we did right. That way, if you find yourself making these mistakes, you know what to do to get yourself out of the mess!

Icons Used in This Book

To make your experience with the book easier, I use various icons in the margins of the book to indicate particular points of interest.

These icons show where I throw in my advice based on things I've learned — usually the hard way. I try to use these Tips only when I know the information is relevant to pretty much anyone reading that section of the book.

This icon is where I throw in friendly reminders of important information you may not always think about. Usually I include them because I've forgotten them myself at some point — and later kicked myself in the butt for having forgotten.

Take these Warning icons seriously, as if I was annoyingly typing in ALL CAPS. If you see this icon, pay attention to it. A Warning lets you know about a potential pitfall, mistake, or problem. Most of these problems can be fixed or avoided, so I also provide that information in a Warning paragraph.

 This icon means my inner geek needed a chance to express herself. Sometimes my inner geek is very helpful. Sometimes she'll make your eyes glaze over. Just sayin'.

Where to Go from Here

Jump into this book wherever you want. Go ahead and read the last chapter first if you want to be a real rebel.

Seriously, this book is my five years of experience squeezed into 360 pages. But there's always more to learn. So feel free to hunt me up on the Web or in real life, because I really, really love to talk about business and blogging. I also have a Facebook page set up just for the readers of this book. That's where I can answer questions, provide specific information, or address new issues and trends affecting blogging and social media marketing. Here's where I spend the most time online:

- ✔ www.WendyPiersall.com
- ✔ www.twitter.com/eMom
- ✔ www.facebook.com/wendy.piersall
- ✔ www.facebook.com/MomBloggingForDummies

Tweet about *Mom Blogging For Dummies* using the #mbfd hashtag.

Part I
Discovering the Fun and Advantages of Mom Blogging

The 5th Wave

By Rich Tennant

"These are the parts of our life that aren't on my blog."

In this part . . .

Part I covers all the blogging basics that will help you build a strong foundation for your blogging business. I talk about what it takes to be a professional blogger from a business perspective *and* a technical perspective so you can determine whether mom blogging is right for you.

I also discuss generating writing topics that will help you kick-start your blog. And — most importantly for mom bloggers — I share some helpful insights on how to share personal information without infringing on the privacy of your family and children.

Chapter 1

Starting a Mom Blog

. . . .

In This Chapter

▶ Understanding what makes mom blogs different

▶ Exploring the range of opportunities you can develop with your blog

▶ Avoiding some of the easiest mistakes to make

▶ Getting to know some of the blog-writing basics

. . . .

*T*wo big questions I was frequently asked while I was writing this book were: "Why a book just for mom bloggers? How is that different from any other kind of blog?" These are actually fantastic questions — in fact, we purposely named the book "Mom Blogging" rather than "Mommy Blogging" because there are tens of thousands of moms who blog, but don't happen to make their family lives and motherhood a big part of the content of their blogs. Mommy blogging is a genre — whereas mom blogging is for any mom who blogs.

That being said, many moms who blog will find that they are treated like a mommy blogger even when they don't discuss mom-centric topics. I found this particularly prominent when I ran my Sparkplugging business blog network. I got pitched all the time to write about laundry detergent, diapers, or kids' snack foods — when my blog was only focused on Internet business and entrepreneurship. Brands have long known that moms are high-impact influencers, and that we control 85 percent of household spending in the United States. We are also natural online socializers and word-of-mouth marketers — 79 percent of moms are active on social networking sites, and 23 percent of these moms said they have purchased a children's product as a result of a recommendation from a social networking site or blog.

In fact, mom bloggers are more likely to be approached by a brand than if they were just everyday bloggers — 33 percent of bloggers have been approached by a brand, but 54 percent of mom bloggers have been approached by a brand. As a mom blogger who has also worked in the corporate marketing world, I can safely say that this high profile as a target of marketers has been both a blessing and a curse for everyone involved. It has empowered moms to transform their influence into rewarding careers as publishers and marketers. Plus it has given brands unprecedented access to directly engage their most important customers and get real-time feedback.

A dark side has also emerged from both bloggers and brands. Some mom bloggers have let their influence go to their heads, thinking they are suddenly entitled to royal treatment — or (worse) using their blogs as extortion tools. Brands have also taken advantage of mom bloggers who have less business experience, exploiting all that eagerness as a way to get free (or extremely cheap) advertising.

There you have two of the biggest reasons I wanted to write this book. I wanted to give you the information and tools you need in order to turn your blogs into real businesses or career opportunities. I get raving mad when I see people whom I consider a part of my own online community getting taken advantage of. But I also want the mom-blogging community and industry to grow and change with the fast-paced changes in word-of-mouth marketing. Acting entitled and using a blog as a weapon hurt both the blogger and the reputation of mom bloggers as a whole. If you're concerned about making sure you get appropriately compensated for your time and your talent, I go into this subject at length in Chapter 10, because I think we can all agree that we don't want to be taken advantage of!

What Makes Mom Blogs Different From Other Blogs

It's very difficult to make any blanket statements about moms who blog. But most of the mom bloggers I know share some commonalities. Mom bloggers are natural networkers and usually extremely helpful and supportive of each other. Mom bloggers also turn to each other for advice — as I said earlier, this is what makes mom bloggers so attractive to brands and advertisers: Brands hope that when moms give advice on their blogs, they advise readers to use the brand's products or services.

Many mom bloggers talk about their personal lives in some way, even when their blogs aren't considered personal blogs. This is another big reason I wanted to write this book. Mom bloggers — especially mommy bloggers who write about parenting — are in a position to disclose highly personal subject matter about themselves and their families. It is this personal, from the heart writing that allows readers to so deeply connect with the blogger. But there are things mom bloggers should all do in this day and age to ensure their families are kept from embarrassment or worse, harassment, threats, and personal attacks. (I cover this in more detail in Chapter 3.)

There are few, if any, bloggers who start out knowing exactly where their blog will take them, myself included. I started blogging simply because I heard blogs would help your website get found in the search engines. I had no idea that blogging was such a powerful medium, that I would go on to create two different blog networks, sell one of them, and then write a book about it all. It sounds like I'm such a big deal when I put it that way, but in reality, I still think of myself more like a newer blogger still learning the ropes. In fact, when I decided to make blogging my business, I had to get over my initial panic attack that I didn't know the first thing about how to make money from a blog. These are the lessons I'm most excited to share — my highs and lows, my biggest mistakes, and how I finally created a blogging business that worked for me as a mom, a writer, and an overly right-brained entrepreneur with full-on attention deficit disorder.

Exploring the Opportunities Blogging Can Offer

Most moms I know who have found success with their blogs started out with a story similar to my own. They didn't have any idea that their blogs would take off, and they too wondered how the heck to turn their success into an income that justified the time they spent. They also started out with somewhat similar blogs, usually sharing posts on motherhood and family. Interestingly, as they got more successful, the blogs became more and more different from each other. They have turned their personal mom musings into consulting firms, brand ambassadorships, blog networks, huge conference events, online e-commerce stores, and even book and movie deals. I see mom bloggers on the *Today Show* and in TV commercials, in national breast cancer awareness campaigns and visiting the White House.

Keep in mind that the vast majority of mom bloggers earn a living not directly from their blogs, but *because of* their blogs (I talk about this more specifically in Chapter 4). Blogs are an extremely powerful way to build a platform for your personal brand. A *platform* is a way of describing your circle of influence online and in the media. It includes how many friends you have on social networking sites, how many people follow your blog, how many times you may have been mentioned on other websites, in the news, or even on TV. Your *personal brand* is how you define and project an image of yourself, so that people come to know you and what you stand for. You can probably guess the kind of personal brand that's behind a mom blogger who goes by a nickname such as Rock and Roll Mama or A Cowboy's Wife.

Bloggers with strong platforms and strong personal brands are the most sought after personalities in the blogosphere. With these advantages, you can attract the opportunities that suit your blogging business the most. These may come in the form of sponsorship and advertising dollars, or (as I mention earlier) book deals, speaking opportunities, and even job offers. Your brand and your platform help you to do whatever you want to do.

But what if you don't know what you want to do? In Chapter 4, I show you how the five main blogging business models work — and what it takes to be successful with each. You may find a business idea that will work for you, or you may want to combine ideas to build a more customized business idea. Then, in Chapter 18, I give you ten examples of mom bloggers who have found success in ten very different ways. They serve as an inspiration to all of us as we each find our own paths to success.

Deciding If Mom Blogging Is Right for You

If you're a mom who wants to blog and earn an income, then this book is for you. Although this isn't a book about personal blogging, you'll find that many of the most successful mom bloggers started out with very personal sites that they never intended to become businesses. (*Remember:* A mom blogger is different from a mommy blogger. A mom blogger is simply a mom who blogs; a mommy blogger writes within a genre of blogs about parenting and family life.)

The mom-blogging community is made up of such a wide range of blog topics that the only thing we all have in common is motherhood. This includes women who are contemplating motherhood (but aren't there yet) or have had the experience of motherhood changed by family tragedies. I'd even say there are many dad bloggers who consider themselves a part of the mom-blogging community. So if this is you and you want to blog, then mom blogging is probably right for you. Here's a practical distinction between mommy blogging and mom blogging: How much of your motherhood and family life do you want to share on your blog? Sometimes this issue verges on irrelevant; other bloggers talk about nothing else.

Deciding where to create your personal boundaries is extremely important when you blog about other people in your family, especially children. There is no one-size-fits-all answer, but Chapter 3 talks about the issues that affect your decision on what and how much to share.

Telling your story

Blogs started out as personal online journals. While they have evolved quite a lot since the early 2000s, it's still true that the most successful blogs are almost all written from a very personal point of view. Consumers can get hard facts and news from hundreds of other sources. There is a true hunger for content written in which the reader feels connected to the writer. Personal stories and creations move blog readers.

This is even true on many business blogs. In the old-school way of thinking, it wasn't appropriate to talk about your children and marketing in the same sentence. Today, more than half of all businesses are started from home. I'd venture to say you can look for this number to soar when the new 2012 U.S. business census data is released. As business life mixes more with home life, it has become completely appropriate to share personal stories in a business setting. In fact, out of the three years I spent blogging about business, every single one of my most popular posts were ones in which I shared highly personal stories about my own entrepreneurial past.

Blogging about subjects you would normally only talk about with close friends may come naturally for some writers. For most bloggers, it takes some time to find a *blogging voice* — your personal style of writing that reflects who you really are while also creating engaging content that others love to read.

You've probably heard this before, but the easiest way to start your blog and tell your story is to write about what you are passionate about. When you come from a place of such excitement and enthusiasm, even everyday stories become engaging content that invokes sharing and discussion. (I talk a whole bunch more about finding your voice and your passion in Chapter 3.)

Connecting with other moms

A mom new to blogging recently shared with me that she perceived the mom-blog community as difficult to break into. I was admittedly surprised by her assessment, because I think of the mom-blogging community as extremely welcoming and supportive. But then I realized that I felt almost exactly the same way she did when I started in 2006.

Being a new blogger is a little like trying to make connections in a room full of people you have never met. And if you've ever been to a formal networking event, you know how intimidating this can be. But the fact of the matter is that most of the people in the room feel just as shy as you do. I put on a good game face at these events, but inside, I hate having to introduce myself and start multiple awkward conversations in the hopes I can find just one friend who can help me get through the meeting. Actually, connecting with other mom bloggers is far easier than this — at least you can do it in your jammies with a cup of coffee next to the computer!

Introducing yourself and starting conversations via blogging is as simple as writing posts on your blog, writing comments on others' blogs, and linking to the bloggers you hope to get to know better. This is exactly how all mom bloggers started, no matter how successful they are today. And frankly, these things never lose their effectiveness. As you get more established, it may become harder to stay on top of these kinds of connections. But even after 5+ years at this, I still set aside time every few days to reconnect with my online friends, find new bloggers, and link enthusiastically to as many bloggers as I can.

There are also more subtle ways to connect with other moms — just by sharing your experiences in a way that resonates with your readers. You'll find that even though you can connect directly with readers through their comments and through their own blogs, you will always have a group of readers called *lurkers*. These are people who return to your blog regularly, but never directly interact with you. You may not be able to get to know these readers, but the fact that they feel connected to you through your writing is a powerful motivator to write more and be accountable to your audience. You can find out a little more about lurkers through your blog analytics — and I talk about that in Chapter 5.

Making a difference

Bloggers have always been great at using their blogs to support their favorite causes. Fortunately, you don't have to be a huge blogger to make a difference. It can be on a personal level, as you communicate one-on-one with one of your readers, or you can use your platform of influence to raise awareness for larger organizations or campaigns you support.

When I first started blogging, the fact that readers specifically said that some of my entries had helped them in their own businesses or lives was really the *only* reward I had for my blogging efforts. It was a powerful reward indeed, and it kept me going when times and finances got tough. And even if all my blogging efforts had failed on a business level, I knew in my heart that I had been successful because of these conversations.

Yet some of the most poignant and powerful ways bloggers have made a difference is by turning their own personal tragedies into the ability to help others through difficult times. Mom blogger Heather Spohr lost her daughter Maddie suddenly to a respiratory infection when she was less than two years old. Maddie had been born premature, and spent the first 68 days of her life in the NICU (neonatal intensive care unit). After Maddie passed away, Heather created Friends of Maddie (http://friendsofmaddie.org), a not-for-profit organization that helps parents when their babies also get admitted to the NICU. She's also funneled her grief into action, using her blogging and social media savvy to raise over $100,000 for the March of Dimes foundation. You can see the good that Heather is doing with her blogging experience on Friends of Maddie in Figure 1-1.

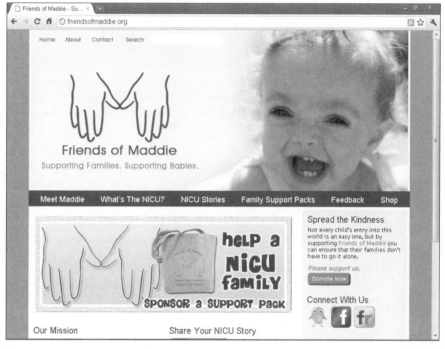

Figure 1-1:
Heather
Spohr
founded
Friends of
Maddie
after the
sudden
loss of her
toddler
daughter.

As your blog and your influence grow, you can also lend your voice to existing organizations for public awareness campaigns. Audrey McLelland, Sharon Couto, and Jane Couto from MomGenerations write a fashion blog aimed at moms, aunts, and grandmothers. Because of their success, The Estee Lauder Companies approached them in the summer of 2010 to request that they take part in the company's ongoing Breast Cancer Awareness Campaign. The three had no hesitation in throwing their support behind fighting a disease that had taken their cousin, Cathy Holden, many years ago. While this meant posing in a very revealing photo shoot, they consider it one of their biggest accomplishments as bloggers and businesswomen.

Building a blogging business

When I first started blogging, everyone talked about how important the people were who were on the A-List. I saw their success, wanted to be successful too, and I vigorously pursued making a name for myself and getting good publicity. When I started my first blog network, I consciously said to myself, "If I could get national TV coverage like the *Today Show,* my site would take off and get all the traffic it needs to be successful." And indeed, two years later, I was on the *Today Show,* talking about my website. My URL went out to the world and the traffic came in. But within 72 hours, I was right back where I had started. No lasting wave of traffic, my site did not become a household name, and I realized how naïve I sounded when I first thought that publicity was the key to my success. Even celebrities get forgotten the instant they turn off the publicity machine.

Building an influential blog is quite different from building a successful business. In fact, several moms who created incredibly well-known — and well-loved — blogs later decided to take them down because their mom blogs were interfering with their business goals. That's why I dedicate Chapter 4 to finding a business model and making it work for your particular blog.

I know it seems like a worthy goal to become a well-known mom blogger. But please don't make the same mistake I did and confuse being well-known with being able to make a living from blogging. In fact, hundreds of well-known mom bloggers don't earn as much as you may think. Your business model *always* needs to come before self-promotion.

Developing an Influential Online Presence

Influence is the ability to compel others to think or act in a new way. For a professional blogger, being influential is very important. But there are different ways that a blogger can be an influencer, and these ways range from very general to very specific:

- Conversation starter
- Instigator
- Inspirer
- Educator
- Leader
- Marketer
- Community builder
- Entertainer
- Informer

Also, you don't need to be an influential *personality* in order to be an influencer. As is the case with my own blog network, Woo! Jr., many of our readers don't know who wrote a particular post; they just know the content is engaging, useful, and relevant to their needs. For other kinds of blogs, it is simply the voice of the writer that is influential. In Chapter 4, as I talk about blogging business models, it will become clearer as to what kind of influence will be most important for you to build. But for all kinds of bloggers, as your influence grows, so will the number of opportunities that come to you.

The best way to increase your influence is to write what you love writing about, not work on increasing your influence. There really isn't some magical way to get people to listen to you. Instead, you want to focus on adding value and being a resource to your readers. Just as it is in life, the more you give, the more you receive. I show you some really effective ways to do this in Chapters 6 and 7. For the rest of this chapter, I talk about some of the basics of blogging that apply to almost everyone.

Creating authenticity and integrity

The reason I wanted to cover authenticity and integrity in the very first chapter is because they are the most important part of blogging. This is true whether you're blogging for personal or professional reasons. Every single successful blog has been written by writers who have been true to themselves and to their readers. Readers don't stay attracted to blogs that don't ring true and writers who aren't genuine.

Writing authentically doesn't mean writing perfectly. In fact, every successful blog also has at least a few early blog posts that the bloggers are downright embarrassed to admit they wrote. Authenticity simply means being honest about your intentions and the information you are putting forward. But it also means writing from the heart — whatever that means to you. I'm not suggesting you need to be mushy-gushy, only that when you write and represent who you *really* are, readers know it. And they love it.

In addition to this, the Federal Trade Commission (FTC) has put forth guidelines for bloggers that aim to ensure that any opinions expressed that have been compensated by an advertiser must be disclosed in certain ways. The Word of Mouth Marketing Association (WOMMA) has similar guidelines for all marketers and writers involved in all forms of social media. These guidelines are critically important to maintain the integrity of the blogosphere and all our long-term interests as bloggers. (I cover these guidelines in detail in Chapter 9.)

Earning the trust of your readers is vital, no matter what business you create with your blog. Readers who trust you are likelier to buy from you, recommend you, or come back to your site. Some ways to earn that trust are obvious — for example, telling the truth and being transparent in your words and actions. More ways you can earn the trust of your readers sound a lot like a mom's good advice, because they are (and they work):

- **Admit your faults and mistakes.** It takes courage to be vulnerable to others and it shows that you are human.

- **Put your readers first.** Always make sure that your readers' best interests are served.

✔ **Be inspiring.** Knowing you have had your own struggles makes you more real to your readers. Passing along that feeling of "I can do it" is irresistible!

✔ **Stick to your word.** Make sure that you do everything you say you will do, even in the smallest measure.

✔ **Be consistent.** People want to know what they can expect from you. When you are inconsistent, it can lead readers to wonder what else they don't know about you.

✔ **Give more than you expect to receive.** Blogging is not the best platform for a hard-sell approach, because of the social nature of the business. Your fellow bloggers will respond to you best when you make adding value a priority.

Building a community

Amusingly, just a few years ago, some people and companies thought that social media was just a fad and would soon be gone. If you told that to the more than 500 million Facebook users, I'm quite sure they would disagree. Forrester estimates that by 2014, 3.1 billion dollars will be spent annually on social media marketing campaigns (see `http://soshable.com/wheres-the-money-being-spent-in-social-media`). The power of the Internet to connect people and form communities is not going away.

In fact, 79 percent of moms with kids under 18 are active in social media, and 57 percent of Facebook users are women (see `http://articles.sfgate.com/2010-12-19/business/25209016_1_social-media-facebook-page-twitter`). Studies have proved that women lead the pack when it comes to participating in online communities — it is very natural for women to want to connect with other women.

Many of the most successful mom bloggers have created a sense of community with their readers. Your community starts with the very first interactions you have with your readers. As your readers interact with each other, your community grows. They will let you know when what you write resonates with them, and may not respond at all when you produce content they aren't interested in. They are absolutely a part of your blog and how it develops over time. In fact, it was because of the community I built around my first blog that I renamed the site — from eMoms at Home to Sparkplugging. My community members included many dads, and they'd specifically told me they thought the old name was off-putting. (Even the moms agreed, much to my surprise.)

Blogs are natural community builders, but here are some more ways you can foster the establishment of a thriving community around your blog:

✔ **Encourage your readers to talk to each other.** You need not be the only source of information on your blog — your readers will love asking each other for advice, inspiration, and information that you might not be able to provide.

✔ **Make your readers famous.** This is some of the best advice that Darren Rowse of ProBlogger has ever given. Link to your readers, invite them to guest post and showcase their talents. You'll be creating connections for others and increasing your own reader loyalty at the same time.

✔ **Be active in social media.** Create a Facebook page so your readers can connect with each other in their own social circles. Interacting with your readers on Facebook and Twitter is important because you want to go to where the conversations are already happening.

✔ **Host regular linking events.** You can do this by posting weekly links to readers' submissions, or you can use a linking tool like Linky Tools (`http://linkytools.com`), which allows readers to create links themselves. This gets people coming back on a regular basis to get their content noticed and to meet new people.

✔ **Respond to reader comments.** While this is an extremely effective way to get to know your readers, it can also quickly become time-consuming. At some point, it can also become downright impossible. But to the extent that you can respond to comments, it will always be highly appreciated by those who take the time to comment on your blog posts.

Writing content readers love

If you are just starting out with a new blog, you might have no idea what kind of content readers will love. You may write about things that you think people will want to read, but the most important thing in blogging is to write about what you are passionate about. This is true even if you think that nobody will read your blog. When you write about what you absolutely love, your excitement and enthusiasm for the subject are absolutely contagious.

I'm a true believer that each of us has a purpose in life, and our interests and passions always lead us to that purpose. I've also learned to trust my instincts. These are the two principles that guide most bloggers when they're first starting out. If you follow them, then as your blog starts to grow, you'll have more tools you can use to find out what readers love the most.

I encourage you to set up analytics software on your blog from Day 1. (I show you how to do that in Chapter 5.) Your blog analytics will tell you exactly how many people come to your site, how they found your blog, and which posts are the most popular. Surprisingly, even when passion and instincts are at work, sometimes the blog post you're sure will be a big hit is a flop. Other times, a post that you think will go nowhere becomes your most popular post ever. Only your analytics software can tell you these things — and the longer you have this set up, the more information you'll have that you can use to your advantage.

Chapter 2

Choosing a Blogging Platform

In This Chapter

▶ Understanding the differences between Blogger and WordPress

▶ Comparing Blogger and WordPress users' opinions on their blogging platform choices

▶ Setting up and customizing a basic WordPress blog

▶ Setting up and customizing a basic Blogger blog

*I*n this chapter, I show you how to set up a new blog with both WordPress and Blogger and give you the basic instructions on how to get started. (For practical purposes, I am only going to focus on WordPress and Blogger in this chapter, because they both squash the competition in so many ways that I really don't recommend using anything else.) I also cover what is great about each platform, plus the drawbacks to using them. Because the heart of this book is in the *business* side of mom blogging, I'm simply not able to give you everything you need to know about the *technical* side of blogging on WordPress or Blogger. For that information, I highly recommend Lisa Sabin-Wilson's phenomenal *WordPress For Dummies,* 3rd Edition, or Susan Gunelius's *Google Blogger For Dummies.*

No matter which platform you choose, you need to purchase a domain name for your blog. I cover tips on choosing a blog name in Chapter 6, and domain name buying tips in Chapter 15. You can use a service like GoDaddy.com (www.godaddy.com) to buy your domain name.

Understanding the Pros and Cons of WordPress

Let me first explain some WordPress basics. Confusingly, there are two different kinds of WordPress blogs:

> ✔ **WordPress.com blogs** are 100 percent free and hosted by the team behind WordPress, Automattic. You're not allowed to use WordPress.com blogs for anything that earns revenue like ads or sponsored content, so this is clearly not a platform for the readers of this book.

Bloggers debate WordPress versus Blogger

As I was writing this chapter, I decided to reach out to my Facebook friends to ask for examples of people who either loved or hated WordPress or Blogger. Honestly, I've never seen a more heated debate, even when I've dared to talk about politics in the past! Turns out bloggers are pretty darn opinionated about their blogging platform choice.

I decided to highlight the two most extreme opposing views, because both of these people articulated quite clearly why they chose their blogging platforms and why they are happy with their decisions. I'll let these two professionals go head to head; you can decide for yourself which side to choose.

WordPress Champion Jesse Petersen, WordPress developer from Petersen Media Group (www.petersenmediagroup.com):

"I personally click off of Blogger sites within 3 seconds because so many of them look unprofessional. If they don't realize the value of owning a domain name and looking professional, why should I gamble that they are worth spending more than 3 seconds of my time? While you can make money and have good content on Blogger, why risk a large segment of professionals taking a look at your site and judging you as irrelevant? Should you decide to move to WordPress later, moving a well-established site off of Blogger onto a self-hosted WordPress installation can be prohibitively expensive, depending how the Blogger site was set up. You can expect to pay between $700 and $2,200 for moving a busy Blogger blog onto WordPress."

Blogger Champion Lisa Douglas, freelance writer, consultant, and blogging at Crazy Adventures in Parenting (www.crazy adventuresinparenting.com) since 2007:

"I fail to understand why a blogging platform should warrant a blogger being taken more seriously. To me, good writing is good writing regardless of platform. Seeing WordPress at the bottom of a blog in the credits does not sway me to consider that person more professional than anyone else. Not everyone wants to worry about servers, hosting, PHP coding, plugins gone awry, servers shutting down, upgrades screwing with their sites, and getting hacked. I know everyone seems to tout WordPress, but honestly, I see it as a giant headache. I'm a writer — one who wants an uncomplicated way to do so. Blogger is a timesaver for me — I have several writing projects, deadlines, and a busy schedule with six kids. WordPress would be added insanity I do not need."

✔ **WordPress.*org* blogs** are still free but are *self-hosted,* meaning you have to supply your own Web hosting through a hosting company. It's WordPress.org blogs that I refer to here and everywhere else in this book.

When your blog is set up on your own hosting account, you have 100 percent control over what you do with your blog. That means as long as you have a good developer, you could feasibly turn a simple blog into a complex content-management system. Yes, 100 percent control *also* means that when something goes wrong, it's up to you to fix it. Luckily, WordPress is pretty hard to break, and it's so widely used that a quick Internet search will usually turn up a solution. And some hosting companies do have tech support that can help with WordPress setup problems.

I mentioned that WordPress is very widely used. This is important to take into consideration; it means that if you need a WordPress programmer, designer, or any other professional help, these people are extremely easy to find. This is not the case with blogging platforms like TypePad, Movable Type, or SquareSpace. WordPress also has a huge developer community that offers tens of thousands of mostly free plugins that will add features to your blog with just a few mouse clicks. (*Plugins* are mini programs that add features and functions to your WordPress blog.) Plugins can help you manage images, add community-building functions, integrate Twitter and Facebook elements, track and analyze your blog readers, or add tons of other features that will make blogging easier and more efficient. Most importantly, WordPress has thousands of professionally designed templates that are free to use. Premium themes are also available for a very affordable price, and these themes are built to include both beautiful designs and high-level features that make them very worth the price you pay. I talk more about free and premium WordPress themes in Chapter 6.

To wrap up my WordPress pitch to you, I'm hoping to impress upon you that once you start blogging, you can never really know where it will take you. I hope you'll have a direction and goals, but sometimes great opportunities arise that you simply can't predict. Most professional bloggers don't start out intending to be professional bloggers — they do it for fun, and then realize they can actually make a business out of it. Kind of like me. So you can never know the kinds of advanced things you may want to do with your blog in the future. You may find, at some point, you want to expand to become a blog network. Trust me; you don't want to do this on Blogger, unless you want to duplicate all your development and maintenance work *and costs* on multiple blogs — instead of doing all that just once, in one place, the way you can with WordPress. You can actually convert your WordPress blog into a multi-user blogging platform in literally just a few minutes. (By the way, I talk more about blog networks in Chapter 15.) Another thing you may want to do some-day is add the capability to create a reader forum, especially if you're great at building community among your readers. WordPress has a companion pro-gram called BuddyPress, which was built exactly for this purpose. As you can tell, WordPress is built to grow with you as your blogging business grows. This may not seem important to you now — but you can certainly hope it will be important to you someday!

Understanding the Pros and Cons of Blogger

If you're reading this section, you might not be convinced that you will need the extra functionality of WordPress someday. Well, you might be right. If you're wrong, it's a great problem to have, so you won't be that bad off.

There really are a few times when having a Blogger blog might be appropriate for you, but I'll say that with a big *only if.* I recommend using Blogger *only if* you use your own domain name, and not the default www.*name*.blogspot.com URL. This is important for several reasons including establishing your brand, perceived professionalism, and the ability to move your blog off of Blogger someday without losing your established readers and search engine rankings in the future. I know I sound preachy on this point, but the importance of getting the message across is worth getting all teacherish on you in this paragraph. But I promise that's the first and last time I do that in this book.

So what is great about Blogger? Oh, it's just so darn easy to use. I'll go so far as to say that it's *beautifully* easy to use. If you're extremely intimidated by technology, Blogger may be right for you. As a professional Web publisher, you'll still have to learn some basic HTML and understand the technology that makes websites work, so you aren't completely off the hook. But Google has created a very simple drag-and-drop interface with Blogger that takes care of almost all the technical stuff needed to publish a blog.

Another great thing about Blogger is that it's 100 percent free and hosted on Google's servers, so you don't have to pay for hosting (which runs about $100 USD a year for a basic blog). As can be expected, Google's servers are powerful enough to handle all the traffic you could possibly attract. If your blog gets featured in the news, on Yahoo!, or gets popular on social bookmarking sites like Digg or StumbleUpon, you could get a *lot* of visitors all at once. Your blog won't break a sweat on Blogger, but if you're self-hosted, it may get swamped, go down, and be unreachable under the temporary heavy load. Again, this is a good problem to have, but it would be unfortunate to get in front of tens of thousands of potential new readers only to have them be unable to get onto your site. WordPress users solve this problem on self-hosted blogs by paying for a dedicated server, which is quite expensive. For Blogger users, everything is still free.

Just because something is free, that doesn't always make it the best option. Most of the time, an investment in your business pays for itself by increasing sales or profits. If you're serious about creating a long-term business with your blog, it's usually wiser to pay for the *right* tools rather than just use the free ones.

Now that that's out of the way, here are a few circumstances when using Blogger won't greatly impact your business:

✔ **When you're using your blog to send traffic to your own products for sale on another site, such as eBay or Etsy.**

The bulk of the technology needed to run your business in this situation is covered by the online marketplace you're using, not your blog. When you're using your blog exclusively as a marketing tool for driving online traffic, then you may never need the added functionality of WordPress. I talk more about selling your own products in Chapter 8.

✔ **When your sole purpose for blogging is to find opportunities that don't require you to continue blogging in the future.**

An example of this would be when you're blogging to position yourself as an expert and get hired by another company. If you're blogging just to gain the experience of understanding how it works as a marketing medium, then there really is no need to go through the longer WordPress setup process. (In Chapter 15, I talk about a few moms who have landed dream jobs because of their blogs.)

✔ **When you're quite sure that you won't want or need a more feature-rich blogging platform in the future.** I hesitate to say *quite sure,* but you know your blogging goals better than I do. Maybe you know exactly what you want to do, and no other outcome will suffice. If that's the case, then go for it!

Since Google hosts Blogger blogs, you must abide by Google rules and terms, especially when it comes to content that could be construed as spam or written to manipulate search engine rankings. Blogger will delete blogs that it believes violate its terms of service. While it's very unlikely this would happen to you, it's important to consider, especially because Google is a company that doesn't offer extensive support for its products.

Setting Up a New WordPress Blog

In an ideal world, I'd be able to walk you through how to set up a hosting account and a new WordPress blog in this section. In reality, every hosting company is a little different, and there are thousands of hosting companies to choose from. The WordPress team has a list of hosting companies that make WordPress easily available to their customers at `http://wordpress.org/hosting`. They frequently feature Bluehost as one of the top recommendations, and I used Bluehost for my first couple of years of blogging, too. I've always recommended them because their team is very knowledgeable and helpful with WordPress setup support, and they offer so-called 1-Click Auto WordPress installation, which is well documented on their site.

When your WordPress blog is set up, you will get an e-mail with your login URL, which is usually `www.YourDomainName.com/wp-admin`. When you log in to your blog for the first time, you see the WordPress Dashboard, shown in Figure 2-1.

From here, you should enter your blog's name and tag line right away before you start blogging:

1. **From your WordPress Dashboard, click the General link under the Settings menu.**

2. **In the Site Title text field, enter your blog's name.**

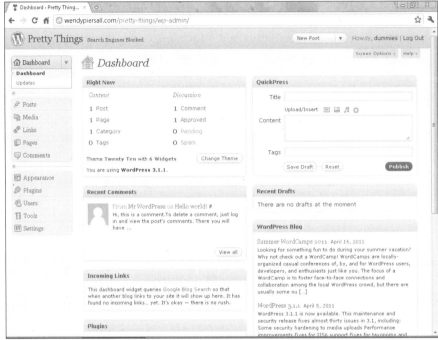

Figure 2-1:
Looking
at the
WordPress
blogging
platform
Dashboard.

3. **In the Tagline text field, enter your blog tag line.**

The tag line is also your blog description. I show you how to write one in Chapter 6.

You also need to know how to install a theme and a WordPress plugin. Be thankful at this point that WordPress has improved so much over the years, because this used to be a hassle for new users. No more! It's now a simple point and click process that I show you how to do in the following sections.

Installing a WordPress plugin

It's easy to feel like a kid in a candy store when you see all the plugins available to WordPress users. Plugins can add so many features to your blog that it may be hard to figure out which ones to use. Mostly, you won't know what you need until you need it. But I want to highlight a few of my favorite WordPress plugins that I think everyone will find useful:

✔ **Google Analyticator:** This plugin makes it easy to install Google Analytics scripts so that you can track your visitors to know how they find your site and what they read the most. I talk more about how to use Google Analytics in Chapter 5.

✔ **Fast Secure Contact Form or cForms:** WordPress doesn't come with a built-in contact form, so you can choose any of several plugins to add one. The Fast Secure Contact Form plugin is quick and easy. cForms is much more robust and for experienced users, but I mention it because it's one of the absolute best plugins available. It's very important to have a contact form on your blog so that your readers and potential advertisers can get in touch with you!

✔ **Google XML Sitemaps:** This plugin creates a sitemap of your blog and automatically sends it to all the major search engines. A *sitemap* is like a directory of all the posts and pages on your blog, which helps the search engines find your content faster and easier.

✔ **TinyMCE Advanced:** WordPress already has a lot of editing features already built into its text editor. But TinyMCE Advanced gives you some features that make it more like a word processor, such as adding tables and a find/replace function. If you do a lot of writing, these tools make your job ten times easier.

✔ **WP Super Cache:** Because WordPress works by pulling information from a database, the more features and content you add, the slower it may run. This can get frustrating for readers, and if your site is too slow, it may even get demoted by the search engines. WP Super Cache speeds up WordPress blogs considerably by limiting the number of times WordPress needs to pull information from your database.

You can also browse for plugins on the WordPress.org site at `http://wordpress.org/extend/plugins` or from your own WordPress blog at `www.`*YourBlogDomainName*`.com/wp-admin/plugin-install.php`.

When you know what plugins you want to install, here's how to do it:

1. **From your WordPress Dashboard, choose Plugins⇨Add New.**

2. **Search for the name of the plugin you want to install by typing it into the text field and clicking the Search Plugins button.**

3. **Review the plugin for usefulness and compatibility.**

   If you want to learn more about the plugins that are available from your search, you can click the Details link to get the plugin description. Some plugins also have additional installation instructions and screenshots of the plugin in action to help you determine whether it does what you want it to do.

   This plugin details page will also contain instructions on how to configure your plugin after you install it. So make a mental note of how you found your plugin in case you need to refer to this information later.

WordPress releases several software updates every year to improve performance and security. Unfortunately, not all plugin authors update their plugins as frequently. Sometimes plugins only work for older versions of WordPress. On this Details page, WordPress lets you know whether the plugin you want to use is compatible with the version of WordPress you're using. Usually, if it isn't known to be compatible, it still might work. If that's the case it will say, "Warning: This plugin has not been tested with your current version of WordPress." A plugin can't break your blog 99.9 percent of the time. If it causes an error, WordPress will automatically disable it. But there are rare times (such as when you have manually edited your template file) when it can cause problems. To avoid this, you can ensure you only use currently compatible plugins, or only use older plugins that don't require you to manually edit your template.

4. **The Install Now link appears in two places:**

   • On the plugin detail page, you see the red Install Now button in the top-right corner. When you click the Install Now button, the plugin is automatically installed on your site.

   • On the plugin search results page, you see the Install Now link directly under the plugin name. When you click the Install Now link, a pop-up window appears confirming you want to install this plugin. Click Yes.

5. **Activate the plugin by clicking the Activate Plugin link.**

   When the plugin is done installing, the screen changes and the Activate Plugin link appears.

6. **Configure your plugin.**

   Every plugin setup is unique, so there is no one way to configure the new plugin. Most of them have instructions or an options page that will enable you to make the plugin work the way you want it to. Usually, the options page can be found in the Settings or Plugin menu to the left of your WordPress Dashboard. You can also find this information on the plugin Details page mentioned in Step 3.

Installing a WordPress theme

Installing a WordPress theme is much the same as installing a plugin. You can find free WordPress themes at `http://wordpress.org/extend/themes` and premium paid themes at `http://wordpress.org/extend/themes/commercial`.

Please read the information on choosing and customizing WordPress themes in Chapter 6 before you download or install a theme. This is because a few themes may contain malware or spam links to other sites, and you definitely don't want to use them! You won't find any of these on the WordPress.org site, so it's safe to browse themes from the Install Themes page in your WordPress blog.

To find and install a theme, follow these steps:

1. **From your WordPress Dashboard, choose Appearance⇨Themes, and then click the Install Themes tab.**

2. **Choose the criteria you want for your theme by selecting the appropriate check boxes on the page.**

   You can narrow your search by selecting the check boxes next to your preferred colors, number of columns, width, features, or subject. Click the Find Themes button to view the themes in your search. You can alternatively browse themes by featured, newest, and most recently updated by clicking those links at the top of the page.

3. **(Optional) Preview a theme by clicking the Preview link.**

4. **When you identify the theme you want to use, click the Install link and then click the Install Now button in the pop-up window.**

   This copies the theme to your WordPress blog but doesn't make it live yet.

5. **(Optional) Upload a theme you've already found elsewhere by clicking the Upload link on the Install Themes page; navigate to the saved `.zip` file and select it, and click the Install Now button.**

   This copies the theme to your WordPress blog but doesn't make it live yet.

6. **Preview the theme by clicking the Preview link.**

   After you've installed the theme, you can preview it with your existing content if you have any. The theme may need some customizing to fit your needs, so the preview is only a guide to determine whether it's close enough to what you want. I talk a little more about customizing themes in Chapter 6. (Remember, this is only a very basic guide to let you know the general things needed to get a WordPress blog up and running. For in-depth information on WordPress setup and theme customization, I again steer you to *WordPress For Dummies,* 3rd Edition, by Lisa Sabin-Wilson.)

7. **Activate the theme by clicking the Activate link.**

   At this point, the theme is live on your blog for all your readers to see.

Using WordPress widgets

WordPress widgets are great little tools for making it super-easy to customize your WordPress sidebar. Widgets act like little boxes of information that you can drag and drop into any position on your blog sidebar. Some widgets come installed with WordPress; others you can create on your own. Widgets are commonly used to display things like your categories, bio, advertising, blog search function, recent comments, page links, or you can drop in your own HTML code as well. You can see the different default WordPress widgets in Figure 2-2.

As you can see in Figure 2-2, you can drag widgets over to your sidebar and drop them into place. You can rearrange them on the fly and the changes will be automatically applied to your blog sidebar. I highly recommend putting a few things on every blog sidebar to make your blog easy for your readers to use:

✔ **Search:** You always want to make your archived content easy to find.

✔ **Categories:** People expect to be able to find information by topic.

✔ **Short Bio:** Most readers prefer to know a little bit about who is writing a blog. It's not mandatory, but it can only help you and not hurt you.

The Search and Category widgets are automatically installed as defaults with WordPress. To add a bio, photo, advertising, or anything else custom, you have to put these into a Text Widget and then add it to your sidebar.

The following steps show you to add your bio (note that the steps are similar to add any text or HTML to your sidebar):

1. **From your WordPress Dashboard, choose Appearance⇨Widgets.**

   Note that if you have more than one sidebar, you need to click the down arrow in each widget area to expand it so that you can drag new widgets into place.

2. **Mouse over the Text Widget in the main widget area until your mouse pointer changes to a Move icon.**

   The Move icon looks like a plus sign with arrows in all directions or a grabbing hand.

3. **Click and drag the Text Widget to the position you want your bio to appear in the sidebar.**

4. **Enter a title or heading in the Title field, and type your bio in the larger field.**

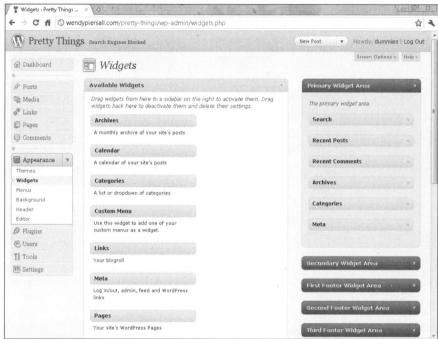

Figure 2-2:
Viewing
the avail-
able default
widgets in
WordPress.

The Text Widget opens automatically after you let go of your mouse
pointer. For a bio, type **About Me** or **My Bio** in the Title text field if you
want to. You can also leave the Title blank. In the larger text field, type
in your bio (or copy and paste it if you already have a short bio saved
elsewhere). If you have your bio formatted with HTML, you can use
that instead.

5. Click the Save button.

You're done! Go to view your blog and see how the widget looks!

Setting Up a New Blogger Blog

If you don't already have a Blogger blog set up, it only takes a few clicks to
get up and running. If you already have a free Google account (which you
have if you use any of Google's other free services, such as Gmail), skip
ahead to the "Setting up your new blog" section.

Signing up with Google Blogger

If you don't already have a Google account, here's how to sign up with Blogger:

1. **Go to** www.blogger.com.

2. **Click the Get Started link under the Don't Have a Google Account heading.**

3. **Enter your e-mail address in the Email Address field, and again in the Retype Email Address field.**

4. **Enter a password in the Password and Retype Password fields.**

   Make your password stronger by using both letters and numbers, because public accounts like this are vulnerable to getting hacked. Google tells you whether your password is too short, strong, or good as you type it in the Password field.

5. **Enter your name in the Display Name field.**

   This would be your first and last name, or a nickname if you prefer that name to be publicly displayed on your blog.

6. **Choose whether to opt in to Blogger announcements, advice and information.**

   At the time of this writing, rumors are swirling around the blogosphere that some cool new features will be added to Blogger soon, so I would select the check box to opt in!

7. **Choose your gender from the drop-down list.**

8. **Enter your birthday in MM/DD/YYYY format in the Birthday field.**

9. **Type the word verification letters into the Word Verification field.**

10. **Select the I Accept the Terms of Service check box.**

11. **Click the Continue button.**

    You now have a Google Blogger account, and you're ready to set up your new blog, as described in the next section.

Setting up your new blog

After you've signed up with Blogger as described in the previous section (or if you already have a Google account, sign in on www.blogger.com), you're taken to the Blogger Dashboard. Here, you set up your blog by following these steps:

1. **Click the Create Your Blog Now button.**

2. **Type in the name of your blog in the Blog Title field.**

   I cover choosing a name for your blog in Chapter 6.

3. **Enter your Blogger URL into the Blog Address (URL) field and click the Check Availability link.**

   This is a mandatory step. Try to choose a short URL that is close to your blog name. (Remember, later you should set up your own domain name as I stated earlier in this chapter.) I talk about choosing a domain name in the section about planning for success in Chapter 15.

   So this URL isn't going to be the one people use to get to your site, anyway. You can set up your own domain name to point to your Blogger blog under the Settings tab in the Publishing section once you're all set up. Instructions on how to do this are on this same page.

   If the URL is already taken, Google will suggest alternate URLs that are available.

4. **If the Blogger URL (*yourname*.blogspot.com) is available, click the Continue button.**

5. **Choose a starter template.**

   Choose a template that is closest to what you want your blog to look like. In the next section, I show you how to install a Blogger template from an outside source, or customize the template with Google's Template Designer.

6. **You can start posting by clicking the Start Blogging button, or continue working on your template by clicking the Customize How Your Blog Looks link.**

   It doesn't matter which one you do first — just explore and play around with it!

Installing a Blogger template

With Blogger, you can either use the built-in template designs, or install a template from an outside source. Finding well-designed Blogger templates is easily done with a search engine. One that I found and liked was `http://btemplates.com`, which had a great selection, was easy to use, and had good support from the site owners.

In this section, I show you how to install a theme you download from another site, and also how to make changes using Blogger's Template Designer.

Just as with WordPress themes, you need to be careful about using free Blogger templates found on the Web. These can also include malware or spam links to other sites. Unfortunately, unlike WordPress, Google has no official site to distribute Blogger templates separate from their Template Designer, so there is no 100 percent safe source for trustworthy themes. My suggestion is that if you see links included in the template that you wouldn't want on your blog, be sure to either remove them or use a different template.

Here's how to install a Blogger template you've downloaded from another site:

1. **Log in to Blogger, and on your Blogger Dashboard, click the Design link.**

2. **Click the Edit HTML tab.**

3. **Click the Download Full Template link and save it to your computer.**

   Make a note of the file name and where you saved it in case you need it later!

4. **Unzip the template file you downloaded from another site.**

5. **Back on the Edit HTML page, click the Choose File button.**

6. **Navigate to where you saved the unzipped files on your computer, and double-click the one that ends in** .xml.

7. **Click the Upload button.**

   If you already have some existing widgets on your Blogger blog, you may get a warning message asking whether you want to keep them or delete them. If you want to preserve the work you've done before, click the Keep Widgets button. If you don't need them anymore, click the Delete Widgets button.

   When the upload is complete, you get a message at the top of the page that says Your Changes Have Been Saved.

8. **Click the View Blog button to ensure that your blog looks the way you want it to look.**

   You may have to remove or move some page elements in order to get the template to display properly; I show you how to do that in the next section.

Oh, the irony. When I did the preceding steps on my own Blogger blog to write this section, the first template I chose did not work, and I couldn't fix it. I believe that some free Blogger templates you find on the Web may be incompatible with the most recent version of Blogger. If this happens to you, you'll either have to find someone very smart who knows how to edit XML, or you'll have to find a different template to upload! You can also reinstall the template you downloaded as a backup in Step 3, or use the Template Designer as explained in the next section.

Customizing a Blogger template

As I mention earlier, Google has a built-in Template Designer; it's extremely easy to use. Here I walk you through making some very basic edits in the Template Designer, plus show you how to use Blogger gadgets, which are also sometimes referred to as widgets.

To change your default template with Blogger's Template Designer, follow these steps:

1. **Go to your Blogger Dashboard and launch the Template Designer by clicking the Design link, and then clicking the Template Designer tab.**

   The Template Designer has five sections, and the first one that appears here is the Templates section.

2. **Choose a base theme to modify by scrolling through the thumbnails and clicking a thumbnail to preview the theme.**

   Scroll through the existing template designs and click various thumbnails to preview the theme on your blog on the bottom half of the screen. There are more selections here than when you first set up your blog. Each template layout also has alternative color palettes.

   You can see the template selections in Figure 2-3.

Figure 2-3:
Viewing Blogger's standard templates in the Template Designer.

When you've chosen a template to use, click it and move on to the next step.

3. **Click the Background tab, and then click the arrow next to the thumbnail of the existing background image.**

   The Select Background Image window appears.

4. **Click a tab along the left side of the Select Background Image window to choose a different image theme, and select the image you want. Click Done when you're satisfied.**

   If you don't like any of these images, you can upload your own. Click the Upload Image button at the top left of the Select Background Image window, click the Browse button, navigate to your image, and double-click it. You will immediately see it previewed on your blog. Click Done when you're finished.

   See the background image selection in Figure 2-4.

5. **Click the Adjust Widths tab and use the sliders to change the Entire Blog and Right Sidebar widths.**

   For best browser compatibility, I recommend keeping the width of your Entire Blog at or under 930 pixels. If you want to add advertising to your sidebar, you will want to make sure that the Right Sidebar is at least 300 pixels wide. You can see the Adjust Widths tab in Figure 2-5.

Figure 2-4:
Changing your back-ground image in your Blogger template.

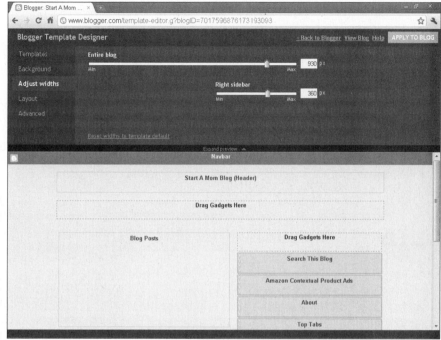

6. **Click the Layout tab and select your blog layout.**

   Blogger has several pre-determined layouts that you can choose from. These will adjust how many sidebars you have, where your sidebars will appear, and how many sections you want in your blog footer.

   My preferred layout is shown in Figure 2-6, with the large box at the top of a right sidebar and two narrower columns underneath it. I like keeping blog post content on the left because it makes it easier to read. And I like the large box at the top of the sidebar because this is a great place to feature important information about you or your blog.

7. **Click the Apply to Blog button at the top right to make your changes live on your blog.**

If that's not enough customization for you, click the Advanced tab in the Template Designer. The options you see are based on which template you chose; some of the items you can change on the Advanced tab are

✔ Body text font and color

✔ Background colors and borders

✔ Color and appearance of text links

✔ Blog title font and color

Figure 2-6:
Choosing
your blog
layout in
Blogger.

✔ Blog description font color

✔ Navigation tabs text font and color

✔ Navigation tabs background color

✔ Post title font and color

Blogger enables you to customize your template further if you have the very advanced skill of knowing how to edit CSS (Cascading Style Sheet) files. Writing and editing CSS is beyond the scope of this book. If you want to find out more about using CSS so you can do advanced template customization, check out *HTML, XHTML, and CSS For Dummies,* 7th Edition, by Ed Tittel and Jeff Noble.

Adding a Blogger gadget

Blogger gadgets work pretty much the same way as WordPress widgets. In fact, gadgets are also sometimes called widgets on Blogger. Gadgets can appear in many different places on your Blogger template, not just your sidebar. You can see in Figure 2-7 you can add them in your header, sidebar, and footer.

Figure 2-7:
Adding a
Blogger
Gadget to
your blog.

Blogger offers quite a few kinds of gadgets, including

- ✔ **Standard blogging features:** These include such niceties as a search box, list of popular posts, list of followers, and pictures and links to your feeds.

- ✔ **Advertising options:** AdSense ads and Amazon affiliate ads (you will need to apply to their programs first — I cover this a little in Chapter 12 on ad networks).

- ✔ **Social networking features:** Share your Flickr photos, Twitter tweets, and Facebook account.

- ✔ **Custom:** Just like with WordPress, you can add your own text or HTML to a custom gadget and add it to any place you would put a gadget.

Most gadgets are very easy to set up, and can be dragged and dropped to rearrange as necessary. The following steps show you how to set up a gadget (I use the Search Box gadget as an example):

1. **On your Blogger Dashboard, click the Design link.**

2. **Click the Add a Gadget link in the position you want the gadget to appear.**

   A pop-up window appears with a list of gadgets to select from.

3. **Scroll until you see the gadget you want, and click the plus sign to the right of it.**

   For example, I scrolled down until I found the Search Box gadget.

4. **Configure your gadget as desired; click the Save button when you're done.**

   For the Search Box gadget, I left the default title in place that says Search this Blog in the provided text field. You can leave it blank, but I suggest making it clear that this is a way that readers can search your blog.

   The Search Box gadget provides the option to allow your readers to search just your blog, the pages that you've linked to in the past, your blog list, your link list, or the entire Web. My personal preference is to keep the search box just for blog content. If your readers want to search the Web, they can use their favorite search engines to do that.

   You can test out how the search box works by typing in a word under the Preview heading and clicking the Search button. This only works if you have blog posts already written that you can search.

Chapter 3

Finding Your Voice and Niche

*I*f you ask established professional bloggers about their first few blog posts, you'll likely notice a hesitation and cringe before they respond. Even if you're already an established writer, developing your personal writing style as a blogger is something that can only come with time. Blogging is different from any other writing medium. Posts need to be relatively short and have a well-defined value proposition for the reader. A *value proposition* is simply making sure your readers know what they'll get out of taking the time to read your blog post. If readers can't determine "what's in it for me" in a short amount of time, they'll leave your blog. Additionally, as a blogger, you have to enjoy what you're writing, or you won't be writing for long. In this chapter, I show you how to balance your need to write for pleasure with the need to give something to your readers in every single post.

To be successful at blogging, you really must enjoy writing for the sake of writing. This is why it's vital to choose a topic for your blog that you're extremely passionate about — a topic that you love so much that you'd be willing to write about for free. Because — let's face it — at the beginning, you *will* be writing for free! (I also give you some tips in this chapter on how to find a topic that you absolutely love.)

On top of all this, the personal nature of blogs makes it next to impossible *not* to write about the people and things that are a part of your life. It also can make it tricky when you want to make a business out of the parts of your life that are typically shared only privately with friends and family. Some of the harshest criticisms leveled at mom bloggers revolve around the ethics of sharing stories about family members — especially children — who don't (or can't) give explicit permission to appear on your blog. While there is no one-size-fits-all answer, I share some of the important things to consider as you find the level of privacy that's right for you and your family.

Understanding How Privacy Affects Your Family and Your Blogging Business

The permanence of blogging puts a different perspective on cute and funny stories about children as they go through stages such as breastfeeding, potty training, and social struggles with their peers. There's no way of knowing what children will think of these writings when they're 16 years old and in the midst of teenage angst. Or how a spouse will feel about what you wrote about an argument you had. Or how your own parents will feel about how you could blog about a childhood experience that you never had the courage to share with them. And Heather (see the nearby sidebar, "Don't cross personal and professional boundaries") specifically cautions: If you think the person you're writing about in a blog post won't find out, think again.

There are also safety issues to consider when you start living your life publicly online. It's next to impossible to conceal your home address and home phone number thanks to public records and online phone books. Additionally, newer cameras are equipped with sophisticated geo-tagging technology that can embed detailed location information in photographs you make public. To date, there have not been any incidents in which bloggers or their families have been harmed due to the findability of personal information. But unfortunately, such harm is still in the realm of possibility.

Ironically, the simple solution to this problem — being and remaining anonymous — isn't a solution that really works for bloggers. Blog readers typically want to know the person behind the words. They care about not only what the blog says, but who says it. So blogging becomes a balancing act between finding ways to share personal stories while setting boundaries about the things you refuse to share publicly. Indeed, even the bloggers who seem to bare it all have certain topics they won't discuss.

Additionally, it's these very personal stories that seem to resonate most with our readers. In fact, writing about taboo subjects (carefully, of course) can be helpful and healing to both the author and the reader. For example, several mom bloggers have shared their personal struggles with anxiety and depression. While this may be a topic that's difficult for their families to discuss, more good than harm has come from shedding light on this condition that affects many women. And the communities that have been created because of these blogs have become an invaluable support system for thousands of women.

WARNING!

Don't cross personal and professional boundaries

When I interviewed Heather Armstrong of Dooce.com for this book, she made a very distinct point to me that she specifically asked that I include in this book. Heather started blogging as a way to vent her frustrations with her co-workers, and to share her critical opinions on her family's Mormon religion. Back then, she certainly never thought any of her family members would ever find her blog online. And she never mentioned names, either of her company or her co-workers, feeling that this level of privacy was all she needed to ensure that her writings wouldn't cause any trouble in real life.

Heather learned the hard way that her co-workers did indeed find out about her blog, and she was promptly fired for it. And around the same time, her family found out about it as well, and was devastated to read the hurtful things she had said about them and their religion.

Remember: Heather's lesson learned is as important now as it was back then — everything that you publish online is *permanent*. You can't delete a blog post and erase it from the Web. Your words don't just reside on your blog — they are spread around the Internet via RSS feeds, search engines, and Web archives. They get copied on server backups and on any computer of a blog reader.

Over the years, I have had to decide whether sharing a particular story is appropriate for both my family and for my readers. Here are some of the questions I've asked myself to help me weigh the value of sharing versus the potential consequences:

- ✔ **Is this information self-serving, or will my blog visitors get something out of reading this post?** Sometimes I've needed to rewrite sections to change my venting into a sharing of lessons learned instead.

- ✔ **Does this blog post say anything that I wouldn't say directly to the persons involved?** If not, then I either chose to speak to that person first, or omitted the information from my blog post.

- ✔ **Does this material violate the privacy of the persons I've written about?** If you would be afraid to have them find the post, then the answer to this question is probably yes.

- ✔ **Is there a way I can get my message across effectively without sharing personal details?** If so, it's probably in your best interests to do so.

- ✔ **How would my children feel about this post if they were reading it as adults?** The best way to answer this question is to imagine that your own parents wrote this blog entry about you. If that leaves you with hesitation or uneasiness, there's probably room for revision.

✔ **Can anything in this post get taken out of context in a way that I hadn't intended? And could that misinterpretation cause harm to me or my family?** If so, be sure to edit your words or add more information. You don't want to risk being misrepresented in a way that creates problems that aren't there in the first place.

Sometimes you just don't know the answers to these questions. Over the years, I've learned to trust my intuition when that little voice says, "don't hit Publish just yet." When that happens, I always walk away from the content for a few hours or days until I can see the situation objectively. And like most other bloggers, I've hit the Publish button too soon on several occasions. Sometimes you don't know you've crossed the line until the line is already crossed. Thankfully, I've erred on the cautious side and I've never inflicted any permanent harm — and I hope that is always the case.

Changing a Personal Blog into a Business

In the first business I started, I created custom hand-painted artwork on furniture and room accessories. Each piece was unique, and I poured love into everything I created. Art is a deeply personal expression of who we are, and I felt that in this business, my heart and soul were on the line. For the most part, people loved what I did, and I sold many pieces of my work. But sometimes someone would say, "Oh, I could do that for way cheaper — why would I buy it from *her*?" And when I decided, after 18 months, that I needed to find a job to bring in more reliable income, it was hard not to feel that I had failed — not only as an entrepreneur, but as a person.

I can't name one successful blog in which the author or owner hadn't also poured her own heart and soul into her blogging business. Blogs aren't just an online journal of personal events — many times they are an expression of who you are as a person. This can make it difficult to be impartial when your highly subjective content must be analyzed objectively from a business point of view. And it makes it even harder to not take criticism or setbacks personally.

If you're taking your personal blog and turning it into a business, two of the most important things you can do are grow thicker skin and consciously start looking at your blog objectively from an outsider's point of view. For many bloggers, that may mean shifting content around into a more user-friendly format and putting up more formal boundaries between personal life and business. It doesn't mean you have to stop being personal — far from it. Blogging is a personal business, and your personality is the greatest asset of your business. But you may find that some things are just too important to you to risk making them a part of your professional life. For me, I've decided that I am happiest with my artwork when I do it just for myself and nobody else. I use my *creativity* in my business every day, but my personal creations are not for sale.

On a larger scale, it's important to pay attention to how exactly you plan on making money off your personal writings. I discuss various blogging business models in Chapter 4, and you want to think carefully about what exactly you're selling on your blog. Even if you aren't selling products, you may be selling advertising or your own services. How will your personal opinions affect your ability to market yourself? In some cases, a blog with controversial content may have a hard time finding advertisers. Other times, you want to put policies in place to ensure that you aren't giving your readers an impression that your opinions are for sale.

Profiting without Selling Out

Selling out is a term used for compromising your integrity, principles, or morals to gain money or success. The problem is, if everyone had the same principles and definition of integrity, there wouldn't be much need for different political parties or religions. People can be accused of selling out if they simply do things like broaden their horizons or develop new interests over the course of time. Additionally, you may have certain beliefs in place that seem important now, but become less important as you gain more experience and knowledge.

A great example of this is the evolution of the very organization that provides standards to bloggers who work with brands: the Word of Mouth Marketing Association (WOMMA). When WOMMA was first established, its founding members came from a very traditional media background and took old-school journalistic standards and applied them to all marketing in the new world of social media. For several years, WOMMA formally said that members were not allowed to pay money to bloggers for writing blog posts, but they could offer products for free. The founding members felt strongly that this led to the perception of buying opinions from bloggers. Yet as the blogging industry evolved, bloggers began to feel taken advantage of. They didn't want useless free products; they wanted to be compensated for their writing and input. The tables began to turn as WOMMA realized this position was enabling brands to get free or cheap advertising at the expense of bloggers' businesses. In a reversal, WOMMA changed its policy (and its board management) to reflect the new needs of social media marketing, and now states that it's absolutely ethical to pay bloggers for writing sponsored content as long as they comply with the FTC guidelines. I go into all these topics in more detail in Chapter 9.

Sadly, mom bloggers are sometimes accused of selling out when they get opportunities to work with brands. The importance of this is not that the accusers are right — usually they aren't. They are projecting their own definition of selling out onto other people. And they are usually coming from WOMMA's old-school perspective that is out of tune with the reality of running a blogging business. Here the crucial issue is that you know what selling out means to *you,* because *true* selling out can only hurt you in the long term if you don't correct your course.

In Chapter 9, I discuss blogging ethics in much more detail. I also show you how to write an editorial policy, which is the key to establishing your own ethical boundaries for you and your business. No matter what you decide is right for you, here are some general topics and guidelines that apply for everyone who wrestles with the idea of what "selling out" means:

- **Unethical advertising:** An advertiser that specifically asks you to write something positive about the company is being unethical. All professional bloggers will refuse any opportunity that requires they lead their readers to believe that an opinion expressed is their own when it isn't.

- **Breaking FTC guidelines:** An advertiser that wants to hire you to write something and asks you not to disclose that the content is sponsored is breaking the FTC guidelines. If you do not disclose that the content was compensated, then you're breaking FTC guidelines, too. Both you and the advertiser would be liable for fines or damages that could arise in the future. This is not ethical social media marketing.

- **Conflicts of interest:** A blogger maintains a respected blog and is a trusted voice in social media only by avoiding opportunities that present very clear conflicts of interest. For example, a mom who writes as a breastfeeding advocate shouldn't become a spokesblogger for a baby-formula company. Most opportunities are not this clear-cut, however, which is why it's a must to create an editorial policy for your blog.

Choosing Topics That Will Help Your Blog Grow

In Chapter 18, I feature ten mom bloggers who have found success in very different ways. Each one has a very different business model from the others. But when I asked each one of them for their best blogging advice they wished to pass along to newer bloggers, almost all of them spoke of the importance of focusing your blog on a tight niche (your chosen blog topic and area of expertise). While you certainly can blog on topics outside your niche, you'll have a much easier time building your audience and revenue if you focus on your most passionate area of interest.

I have an unshakable belief that there will always be room in the blogosphere for new bloggers to make it big. Just because there are a lot of blogs doesn't mean that the market is saturated and that there are too many voices. That would be like saying there are too many books in the world and there's no room for new authors. But as in the traditional publishing industry, general unfocused content isn't as valuable as content created with a specific audience in mind.

In the next section, I talk about identifying subjects you're passionate about and identifying your target audience. But when you're first starting out, you may need some help figuring out how to direct your efforts. It may seem obvious to simply get ideas from the blogs you love that are successful. The problem with that approach is that just because a blog seems to have a lot of traffic doesn't necessarily mean that the blog is making any money. In fact, this lack of income is the case more frequently than you might guess. Additionally, it isn't a good business model to build a blog that's a thinly veiled copy of someone else's blog. Instead of building your own business and brand, you become known as *the blog like so-and-so's,* and you're actually helping to build the other blog's brand instead of your own.

If you truly want to gauge demand of topics you're considering, you can try out a few free and easy tools. The first thing you'll need to do, though, is brainstorm a list of ideas to research. I include a list of ideas in the online Cheat Sheet at `www.dummies.com/cheatsheet/momblogging` to get you started. Then the fastest and easiest way to get an idea of how much interest there is in each of your ideas is to turn to something you use frequently — search engines.

When you type your search terms into a search engine, somewhere at the top of the page, you'll find a number that represents the number of all the results available for that term. For example, a search for *recipes* on Yahoo! returns nearly 80 million results.

While that's a huge number, and it indicates that recipes are pretty darn popular, it also means that there could be a lot of competition on the Web for this topic as well. Indeed, your blog would be going up against powerhouses like the Food Network and Betty Crocker. I encourage you at this point to explore more focused ideas instead of such a broad category like *recipes.* A second search for the more specific term *vegetarian recipes* brings up 24 million results. That's still a healthy number, and it also shows there's plenty of interest in the subject while also being a little easier to get found.

Getting just a tiny bit more specific, if you search for *vegetarian recipes for kids,* you'll find two really great things: First, there are still nearly 15 million results. Second, there's a mom blog on page one.

I actually find this process both fascinating and a little addicting. Sometimes I am completely surprised by the amount of information available on a topic I had assumed to be very obscure. Search engines are the market-research tools I use most frequently for all my blog network sites. They also have some fun tools that help you uncover more ideas about what people like:

✔ **Suggested terms:** I always pay attention to the terms that the search engine suggests for me as I type. These terms are generated automatically by frequency of use, so they can indicate consumer interest, too.

✔ **Related searches:** All three major search engines have a section on the home page in which they suggest related search terms. I also pay attention to these terms for ideas that I might not have thought of on my own.

✔ **Google Keyword Tool:** Google has a keyword tool found at `https://adwords.google.com/select/KeywordToolExternal`. The tool is free, but you need to sign in with your Google account to use it. By typing in a term to this tool, you can find out the number of actual monthly searches that Google processes for that term. It also greatly expands on words and phrases that are related to your original query. As you can see in Figure 3-1, the more specific the search is (like in the previous example), the fewer number of searches occur. Plus the tool suggests phrases that are related, which can give you more clues as to how popular the topic is.

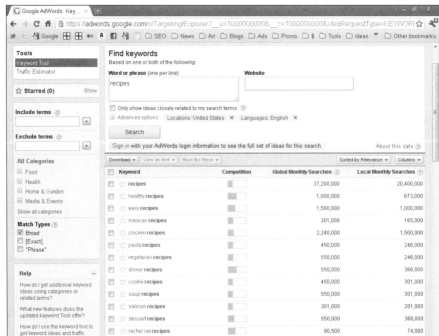

Figure 3-1:
Using the Google Keyword Tool to do research on blog topics.

While crunching numbers — in particular, quantities of search phrases — isn't the only way to assess potential demand, it's easy, free, and a fairly reliable indication of how much interest there is in your chosen blog topics. In Chapter 5, I discuss data and analytics in more detail, and show you how to use analytic tools to find out what content is most popular as your blog grows. Don't worry, it's not really dry information — it's actually a great way to get feedback from your readers who don't comment or interact with you personally!

Using a search engine, analytics, and market research to come up with topic ideas is a great way to understand how many people may be interested in the content you want to write about. But they aren't the only tools you should use to decide what to write about. Until just a few years ago, nobody knew what a cake pop was, let alone how to make one. But thanks to Angie Dudley of the Bakerella blog (www.bakerella.com), cake pops are such a hit that Martha Stewart is featuring them and Starbucks is selling them. So use this numbers-based analytic approach as only one of the ways you identify your niche. I talk about writing about what you are passionate about in the next section. Ultimately, if you are super-excited about an idea that you can't get out of your head, don't worry if there doesn't seem to be a lot of demand for it now. Your enthusiasm means more than search engine numbers.

That being said, if you *really* want to start out writing about a topic that has an established audience, try to find keywords that generate at least several hundred thousand results. If at some point you feel like you want to expand, you can always expand to cover related topics.

Identifying Subjects You're Passionate About

While it's a nearly exact science to determine how many people are interested in a given topic, identifying your blogging passion is anything but an exact science. I know this sounds esoteric, but after studying what makes a blog successful for over five years, I can honestly say that the most successful blogs have only one thing in common: Their writers have chosen a topic so close to their hearts that they are doing what they were truly put on this earth to do.

Sometimes their blogs represent that end result. I know (for example) that Darren Rowse of ProBlogger doesn't write about making money online just for the sake of earning money. He has empowered thousands of bloggers to earn a living doing something they love — myself included. And Heather Armstrong of Dooce doesn't blog just for the advertising revenue and page views. Her honest and raw account of dealing with postpartum depression has helped thousands of people come to terms with their own mental-health issues or those of family members.

Other times, the blog is a step toward a greater end goal. Michelle Lamar started blogging many years ago as the *White Trash Mom*. While it landed her a book deal and popularity among her peers, she found that it ultimately didn't really represent her talents as a marketing executive with 15 years' experience in the industry. She ended up taking her blog down in 2010 in order to enhance her professional profile as an experienced social media marketer. Yet it was her experience as a mom blogger that landed her a dream job with the V3 Integrated Marketing agency as the VP of Integrated Marketing. You can find out more about her blogging journey in Chapter 18.

So how do you figure out what you're passionate about? I state the simplest way to know at the beginning of this chapter: You have to love the topic enough to be willing to write about it for free. Beyond that, what do your friends and family always come to you for? Creative ideas? Political analysis? Fashion advice? What are you known for? Because as you get more established as a blogger, you want to become that go-to person for that same area of expertise. Dawn Sandomeno is a blogger who absolutely loves party planning, and started a party-planning blog with her friend Elizabeth Mascali in 2007. As their blog grew, their reputation as *the* party-planning expert bloggers grew as well. A conversation on Twitter with a publisher led to a book deal in 2010. Now they are regulars on national television shows like the *Today Show* and *Good Morning America* when producers need someone who can talk about subjects such as Super Bowl parties and holiday celebrations.

Focusing Your Blog on a Target Audience

As I explain in Chapter 10, focusing your blog content on a specific target audience makes your blog very attractive to potential advertisers. In fact, they are more interested in a *focused target audience* than they are in very large numbers. Being focused also works to your advantage as you work to make a name for yourself and build your blogging business. It's always easier to become a big fish when you're working in a smaller pond.

It's a misconception that you're limiting yourself unduly by focusing on a niche. No one blog can be everything to everyone. In fact, as you get more successful in your niche, you start to become better known to bloggers in other niches as well. Ironically, it's quite difficult to choose a niche that's too small. But if you do, it's an easier mistake to correct than choosing a topic that's too broad. If you can conquer one topic, you know what to do to expand into related topics. If you've started out with too general a focus, it will be harder to find success at all, and you may get discouraged and stop altogether.

What's interesting about being focused on a specific topic is that you can have two blogs considered to be in the same category, yet attract very different readers from each other. Todd Fratzel writes the Home Construction and Improvement blog, which offers his expert advice on installing window wells and basic sump pumps. His blog conveys a very authoritative image and a design that appeals to other readers much like himself: middle-aged males. You can see what I mean in Figure 3-2.

Now look at Remodelaholic, written by a mom named Cassity: She features reader-submitted "before" and "after" photographs of home-improvement projects, room decorating ideas, and project tutorials. Her blog clearly attracts young and middle-aged women, many of whom are moms. You can see how different her blog looks in Figure 3-3.

As you develop your blog idea into a solid business, it'll be advantageous — not only to attract readers who are interested in specific topics, but also to appeal to a specific demographic. (A *demographic* is a group of people who have similar lifestyles. I talk more about demographics in Chapter 10.) Why?

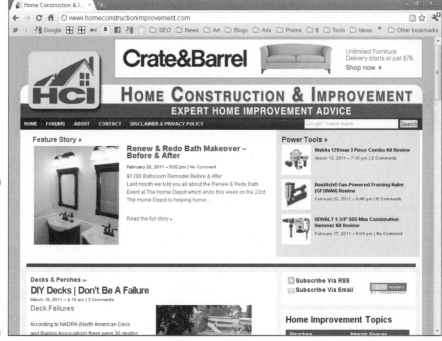

Figure 3-2: Todd Fratzel's home-improvement blog attracts an older male audience.

Figure 3-3:
The
Remodel-
aholic home
improve-
ment blog
attracts
women and
moms.

Because these are the kinds of things that make blogs attractive to advertisers and sponsors. Identifying your target demographic also makes it easier for you to identify and find opportunities that can help your blogging business grow.

Part II
Building Your Blogging Empire

The 5th Wave   By Rich Tennant

"Remember – if you're updating the family blog, no more animated Gifs of your sister swinging from a tree, scratching her armpits!"

In this part . . .

In Part II, I start getting into the nuts and bolts of creating a business out of your blog. In Chapter 4, I explain exactly how blogs make money so you can figure out a formula that will work for you. (This is one of my favorite chapters in this entire book.)

I share with you how to lay a foundation to measure your success, attract readers to your blog, and begin to build a strong personal and professional brand online. These things are critical to your long-term success.

In this part, I start covering some more intermediate topics, such as how to get media coverage (or even get on TV!). And for those of you who have products or services to sell, I have a whole chapter dedicated to helping you do just that.

Chapter 4

Determining the Best Business Model for Your Blog

In This Chapter

▶ Understanding how different blog topics earn money in different ways

▶ Choosing a business model based on your strengths and weaknesses

▶ Knowing what it takes to be successful depending on your type of blog

▶ Developing a plan for how your blog will earn money

▶ Setting blogging goals in a way that motivates you

*T*his chapter is one I most looked forward to writing. I absolutely love talking about how businesses work, especially when it comes to blogging. The ways a blog can make money are almost as numerous — and varied — as the blogs out there in the blogosphere, but all those ways fall into just a few defined categories of business models.

I learned very early on from Darren Rowse of ProBlogger.com that the two main ways blogs make money are directly and indirectly. A blogger can earn money directly *from* the blog, or indirectly *because of* the blog.

Examples of how blogs earn money directly are

- ✔ Advertising and sponsorships
- ✔ Affiliate marketing
- ✔ Product sales
- ✔ Selling their blogs to other owners

Examples of how blogs earn money indirectly are

- ✔ Getting freelance or full-time jobs
- ✔ Book deals
- ✔ Becoming a brand spokesperson
- ✔ Speaking gigs

In this chapter, I show you the five most common blogging business models and explain how best to implement them. I also share my personal story of how I found the right business model that fit my own strengths and weaknesses. This was definitely a lesson learned the hard way. I love sharing the story because I think it's helpful to nearly any blogger who wants to build a business.

Understanding How Blogs Make Money

After I had blogged for about a year or so, I felt like I knew quite a lot about making money from a blog. I was earning a modest but steady income, I was already starting to speak at conferences, and I was on top of my game. I started writing for Entrepreneur.com, started up a second blog, and suddenly found myself working 50-hour work weeks in order to keep up with it all. Because I still hadn't replaced my old corporate-job income (I wasn't even close!), I knew I had to do something different. Yet I had hit a wall — I couldn't take on any more work. The freedom of working at home — and for myself — was getting lost in the process.

I decided to change my mom-entrepreneurship blog called eMoms at Home into a blog *network*. It was an incredibly risky and bold move; no other woman had done anything like it at the time. But I believed in myself and I created a plan. I specifically wanted to create a high-traffic website that would be primarily monetized by direct advertising and affiliate marketing. I intended to add six new blogs on the topics I knew my readers were most interested in. I went through a lengthy hiring process, and found six new bloggers to write for me. I invested a lot of time and money in building up a website and template system to accommodate the new writers and content. And I created a spending budget based on my most reliable monthly income. In September of 2007, I launched my blog network, and it was incredibly well received.

I was dang proud of myself. For about two weeks.

The first hiccup I experienced was that monthly "reliable" income suddenly vanished. Due to a change in Google's policy about paid links, I lost ten monthly advertisers overnight. I was still making enough to cover my expenses, but it left next to nothing for my own income. Yet I persisted.

The second hiccup I experienced was that I soon realized that I knew a ton about blogging — as long as that blog was on the topic of mom entrepreneurship. My six new blogs were on different but related topics. I realized fast that I didn't know so much about blogging about freelancing, craft businesses, kids' activities, work/life balance for dads, eBay selling, or product reviews and giveaways.

I had about a week of sleeplessness as I panicked about what I had gotten myself into. The blogs were each drawing readers from completely different sources. New advertisers were interested in some of the blogs and completely ignoring others. Some blogs got tons of comments. Others got none, even though all the writers were talented and engaging. Even my Google AdSense ads were earning different rates on each blog, and receiving a very uneven number of clicks.

What followed over the next year and a half was a struggle to find a way to make my blog network profitable. I changed the name of the site to Sparkplugging. I tried selling my own downloadable training courses. I added another group of blogs, having as many as 15 at one time. I developed a big sponsorship campaign with Epson, bringing my entire writing team to the BlogWorld Expo conference in the fall of 2008. I even got on the *Today Show,* thinking that with 5 million morning viewers, my site would finally attract the traffic I needed to earn a living.

My social influence was at an all-time high. My bank account was at an all-time low.

None of it worked. In the spring of 2009, I was faced with a health problem that at the time was terrifying. I was going in for tests, getting needles stuck in my neck, and was ordered to have a biopsy. When you're faced with your own mortality at the age of 40, suddenly your priorities can do some drastic rearranging.

In the meantime, I had started another kids' activities blog network called Woo! Jr., based on the success of one of my all-time most popular blog posts and one of the more successful blogs on Sparkplugging. Even though the new network was only five months old, it was already getting more traffic than Sparkplugging. Everything I did that didn't work to grow Sparkplugging was working ten times better than I had expected it to on Woo! Jr.

Sparkplugging offered me a major platform to get speaking gigs, get marketing clients, be a published writer, and be a thought leader as a business blogger. Woo! Jr. offered me little visibility, little opportunity for peer recognition, and a huge risk of losing everything by walking away from an established brand. But when faced with potential thyroid cancer, I had to make a choice between the two business models:

 ✔ Sparkplugging had had the most success with indirect methods of making money. I would have to abandon my goal of building a blog network that directly earned revenue from advertising and affiliate marketing if I was to continue. And I would have to go back to taking on clients and selling training products.

> ✔ Woo! Jr. was small but growing rapidly, and was earning all its income directly from advertising. But I would have to give up a three-year blogging career and pretty much start from scratch all over again in order to make this choice work. The blogging fame I had worked so hard to establish wouldn't do me much good in my new endeavor.

It may sound crazy, but it was a pretty easy choice for me to make. In all due modesty, I am great with clients, and I am an amazing trainer. But I'm terrible with follow-up and customer support. I always have e-mails waiting to be answered. And my voice mail is always full. (This is why Sparkplugging never worked for me.) But I am awesome at writing great content, driving blog traffic, and developing creative activities for kids. I can do this stuff in my sleep. And I *love* it. Woo! Jr. easily won the battle — and I sold Sparkplugging less than six months later.

Choosing the Best Business Model for Your Blog

I don't know why it took me so long to figure out that I was trying to fit Sparkplugging into the wrong business model, like a square peg in a round hole. It's possible that my ability to see the potential in everything blinded me to what was really there in front of me. My mistake is one I hope you don't have to make. I see many bloggers doing what I did — struggling with a lot of different ways to make money off their blogs, never finding the one that fits.

In an ideal world, bloggers would be able to determine their business models before jumping in and starting a blog. You could base your choice of topic and content on the way you want to earn revenue. But blogs don't start out that way. Blogs start out with a passion for something and a desire to share that passion with the world. But just because you're great at blogging about your passion doesn't mean that you're automatically great at making money with that particular kind of blog.

In the following sections, I show you five common ways that the most successful blogs earn their revenue. I also show you what it takes to make each work so that you can evaluate whether your personal strengths will be a good match.

Selling your own or others' products

If you have your own products to sell, or are primarily dedicated to selling others' products via affiliate marketing, then using a blog to drive sales is very effective. Blogs naturally do well in search engines, and can make it easier for you to rank well in the quest for effective search terms (and that can be *quite* competitive). This kind of blog is also an excellent way to communicate directly with your customers and put a personal face on your business.

Your most effective content will be tutorials and how-tos that utilize the products you're promoting. If those approaches aren't applicable to your product line, then reviews also work well. Additionally, quality product photography is absolutely critical and should be professionally done. When it comes to online retail sales, your goal should be to get your readers to your sale confirmation page in as few clicks as possible.

This kind of blog is very similar to one you would use to promote your own services, but there is less focus on building working relationships with your potential customers. Instead, your main goal is to get people to your product page and to get them to make a purchase right away. Most blogs that are devoted to product sales don't carry any advertising, because they don't want to distract visitors from making a purchase.

This kind of blog is the most difficult to diversify in terms of where your income comes from. That limitation leaves you a little vulnerable to changes in the industry, economy, or even changes in how the search engines rank your site, which can and does happen. Two possible defenses are

- ✔ You can diversify what you sell; for example, you can teach classes or host events that use your product line.

- ✔ You can pursue complimentary sponsorship opportunities; for example, you can promote your favorite sewing machine brand if your online store sells fabric and notions.

The best way to promote this kind of blog is by creating valuable content that other bloggers will want to share with their readers. This means your blog posts can't just be about selling products. Instead, they should focus on being informative, entertaining, or educational. Additionally, intermediate to advanced level search engine optimization skills are going to be very important to your success. You will want to optimize your content for the right keywords, and also optimize your product images so that your blog can be found via Google's Image Search. You don't need large amounts of traffic to be successful with this kind of blog — instead, you need small amounts of traffic but visitors who are highly interested in your products. And finally, occasional giveaways of free products will draw attention to your blog and help you find new readers.

To summarize, here are four recommended ways to be successful with a blog that promotes product sales (such as the blog shown in Figure 4-1):

- ✔ Create useful content that your potential customers will value and want to share with others.

Figure 4-1:
The Paper
Crave blog
promotes its
own online
shop of sta-
tionery and
paper craft
supplies.

✔ Learn intermediate- to advanced-level search engine optimization.

✔ Pursue sponsorship opportunities as long as they are complimentary to your business and offer value to your customers.

✔. Focus on finding the right kind of traffic rather than large amounts of traffic.

For a good example of this kind of blog, check out Paper Crave at http:// papercrave.com. They not only feature their own products, but products from other websites as well — even from sites that would actually be considered their competition. Paper Crave focuses on stunningly beautiful paper products, so they have built a loyal following thanks to their great taste in design (see it in action in Figure 4-1).

Promoting yourself as a freelancer or consultant

If you are a freelancer or consultant, then using your blog to attract new clients is one of the most powerful ways you can do so. Your blog should become a part of your *sales funnel,* which is how you lead people from being interested in hiring you to becoming full-blown clients. You do this by offering free or low-cost resources and gradually encouraging your customers to purchase larger products or services from you. (I explain sales funnels in detail in the later section, "Create a sales funnel.")

Your most effective content will be articles that demonstrate you can fix the problems your clients need help with. Consider building a mailing list to develop relationships with people who prefer e-mail over RSS. And make it easy for readers to contact you — feature your contact form or information prominently on your blog template.

Because the goal of your blog is to get new clients, advertising can sometimes detract from this goal. While I do advocate diversifying where your income comes from, most professional blogs in this category don't have enough daily traffic to make advertising worth the time, anyway. There certainly are exceptions to this, especially when you can find advertisers or affiliate programs for products that enhance and don't compete with your services.

One of the most effective ways to diversify your income on this kind of blog is to create your own training products that make your expertise available at a lower price than in a traditional client relationship. This way you create new revenue while also giving potential clients a way to test the waters with you. You can also create simple service packages of frequently requested projects like Shannon from EightCrazy Designs. Her Design Services page features bundled packages such as an Etsy store banner, avatar, and custom-order image for a flat fee. It's an excellent example and can be found at `http://eightcrazydesigns.com/design-services`.

The best ways to promote this kind of blog online involve social media interactions and search engine optimization. I explain both in more detail in Chapter 6 — especially their role in attracting readers to your blog.

To summarize, recommended ways to be successful with a blog that promotes your freelance or consulting services (such as the blog shown in Figure 4-2) are to:

- ✔ Generate high-quality content that showcases your expertise.
- ✔ Know your niche so you don't need heavy traffic in order to be profitable.
- ✔ Minimize advertising so you don't distract readers from hiring you.
- ✔ Build a sales funnel in which you lead customers into a working relationship with you.
- ✔ Consider starting an e-mail newsletter.
- ✔ Diversify the way you earn money by creating your own products to sell.
- ✔ Set aside time every week to build relationships on LinkedIn, Facebook, and Twitter.

Figure 4-2:
Pam Slim uses her Escape from Cubicle Nation blog to find coaching clients, line up speaking opportunities, and to sell her book.

A good example of this kind of blog is Escape from Cubicle Nation, written by Pam Slim (www.escapefromcubiclenation.com). Pam exemplifies all the things that make this kind of blog successful, and it shows. She has a wide range of products and services to sell, an engaging blog, an award-winning book, and a textbook-perfect sales funnel. You can see it all in action in Figure 4-2.

Earning from advertising and sponsorships

Advertising and sponsorship revenue suits a blog best in two situations:

- ✔ **When the blog gets a lot of traffic:** This is the "strength in numbers" approach. If you have a product or service that a lot of people want, an advertiser gets to put a message in front of a lot of eyes.

- ✔ **When the blog attracts a very specific interest group:** This is the "target marketing" approach, and it's all about catering to specific needs. For the record, "moms" is not a very specific interest group. Instead, "moms with newborn infants under 6 months" or "moms who are interested in photography" are good examples of the kind of specific groups advertisers are looking for.

Blogs focused on advertising revenue should be built to encourage people to stay on the site and view as many pages as possible. There is a reason there are so many slide shows on very large websites — those slide shows serve up an ad impression for every photo in the series. Other ways that blogs have increased their ad views is by adding forums, multimedia content, or by hiring more writers. This increased interaction makes the website more profitable.

Your most effective content will be on topics that are popular and generate a lot of consumer interest. Advertisers love to have their ads appear by related content, so it helps if your blog topic is related to the consumer goods and services that advertise frequently on the Internet. Quantity is just as important as quality on these blogs, because the more content you have, the more advertising you can display. That means that you need to be willing to write a lot or hire writers. If you have a smaller blog, advertisers will be most interested in you if you're very tightly focused on a niche topic that attracts a large percentage of their potential customers. If not, most advertisers prefer to work with larger sites with a more influential presence.

Because the goal of this type of blog is to increase ad impressions, it's helpful to have an eye for design. The idea is to place as many ads on your pages as possible without letting them become overbearing or distracting. You will also want to encourage readers to view your related blog posts with suggested links at the end of your entries and/or in your sidebars.

One effective way to diversify your income on this kind of blog is to work with an ad network that will allow you to sell your own ads, too. Plus, take advantage of affiliate marketing techniques to create new ways to generate revenue from your existing content. Depending on your blog topic, syndicating your content might be an option for you as well.

One of the best ways to promote this kind of blog is to spend the time necessary to learn intermediate level search engine optimization, because it can be a very huge source of traffic. Additionally, you'll need to set aside time regularly to build incoming links to your blog. Ensure that there are plenty of ways for your readers to share your content with their friends. Add Facebook Share and Like buttons, Tweet This buttons, or use a service like AddThis (www.addthis.com) to give an even wider range of sharing options. And work on building a loyal following that returns to your blog again and again.

Here's the short list of ways to be successful with a blog that earns revenue from advertising and sponsorships (such as the blog shown in Figure 4-3):

- ✔ Maintain a high quality and quantity of content that appeals to a large audience and gets updated frequently.
- ✔ Aim for a very high-traffic site or a smaller site that attracts a very dedicated niche audience.

Figure 4-3:
Money
Saving
Mom.com
is a good
example
of a blog-
advertising
business
model.

✔ Use various sources of advertising including ad networks, selling your own ads, and affiliate marketing.

✔ Learn search engine optimization.

✔ Set aside time to promote your content to other bloggers and websites.

For a good example of this kind of website, look at MoneySavingMom at http://moneysavingmom.com. Blogger Crystal Paine earned enough from her blog advertising to pay for her home in cash in 2009. Her blog fits all the criteria I just mentioned, and you can see her well-designed blog in Figure 4-3.

Leveraging your blog into career opportunities

As more and more companies realize the value that mom bloggers bring to the table, many moms are getting outright job offers from companies that want an employee who is on the inside of the mom-blogging community. These can range from regular corporate jobs to flexible work-at-home positions that offer stable income with great work-life balance.

If you are hoping to find a job because of your blog, your most effective content will be resourceful and insightful articles that showcase your knowledge and expertise. You'll want to find a good balance between sharing personal information and professionalism. Your influence in the mom-blogging community will be a true asset for a potential employer, so you'll want to nurture your online relationships and be a resource to your fellow bloggers as well.

Because the goal of this blog is to get hired, you want to get as much brand experience under your belt as possible to build your résumé. It's important for you to develop your online connections into offline relationships. So you want to get out to as many blogging and industry events and conferences as your schedule allows. This is your best opportunity to get in front of brand representatives and impress them with your expertise. You also want to pursue any freelance or consulting opportunities you can find, because often temporary work leads to permanent positions.

The most important way to promote this kind of blog is through social media. Potential employers will most likely need you to handle their social marketing initiatives, so you need to be well established on Facebook and Twitter, and perhaps Foursquare or Groupon, especially if the employer is involved in marketing at a local level. Any experience with Facebook pages, Twitter parties, or coordinating other social media marketing projects will be proof that you can turn your online marketing knowledge into actual campaigns. Writing for larger publications will also help to build your credentials and get your name in front of a larger audience.

To summarize the recommended ways to be successful finding a job with your blog:

- ✔ Write resourceful blog posts that showcase your expertise.
- ✔ Get out to blogging and industry conferences to network with potential employers.
- ✔ Demonstrate your social media marketing experience by developing and participating in successful marketing campaigns.
- ✔ Nurture your relationships with the blogging community by being active on Facebook, Twitter, and other social networks.
- ✔ Work on finding freelance or temporary work with clients because they may lead to full-time work.

Amber Watson-Tardiff is a great example of this scenario. She was able to take her experience in the legal field and as a mom blogger and get hired as the Content and PR Director for Legal Marketing Maven. She now works at home making a very respectable full-time income. You can check out the Legal Marketing Maven site (`http://legalmarketingmaven.com`) in Figure 4-4.

Figure 4-4:
Amber
Watson-
Tardiff
works
for Legal
Marketing
Maven
because
of the
marketing
experience
and cre-
dentials she
built as
a mom
blogger.

Building a platform as a well-known influencer

I hesitate to suggest that any blogger make a goal to be famous without first creating a plan for what to do with the fame you seek. Pursuing blogging fame is tempting because it seems so rewarding and so many people are doing it. But if you don't have a concrete way to turn that fame and influence into dollars, it's an empty goal that takes up more time than you can possibly imagine.

Your most effective content will be entertaining, honest, and real. You need to be a charismatic person that people can relate to — or perhaps instead you may be a polarizing blogger with controversial opinions. Either way, you need to prove that you have what it takes to draw a large audience that thrives on reading your content. Plus, in a crowded blogosphere, you really have to be unique to get noticed. This kind of blog can be a compelling personal journey, such as Heather Armstrong's Dooce blog at www.dooce.com, or it can be a professional platform such as Penelope Trunk's Brazen Careerist blog at http://blog.penelopetrunk.com.

If you're the kind of blogger who thrives in the spotlight, then your blog should be all about broadcasting your message to the world. You are building a platform from which you can promote yourself and any endeavor you pursue. The platform isn't the end goal — it is the *means* to an end. From your platform, you can become a book author, be a paid speaker, become a spokesperson for a brand, or sell your products and services. A handful of bloggers have even landed movie deals, the first one being Julie and Julia in 2009. It usually doesn't come without a cost — as bloggers become more influential, they also become larger targets for criticism. Whether or not the criticism is valid, you need to have a thick skin to manage any response on your part with dignity rather than with retaliation.

Effective ways to make money off this kind of blog are to combine several direct and indirect methods of monetization. With a popular blog comes traffic, so selling ads or working with an ad network are important. But only in rare cases is it enough to earn a living just on advertising. Additionally, you need to pursue relationships with book publishers, top brands, or event planners, and build up your personal brand and fan base enough that you stand out from the crowd. All the while, you still need to be writing content and maintaining your blog so you continually engage your readers. Should you get a book deal or spokesperson gig, these can instantly double your workload. If you are seeking speaking gigs, plan on traveling frequently — around six to ten times a year.

The best way to promote this kind of blog is by word of mouth, so you want to get people talking about you. That means you have to spend a lot of time on social networks and on other blogs, because first you need to go where the audience is. You have to establish a strong personal brand that's unique and compelling, and your blog design has to reflect the level of professionalism you're aiming for.

To summarize, here are the recommended ways to be successful with a blog that serves as a platform for fame (such as the blog shown in Figure 4-5):

- ✔ Your writing style has to be charismatic, unique, and appealing to a large audience.
- ✔ You have to work consistently on getting exposure for yourself while you're also maintaining a rigorous writing schedule.
- ✔ Establish a strong personal brand.
- ✔ Be able to sell yourself to book publishers, event managers, and large company brands.
- ✔ Invest in a professionally designed blog theme.

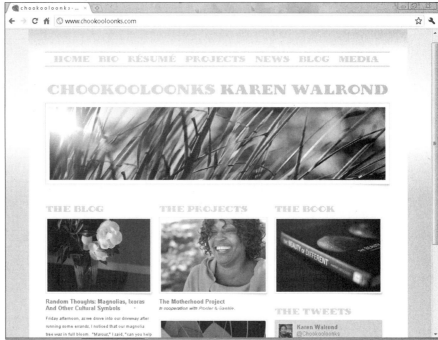

Figure 4-5:
Karen
Walrond
blogs at
Chookoo-
loonks,
works with
big name
sponsors,
and has
published
her first
book, *The
Beauty of
Different.*

A great example of this kind of blogging success is Karen Walrond of Chookooloonks (`www.chookooloonks.com`). Karen has built up a strong personal brand as a talented photographer, writer, and blogger. She's worked with brands such as Nikon and Procter and Gamble, and authored the best-selling book, *The Beauty of Different.* Check out her gorgeous, award-winning blog in Figure 4-5.

Writing a Monetization Plan of Action

Choose a blogging business model that best fits your work style and blogging ambitions. Though blogging is largely about doing what you love and playing to your strengths, it's okay to start thinking about monetization by noticing what you *don't* like:

- If you hate working with clients, then choose to pursue the advertising and sponsorship model or the product-sales model.

- If you hate the thought of learning search engine optimization and don't feel like you can bring in hundreds of thousands of page views a month, then set up shop as a freelancer or pursue a full-time job with your blog instead.

Prioritize your action steps

It can be easy to get overwhelmed with all the work it takes to get your blog to the level of success you want. Instead of learning everything you can learn about blogging techniques in general, choose two or three top priorities that you know will make the biggest impact on your income. As you start to master these skills, add new initiatives one at a time. You may never have to learn anything about (say) e-mail marketing to be successful; most bloggers don't. But if your business model requires it, then make it a priority.

After you decide on the direction of your blog, and choose the actions you want to take to earn revenue, break down the tasks you need to do into chunks and write them down in a simple one- or two-page document. I show you a very simple example in the next section. I know you probably want to skip this step, but I do highly recommend it. Translating your business ideas into action steps usually makes the process of getting from here to there much more attainable than if you just let the ideas swim around in your head.

Create a sales funnel

For bloggers who are selling services, I highly recommend building a formal sales funnel. Okay, that takes a bit of work, but it builds the most solid online business possible. A *sales funnel* works by attracting potential customers with free or very-low-cost items, and then convincing these potential customers to sign up on your mailing list or subscribe to your RSS feed. When you have their contact information, you can start to build a relationship with them, ensuring that when they're ready to make a purchase, they come to you. Offering your potential customers a range of products at different prices helps build up their trust, eventually making it easier for them to invest in your higher-priced items or services. If you normally earn your income by charging by the hour or by the project, a sales funnel also serves to create diversity in how you bring in your income. That protects you against putting too many eggs in one basket.

See how the sales funnel works in Figure 4-6: You have your largest number of potential customers on your mailing list, and gradually smaller numbers of actual customers as the price of your services increases.

After you create your plan of action and put it into attainable goals (see the "Setting Your Blogging Goals" section for details), you can then focus on the chapters in this book that you know will be the most helpful as you grow your blogging business.

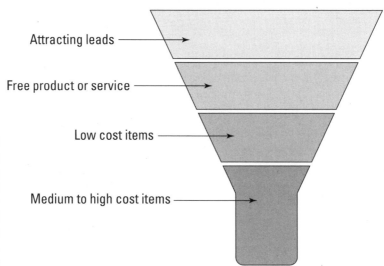

Figure 4-6:
Create a
sales funnel
to sell your
professional
services as
a blogger.

Attract leads

This is how you attract clients interested in your services to your website:

- ✔ Post blog entries that offer free advice.
- ✔ Get mentioned in the press.
- ✔ Meet potential clients on Facebook and Twitter.
- ✔ Ensure your content can be found in search engines.
- ✔ Publish articles on other websites.

Free product or service

In exchange for your potential clients' contact information, offer items such as:

- ✔ Audio recordings
- ✔ White papers
- ✔ Newsletters
- ✔ e-courses
- ✔ Mini e-books
- ✔ Resource lists and forms
- ✔ Free graphics
- ✔ One-time teleseminars
- ✔ Free consultations

Low-cost items

Offer a range of low-cost products you develop that offer your expertise without having a client work directly with you. These products let your clients know what it would be like to work with you without risking a large amount of money. They include

- ✔ Workshops
- ✔ Consulting packages
- ✔ e-books
- ✔ Group coaching
- ✔ Membership sites
- ✔ Video or audio series

Medium- to high-cost items

When people hire you for large projects or ongoing work, you're selling them your medium-to-high-priced items. These are the clients you want most of all; they pay you well for your expertise and also give you valuable experience to build your portfolio of work experience. Your medium-to-high-priced items might include

- ✔ One-on-one coaching or consulting
- ✔ Monthly retainer clients
- ✔ Project management work

Setting Your Blogging Goals

After reading about these five different blogging business models, you can see that not all blogs are created equal — a hard lesson I learned when I started my first blog network. One blog was perfect for selling freelance services; another one was perfect for selling advertising. Having so many blogs needing so many *different* marketing and sales strategies ended up splintering my efforts. But eventually, I was able to take that knowledge and create five blogs in my *next* blog network that all earned money in the same way. When I did this, all my marketing and blog-building efforts helped the entire network grow.

I got where I am today through a combination of hard work, learning from my mistakes, and by setting short- and long-term goals to direct my actions. The most effective way I've found to approach goal-setting is to decide where you want to be in three to five years and work backward from there to where you are right now. Filling in those stages is how you create your blogging business plan.

For example, say you eventually want to have a thriving social media consulting business in which you speak professionally and also write books on marketing to women. You want to reach this level of achievement in three years' time. Decide on the things you need to do to get there, being specific about the kind of work you have to do to achieve your end goal. Then start from the end goal and create milestones, working from the future back to the present and creating quantifiable action steps, like this:

✔ **End of three years: ten regular weekly clients, one speaking engagement every quarter, and first book completed.**

    a. My blog will have 15,000 monthly visitors.

    b. My mailing list will have 5,000 subscribers.

    c. I will have written articles for five prominent publications.

    d. I will have created five downloadable e-products that potential clients can purchase without hiring me directly.

✔ **End of two years: five regular weekly clients, and book proposal written.**

    a. My blog will have 10,000 monthly visitors.

    b. My mailing list will have 2,500 subscribers.

    c. I will have written articles for two prominent publications.

    d. I will have created three downloadable e-products that potential clients can purchase without hiring me directly.

✔ **End of one and a half years: three regular weekly clients.**

    a. My blog will have 7,000 monthly visitors.

    b. My mailing list will have 1,750 subscribers.

    d. I will have applied to write for five prominent publications.

    c. I will have created two downloadable e-products that potential clients can purchase without hiring me directly.

✔ **End of one year: one regular weekly client.**

    a. I will have completed ten short-term projects with clients who could turn into regular weekly clients.

    b. My mailing list will have 1,200 subscribers.

    c. I will have chosen the five publications that I want to apply to write for.

    d. I will have created one downloadable e-product that potential clients can purchase without hiring me directly.

At this point, imagine you've been at this process for six months, and have worked backward to the present. Here's what the short-term here-and-now entries look like . . . .

✔ **End of six months: hired for two short-term client projects.**

    a. I have tested my mailing list subscription form, in several placements on my blog template, to determine which brings in the most subscribers.

    b. I have created one free e-product that is only available to mailing list subscribers.

    c. My mailing list has 500 subscribers.

    b. I have learned basic search engine optimization techniques and have written 20 blog posts that my potential clients would find useful.

✔ **End of three months: Ready to find clients.**

    a. My professional blog template is completed.

    b. My mailing list is set up and ready to add subscribers.

    c. My e-mail newsletter is formatted and ready to send.

    d. I have created a free download to attract subscribers to my blog and mailing list.

    e. My Services page has specific service packages that potential clients can hire me for.

✔ **This month:**

    a. I will get my Facebook page and business Twitter accounts set up.

    b. I will review various e-mail marketing vendors and choose one.

    c. I will hire a designer to customize my blog template, or I will learn enough about template design to customize it myself.

Of course, this list would be completely different for someone who wants to build a blog that earns money from advertising. Instead of mailing list objectives and developing e-products, this blogger will set goals for number of posts written, creating a media kit, number of regular monthly advertisers, and increasing number of page views per visitor.

Setting goals and working out the action steps by "walking backwards" will help you to determine whether what you want to accomplish is realistic or not. If you want 50,000 e-mail subscribers in two years, breaking it down from end to beginning will force you to realize that you'll need to get about 10,000 new subscribers in your first six months. Unless you're already a master at e-mail marketing, this number just isn't going to be attainable — but it gives you a set course for the work you need to accomplish over the long term. This will help you tremendously as other opportunities inevitably arise over the course of time. It is easy to get distracted by fun new projects, but if you evaluate them in the context of how they'll help you get to your end goal, it will be easier to decide whether each one is a worthy project to pursue.

Just because you plot a course for the next few years doesn't mean that you're locked into an inflexible plan of action. Sometimes you can't anticipate a future fork in the road. For example, just two years ago, I never would have guessed I would be running a kids' activities blog network. But all the work I did on my previous projects is what enabled me to be so successful with my current project today.

Chapter 5

Measuring Your Success

*W*hen I was in college, taking a statistics and data class was a requirement for me to graduate. But I hated, and I mean *hated,* statistics and data. I never understood how they could ever be important or relevant to any career I would ever be interested in pursuing. So I talked my guidance counselor into letting me skip the class. I honestly can say that is one of my biggest educational regrets — you may not believe me now, but statistics can be creative, insightful, and downright fascinating.

Understanding the statistics behind your blog can make a huge impact on how much you can earn from the blogging work that you do. Your statistics will let you know where your readers find you, the content they like the most, how much they engage with your content, and what kind of people are reading your blog.

In this chapter, I introduce you to the tools you need to generate those statistics. Don't worry, they are super-easy to set up and will take you less than 30 minutes to do so — plus they're free! Then I dive into explaining those statistics and show you how to make practical use of those numbers. I also break down what these numbers mean to you as a publisher — and what they mean to potential advertisers.

Appreciating and Using Statistics

Until now, you've probably been relying on your readers' comments for feedback on your writing. But your blog analytics will give you feedback from *all* your readers — and you may be surprised as to what people really think. Sometimes you'll find that posts can be very popular and viewed frequently, but have the fewest comments of all. Other times you can spend all day writing a post that you think is good enough to land you a book deal — and it becomes your least-viewed post of all time. I say this because I've experienced both firsthand. Even after five years of blogging, I still can't accurately guess (at least not 100 percent of the time) what content is going to be a hit or a miss. Whenever I'm in doubt, I turn to my analytics to help me decide what content has the best possible chance of success.

Your blog analytics are a treasure trove of insights into what your readers are looking for when they visit your blog. The keywords people use to find your site via search engines are particularly helpful. These words and phrases are the questions they're seeking answers to. When certain keywords start showing up more frequently, they are content suggestions handed to you on a silver platter that are sure to be a hit and increase your traffic.

Choosing the Right Measurement Tools

Getting great analytics software on your blog can be expensive — really expensive. The good news is that you probably won't need such robust tools until you make enough money to pay for them anyway. In the meantime, fantastic free tools such as Google Analytics and Quantcast are easy to set up and use. The accompanying sidebar briefs you on how these programs work.

Tools to measure your blog traffic

When choosing analytics software, keep in mind that you want the software to keep track of as much data as possible — but you also need it to present the data in a way you can understand. Many options are available, but for simplicity's sake, I'm going to focus on the few that I think are the best of the bunch — the ones considered industry standards: Google Analytics and FeedBurner. If you want to explore other options, Wikipedia maintains a list of current Web analytics software at `http://wikipedia.org/wiki/List_of_web_analytics_software`.

Setting up Google Analytics

The tracking software most widely used by bloggers is Google Analytics. The reason it's so popular is that it's comparable to some of the most expensive analytics solutions available — but it's free! Google Analytics is also a very widely accepted tool to use when you're reporting your traffic statistics to potential sponsors and advertisers.

Google Analytics will measure things such as the number of monthly unique visitors that read your blog, where your readers come from, how they find your site, and what content they're most interested in reading. Other things that sponsors or PR firms may be interested in are your bounce rate, pages per visitor, and average time on site.

To set up Google Analytics on your blog:

1. **Go to** `www.google.com/analytics`.

2. **Click the Access Analytics button and sign in with your Google account.**

   If you don't have a Google account, you can sign up for free.

3. **Click the Sign Up button under Sign Up for Google Analytics.**

   The Analytics: New Account Sign Up page appears.

4. **Create a new Google Analytics account by entering the URL of your blog in the website's URL text box.**

   Leave off the `http://` because it causes an Invalid Input warning.

   The Account Name will automatically populate with the same URL you just entered. You can leave it this way or change it to a different name. This name is for your organizational purposes only; the name you choose has no bearing on how it works.

5. **Choose your country of residency from the Time Zone Country or Territory drop-down list.**

6. **Choose your time zone from the Time Zone drop-down list.**

7. **Click the Continue button.**

8. **Enter your first and last names in the name fields, select your country (again), and click Continue.**

9. **Select the Yes check box to agree to the Google Analytics Terms of Service and click the Create New Account button.**

   Your Data Sharing Settings are set by default to share your Google Analytics data with other Google products and to share the data anonymously with other Google users to gather benchmarking data. I recommend leaving the settings this way. It's helpful to be able to link your Google Analytics with other Google products, such as AdSense. And the benchmarking data is simply helpful to all other website owners who want to see how their sites compare with others on similar topics. Click the Edit Settings link if you wish to change this, or click the Learn More link to get a more detailed explanation of what these things mean.

   Google Analytics generates a unique code for you to copy and paste into your blog template, as shown in Figure 5-1.

Figure 5-1:
Google
Analytics
tracking
code.

A unique Google Analytics tracking code is generated; to copy it to a Blogger blog, copy the unique code to your clipboard and paste it into an untitled Blogger gadget, as explained in Chapter 2.

To add the Google Analytics tracking code to a WordPress blog, copy the unique code generated to your clipboard, paste it into an untitled WordPress widget (as explained in Chapter 2), and drag it onto your sidebar.

These methods of adding the tracking code to your blog won't visibly show up on your blog template; the code is not viewable on your blog pages.

If your WordPress blog uses a template that uses a different layout for different pages (for example, a template that has a different layout for the home page and the rest of the pages), make sure you place the Google Analytics widget so that it appears on all your template layouts. In this example, that would mean adding the widget to both your home page sidebar and your blog sidebar. You can get around this by using the Google Analyticator plugin, which will add the code for you. You can find it at `http://wordpress.org/extend/plugins/google-analyticator`.

Later on in this chapter, I show you how to use Google Analytics. But while you're setting things up, I show you how to set up a FeedBurner account.

Setting up FeedBurner

Every blog generates what's called an *RSS feed.* RSS stands for Real Simple Syndication. An RSS feed allows your blog visitors to follow your content in a *feed reader,* like Google Reader (`www.google.com/reader`) and My Yahoo! (`http://my.yahoo.com`). When a blog visitor subscribes to your feed, they can read your blog posts in a feed reader instead of on your site. This is a great benefit for your visitors, because it makes it easy for them to read all their favorite blogs in one place. Additionally, it offers some of the same benefits of e-mail newsletters (described in Chapter 8), primarily by reminding your visitors to come back to your site more frequently.

Your blog's feed statistics are just as important as your traffic statistics. Your RSS readers may not visit your site in order to read your blog posts, because they will be reading them in a feed reader. Google Analytics can't track visitors unless they visit your blog's Web page. Using a service such as FeedBurner allows you to track *all* readers of your blog, whether they come to your site or read it in a feed reader.

To set up FeedBurner on your blog:

1. **Go to** `http://feedburner.google.com.`

2. **Sign in to FeedBurner with your Google account.**

   You can sign up for a Google account for free if you don't already have one.

3. **On the My Feeds page, type your blog URL into the Burn a Feed Right this Instant text box, and click the Next Button.**

4. **Some blogs will generate two or more different kinds of feeds, Atom and RSS. It doesn't matter which one you choose to use here, so you can leave it at the default selection and click the Next button.**

5. **Check to make sure that FeedBurner created the account with your accurate blog name, as shown in Figure 5-2.**

   Your blog name and description can be changed later if necessary. But it's very important to also *make sure you approve of the feed URL that it generates for you.* This *can't* be changed later, so make sure it's one you want to keep for the life of your blog. If you want to change it, type your changes into the Feed Address text box and click the Next button.

   FeedBurner only distributes unique URLs, so if you try to take a feed address that is taken, you'll get an error that says "The feed was cancelled and not activated." Just type a different address into the Feed Address text field and click the Next button again until you find an address that is available.

If you have problems with FeedBurner identifying your proper feed address, make sure you have at least one blog post up on your blog. If that doesn't fix the problem, try going to the W3C Validator service at `http://validator.w3.org/feed`. Enter your full blog URL (including `http://`) into the Address text box and click the Check button. On the next page, the service lets you know if it found a valid feed address on your blog — and if so, displays it in the text field at the top of the page. You can retry setting up FeedBurner with the feed address you get from the W3C Validator site.

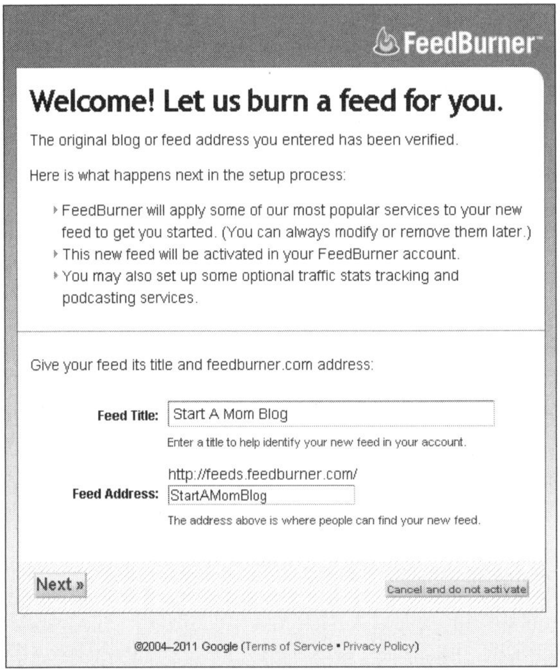

Figure 5-2:
Google
FeedBurner
feed name
and address
confirmation.

You can and should promote your RSS feed to your readers prominently on your blog. You can do this by putting a feed icon in your sidebar and linking it to your new FeedBurner feed address (here's another use for WordPress widgets and Blogger gadgets!). There are a ton of beautiful free RSS icons on TemplateLite at `www.templatelite.com/feed-icons-buttons-collectionpart-2`.

As your blog RSS feed gathers subscribers over time, FeedBurner will become more useful to you. When you log in to your FeedBurner account, it will let you know how many subscribers you have, and how it grows over time. Your FeedBurner Feed Stats will also let you know how many subscribers viewed your blog posts in your feed, and how many subscribers clicked on links in your feed.

To view your FeedBurner Feed Stats, log in to your FeedBurner account at `www.feedburner.com`. Click your Feed Title. Your Feed Stats Dashboard appears. Under today's date, the Number of Subscribers appears first. The *Reach* number appears next — this number refers to the total number of people who have viewed or clicked the content in your feed. Below that, you see a short list of popular feed items. This information will only appear if you have existing subscribers who have taken actions on your feed in the last 30 days.

Tools to measure your readers' demographics

Potential sponsors and advertisers need to work with bloggers who reach their target market. A *target market* is simply marketing jargon for a specific group of people whose characteristics fit them into a very general stereotype. It's also known as a *target audience.* By virtue of being a mom blogger, you probably are already attracting one broad target market to your blog: other moms. But you need to know more than that in order to attract potential sponsors and advertisers.

Does your blog attract new moms with infants? Empty-nest moms with kids in college? Working moms? Green moms? Crafty moms? Libertarian moms? Or maybe you're a mom writing a blog for new dads? For teachers? For marketers who want to reach moms? The list is infinite.

There are two ways to measure the general makeup of your blog's readership. The hard way is to ask them via a survey, which can be difficult to administer and a struggle to attract participation. The easy way is to use Quantcast, a free tool that will measure your audience demographics for you automatically, using estimates based on sample users who share their surfing information with Quantcast via a toolbar.

To set up Quantcast on your blog, follow these steps:

1. **Go to** `www.quantcast.com` **and set up a new account.**

   Quantcast sends you a verification e-mail. After you've confirmed your e-mail address with Quantcast, you can sign in to your account and continue to Step 2.

2. **Click the Generate Tag button.**

   There are two Generate Tag buttons on the page — they both do the same thing.

3. **Copy and paste this code into your blog template.**

   It can go in the same place as your Google Analytics code as explained earlier in this chapter. You can ignore the Multiple P-codes option unless you have an advanced setup with multiple blogs in a blog network. If that's the case, then read the instructions by clicking on the What's This link for your custom setup.

4. **Click the Scan the Site button.**

5. **Enter your blog URL into the text box, as shown in Figure 5-3.**

6. **Click the Scan Site button.**

By default, Quantcast makes your traffic and audience demographics public information on its website. If you prefer to keep this information private, be sure to go into your Quantcast account settings and change your privacy settings. This will not interfere with its ability to measure your site traffic. But just so you know, potential advertisers may also be looking for you on Quantcast. You may want to make this information easily available to them if you plan on selling your own advertising.

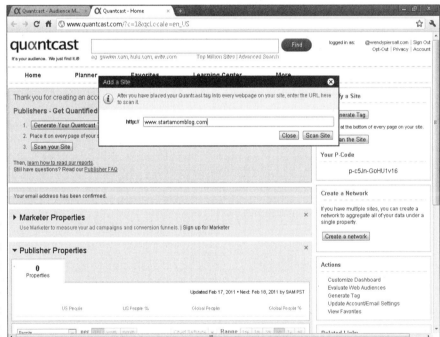

Figure 5-3: Setting up your Quantcast account.

You can change your privacy settings by logging into Quantcast and clicking the Settings link next to your website name. Under the Public Access section on the next page, you can select the check boxes for the items you wish to make public and deselect the check boxes for the items you wish to make private. To save these changes, click on the Save All Settings button.

Making Your Analytics Easy to Understand

After your measurement tools are set up, you'll need to let them gather data for a while so you actually have something to view in your reports. For a true representation of your audience, I recommend waiting at least one month before you make any conclusions about your site visitors — three months is even better if you're extra-patient (which I am not, so it's okay if you aren't, either!).

Your Google Analytics account may seem a little confusing and intimidating at first, especially if you don't know how to read the reports. But don't worry — the following sections give you the essentials of how to read your data so that you can improve your blog content, grow your traffic, and pitch your blog effectively to brands and PR firms.

To view your Google Analytics reports, log in to your account and simply click the View Report link next to your blog name on your Google Analytics home page. This will bring you to your Dashboard, which gives you the highlights of the most important information in your analytics account.

In the next sections, I walk you through the most important reports in Google Analytics. These reports give you the most insights into your blog readers, and also give you the most important information you need when you're preparing your blog to work with advertisers and brands. In each section, I explain why the information is relevant to you, and why brands care about the information in that specific report.

Absolute Unique Visitors report

The *Absolute Unique Visitors report* by default shows the number of people that visited your site over the last 30 days. If one visitor comes three times over that month, that person is only counted once.

To view the Absolute Unique Visitors report, go to your Dashboard and click Visitors on the left menu. Then in the main area of the page, click the Absolute Unique Visitors link. Figure 5-4 shows how the Absolute Unique Visitors report is displayed in Google Analytics.

The following list explains why brands want to know the number of your monthly unique visitors and how you can use this number to track your success:

- ✔ **Why brands care about your Monthly Unique Visitors report:** They need this number to base their calculations on how many true qualified leads they may get out of working with you. Brands want to know how many individuals they can reach if they work with you. If you have 100 Monthly Unique Visitors that visit your site every day for 30 days, you will have 3,000 Visits. If you give them the latter number, it misrepresents the actual number of unique visitors your blog attracts.

- ✔ **Why you should care about your Monthly Unique Visitors report:** This is your baseline measurement for growth. You'll want to track this number over time to ensure you're drawing new visitors to your blog, as well as retaining your current readers.

Figure 5-4:
The
Absolute
Unique
Visitors
report in
Google
Analytics.

Pages Per Visitor and Average Length of Visit reports

Your Pages Per Visitor report is the average number of pages a visitor views with no more than 30 minutes between page requests. Your Average Length of Visit report is the average actual length of time a visitor spends on your site. If you have a high pages-per-visitor count (over 3 to 4), or average length of visit (over 2–3 minutes), it means that readers come to your blog and want to stick around.

To view the Pages Per Visitor and Average Length of Visit report, go to your Dashboard and click Visitors on the left menu. Then, in the main page area, click Average Pageviews to see your pages per visitor; click Time on Site to see your average length of visit. Figure 5-5 is an example of your Visitors Overview that reports both of these numbers.

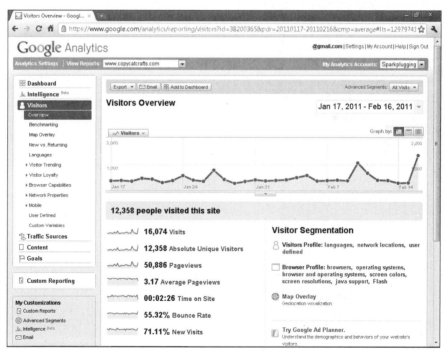

Figure 5-5: Visitors Overview in Google Analytics.

Here's how these reports give both you and your potential advertisers an understanding of how engaged your readers are.

- ✔ **Why brands care about your Pages Per Visitor and Average Length of Visit reports:** If those figures are high, they suggest that you have an engaged audience that interacts with the content you create, and you probably influence their purchasing decisions. A high number is very relative — on a community forum, a well-engaged visitor will view ten or more pages and stay for more than five minutes. On a news site, an average visitor may view only two pages and stay for a little over a minute.

  A blog that gets a lot of comments certainly shows you have an engaged audience. But for the kinds of blogs that aren't big drivers of conversations (for example, a coupon blog), these numbers show your reader engagement in another way.

- ✔ **Why you should care about Pages Per Visitor and Average Length of Visit reports:** Growing these numbers is evidence that your readers are increasingly satisfied with your content and makes it more likely they'll recommend your site to others. Your readers are probably finding what they're looking for on your site instead of elsewhere on the Web, which means they'll likely return in the future. Plus: If you're selling advertising, more page views can mean more revenue in your pocket. The more advertising views you can generate, the more you have to sell.

  If you can increase the number of pages viewed per visitor, you can sometimes increase your advertising revenue, even without more people visiting your site. This is possible when you are getting paid for every ad view you can display — see Chapter 11 for more about this kind of advertising. You can increase your pages per visitor by writing longer posts and breaking them up into several pages, or by recommending related content to your readers at the end of every post.

Traffic Sources report

Your site traffic will come from four sources: search engines, other websites, direct traffic (people who have bookmarked your site or typed in your site address), and your RSS feed. A healthy site will have a good balance of traffic from all four sources. You never want to have all your eggs in one basket unless you're the Easter Bunny, and frankly, not even then.

To view the Traffic Sources report, go to your Dashboard and click Traffic Sources on the left menu. See Figure 5-6 for a sample breakdown of the Traffic Sources report for a blog.

The following list describes your search engine traffic. You can find this specific report from the Traffic Sources report by clicking the Search Engines link.

report: If you have a high percentage of you're acquiring new readers on a regular es determined by your keywords.

Engine Traffic report: Search engines of traffic over the long term, and provide f your website.

arch Engine Traffic report: Search mendous amounts of traffic, but you don't high. Google can (and sometimes does) ou could lose more than half of your visi- engine traffic more in Chapter 6.

that comes to your blog by clicking no specific RSS Feed report in Google Analytics, because feed traffic is categorized under Other. You can still find this specific information from the Traffic Sources report by clicking the All Traffic Sources link in the left menu, then type **Feed** into the Filter Source/ Medium Containing text field.

Figure 5-6:
Traffic
Sources
Overview
in Google
Analytics.

- ✔ **Traffic Source: Your Feed report:** If you have a high proportion of traffic coming to your blog by clicking through your blog feed, this means you have highly engaged readers who trust you and listen to what you say.

- ✔ **Why brands care about your RSS Feed Traffic report:** Again, an engaged audience will likely listen to what a blogger has to say.

- ✔ **Why you should care about your RSS Feed Traffic report:** Your feed is kind of like a mailing list, and is a true asset to your business to reach your readers off of your website on a regular basis.

The following list describes your Referring Sites traffic. You can find this specific report from the Traffic Sources report by clicking the Referring Sites link.

- ✔ **Traffic Source: Referring Sites report:** This means that other bloggers and websites respect you and your content enough to talk about and link to you.

- ✔ **Why brands care about your referral traffic:** Your blogging influence likely spills over beyond your blog onto others' blogs. And that means a brand that places ads with you might reach not only your readers but other bloggers' readers, too.

- ✔ **Why you should care about your referral traffic:** Visitors from other blogs and websites similar to yours are the ones most likely to subscribe to your feed, comment on your posts, or become repeat visitors in the future. Plus: Link building is important to get your blog better ranked in the search engines.

Top Content report

Your Top Content report shows the most popular posts on your blog. Your popular content gives you insight into why your readers come to you. The topics of these posts tell you what people like, even when they don't comment.

To view the Top Content report, go to your Dashboard and click Content on the left menu, and then click Top Content. See an example Top Content report in Figure 5-7.

The following list describes why the Top Content report is indispensable to the long-term success of your blog:

- ✔ **Why brands care about your Top Content report:** Your *top content* defines your blog for both your readers and your advertisers. You can tell them, "My readers come to me for great quilting tutorials" or "My readers come to me to discuss the political issues important to parents of disabled children" or "My readers come to me to share the humor in potty training a three-year-old."

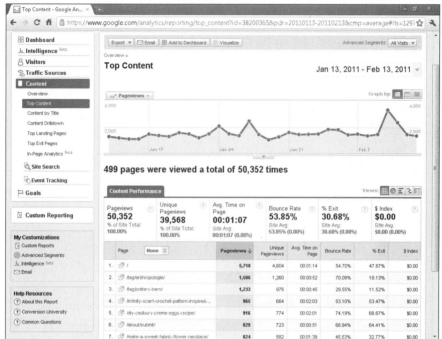

Figure 5-7:
Top Content
Report in
Google
Analytics.

✔ **Why you should care about your Top Content report:** You'll find over time that occasionally the posts you think will be extremely popular will flop, and other posts that seem like an afterthought become your readers' favorite content. This is incredibly important feedback that you should be using to guide your content strategy.

Every blog I've ever created (except for the first ones) were spinoffs of extremely popular blog posts. Each of these blogs has been more successful than their predecessors, so it literally "pays" to pay attention to what your readers want from you.

Top Keywords report

Your Top Keywords report shows the words and phrases that search engines have associated with your content and used to find your site.

To view the Top Keywords report, go to your Dashboard and on the left menu click Traffic Sources; then click Keywords. Figure 5-8 shows you what the Top Keywords report looks like in Google Analytics.

The following list describes important aspects of the keywords people use to find your site:

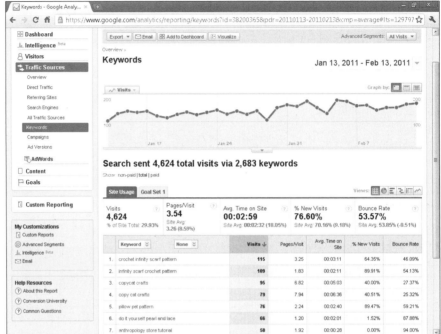

- ✔ **Why brands care about your Top Keywords report:** If you rank for keywords related to their products or services, they'll want their name appearing on your site.

- ✔ **Why you should care about your Top Keywords report:** You want to make sure that the keywords that appear in this report are the ones you want to be associated with you and your content. If you dig deeper into these phrases, you should also be able to uncover reader questions that they may not be asking you in your comments.

Important audience demographics

Your audience demographics define your typical blog reader in general categories. Google Analytics doesn't measure this information as well as Quantcast does — or at all. In your Quantcast profile under U.S. Demographics, you can see whether your typical reader is male or female, of what age group, and the general ages of the children in the home — as well as his or her nationality, household income, and even level of education. Don't worry — none of it is personally identifiable information. Demographics can't tell you all this stuff about specific readers; they just aggregate the information. Take a look at the demographic breakdown in a sample Quantcast profile in Figure 5-9.

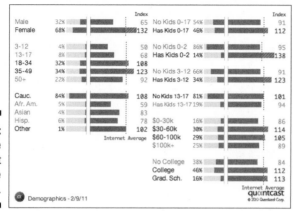

Figure 5-9:
Sample
Quantcast
audience
profile.

Here's why this information is such a big deal to brands — and how the information helps you:

- ✔ **Why brands care about your audience demographics:** Brands are most interested in the gender and age range of your readers, whether or not they have children in their home, and their household income. They also may want to know what percentage of your visitors is U.S.-based. They need to know whether the readers of your blog fit their pre-determined target market.

- ✔ **Why you should care about your audience demographics:** Knowing who your readers are makes it easier for you to create content that they'll love. You can do this by making educated guesses about the general interests of the typical reader that visits your blog. For example, if you know that you have a lot of readers who are young mothers and live in households that earn less than $30,000 a year, you can guess they will be interested in money-saving tips for their families. Well, *anyone* might be interested in this kind of information, but you can be more confident about that assumption with an audience like in this example.

Highlighting Your Assets No Matter How Much Traffic You Have

The Google Analytics and Quantcast analytic tools have already measured your influence and have translated it into the numbers and data brands need to see. Don't worry if you don't have a lot of traffic. There are gems to be found in your data, no matter how many readers you have.

Mining your analytics data for insights on your audience

When you know how to read your Google Analytics reports and Quantcast data, you can start looking for information that you think brands would be interested in. For example, if your top content happens to be on the topic of being a mom entrepreneur, an office-supply chain would probably want to get its message in front of your readers. If you rank well on Google for bread recipes, a maker of kitchen appliances — especially bread machines — would be a smart prospect to pursue as a sponsor.

When you're gathering your numbers together to build a media kit or as part of a pitch, get the hard part out of the way first. There's no two ways around it: Brands will want to know how many visitors you have. If you skirt around the issue, they could assume the worst — that you have 10 visitors, when in fact you have 10,000. So just get over any embarrassment you may feel about how many readers you have, and just tell your prospective sponsor up front. Because it's not all about quantity — the quality of the attention your blog gets is important too.

For someone with a half a million visitors a month, the numbers seem impressive. But some brands may, in fact, prefer to work with the person who only has 1,000 visitors. The reasoning is that the huge audience might be too varied to fit into the brand's target market. But the brand might know for certain that the smaller audience would be interested in its product. Brands would get a better sell-through from 10 percent of 1,000 viewers than from .001 percent of 500,000 readers.

Building your credentials with your social media presence

Most bloggers also have a presence on other social media sites such as Twitter and Facebook. You can discover how to use these important tools in Chapter 6. But don't forget that your influence on social networking sites is important to brands, too. Why? It means that if they work with you, they aren't just reaching the eyeballs that read your blog. They also have the potential to reach your extended community, which is very valuable to them.

That said, I don't recommend just building followers and adding friends simply for the sake of boosting your numbers. That approach can end up diluting your influence instead of building it. But brands are definitely interested in bloggers who have a large social circle. They use it as another measure of your influence.

Chapter 6

Attracting Readers to Your Blog

In This Chapter

▶ Creating a personal brand and a brand for your blog

▶ Getting a professional-looking blog on a budget

▶ Understanding the benefits of networking with other bloggers

▶ Using social media to drive traffic to your blog

▶ Attracting visitors with well-run giveaways

*W*ith 4 million mom bloggers, there really is no topic that hasn't been blogged about already. Yet I continue to be surprised by the ability of two blogs to be so much alike and yet so much different. For example, last year I started up a blog called CopycatCrafts as a way to highlight craft bloggers who were putting together tutorials to make DIY versions of high-end products they were finding in their favorite stores. In an initially disappointing coincidence, another blog called KnockOff Decor started soon thereafter with the same goal. Yet it took less than a month for our two blogs to become unique websites that complemented each other rather than competing against each other. My readers expressed more interest in jewelry, clothing, and copycat recipes. Her readers wanted home décor ideas, and our blogs rarely overlap content at all. We have even found a few ways to help each other grow, because we both believe there's enough room in the blogosphere for everyone. In this chapter, I show you exactly how to create your own unique blog and brand that will showcase your natural talents and stand out from the crowd, even when another blogger has the same idea as yours.

I believe the blogosphere will never have too many bloggers, just as there can never be too many books in the world. But I will add that there *can* be too many mediocre blogs. Because books take a significant investment to publish, editors are very picky about the titles that actually make it into print. Blogs are free or extremely cheap to start up, so there's nothing stopping even very poor writers from becoming bloggers. The only way to start a blog and make a living with it is to stand out from the crowd and create a unique identity for yourself online.

Setting Yourself Apart with Your Personal Brand and Blog Brand

It's important to differentiate between creating a unique blog brand and a unique personal brand for yourself. A *blog brand* is the combination of several factors such as the name, design, topics, and writing style of a blog, which all send signals about what readers can expect from reading a blog. A *personal brand* is the combination of your areas of expertise, your personality, and your interests, which combine to project a unique image to the world.

Your blog is not you, but it is an extension of your personal brand. It resides in one place, while you can appear anywhere — on other blogs, on Facebook or Twitter, or even in magazines and on TV. Of course, the two are always interconnected, but they are and should be treated as separate entities. Your personal brand is what you stand for and want to be known for. It follows you everywhere and stays consistent no matter what you do and who you interact with. Your blog's brand, on the other hand, is a specific business entity that may or may not always be a part of your career.

Crafting an extraordinary personal brand

You can't simultaneously fit in and stand out. So as you work on defining your personal brand, you want to emphasize your personal strengths and the things that make you uniquely you. More aspects to consider are

- **What you're known for:** These are things you do well or the topics on which your opinion is already sought by family and friends.

- **Your interests and passions:** In order to rise above the crowd, your enthusiasm for your field will be your biggest asset as you gain readers and visibility.

- **Building trust:** Because your personal brand will be a big part of your online presence, you need to build trust in your community as a person who has integrity, is honest, and has her readers best interests' at heart. Being incongruent and losing the trust of your readers and colleagues will immediately undermine any success you've gained.

- **Positioning yourself as an expert:** No matter what your chosen field is, your personal brand should serve to boost your professional credentials. It also signals what opportunities you want to be considered for once you attract enough readers to pursue sponsorships and advertisers.

Personal branding expert Dan Schawbel makes a very important point about how your personal brand can affect your professional success: "When it comes to the Web, you're graded based solely on what's observable. What others say about you can be more influential than what you say about yourself." For more information on personal branding, I recommend Dan Schawbel's blog at `www.personalbrandingblog.com`.

For example, a mom who has developed a very powerful personal brand is Liz Gumbinner. Her personal blog, Mom-101 (`www.mom-101.com`), talks about her family life living in New York City, having a birthday on 9/11, and being a working mother; it also mentions of her left-leaning political views. She also has a career in advertising and co-founded one of the most successful blogs in our community, Cool Mom Picks (`www.coolmompicks.com`). Liz and one or both of her blogs have been named to numerous lists of the best of the best bloggers and social media moms. But when many people think of Liz, they don't just think of her as Mom-101 or Cool Mom Picks, though they know these are some of her projects. People also think of her as a leader in the mom-blogging industry, an advocate and educator helping other mom bloggers, and as an extremely savvy businesswoman. She's established herself as such a well-known social media mom that she was invited to discuss hot-button parenting topics on the @KatieCouric online news program.

Your personal brand isn't something that you put together and set in stone. It's an evolving process that can change course drastically as your blogging career progresses. Lucretia Pruitt started her blogging career as GeekMommy. She took the Twitter name @geekmommy as well, and began establishing herself as an expert voice discussing marketing, technology, and business. Her initial inspiration was to utilize her background in IT and as a college professor to discuss what it was like to be a parent in a world filled with new technology. The brand GeekMommy stuck well — too well, she says now. She became an extremely influential voice in the mom-blogging community, becoming one of the first Walmart Moms when they were still the 11moms. Her readers knew she was a tech blogger, but when she met new people, they automatically assumed that her personal brand meant that she was a mommy blogger. As her career as a consultant to brands and companies began to get more established, she found that the GeekMommy brand led to perceptions that didn't accurately portray her business. Her potential clients saw her as a mom blogger, not as a consultant who could help them put together social media campaigns, do corporate training, or create new business processes that integrated social media strategy into every department of a company.

Lucretia finally closed down her GeekMommy blog and is rebuilding her personal brand separately from her blog at TheSocialJoint. At first it felt like she was throwing away years of hard work building a brand that didn't help her grow. What she has found, though, is that her time spent as GeekMommy was absolutely critical to her success in her business today. Her clients rely on her firsthand experience as a social media mom. And she frequently works with her large network of blogging friends in the community; they trust her for the same reason — she knows exactly where mom bloggers are coming from. Her personal brand as GeekMommy isn't active anymore, but it still works to her advantage.

Creating an appealing brand for your blog

The topic of branding your blog is one of the most talked-about topics among professional bloggers. That's not just because it's one of the most crucial aspects of how you get successful. It can also be an extremely subjective process that never seems to be 100 percent complete. Your blog's brand is as unique and personal as you are, and what works for one blogger may not work for another. Like your personal brand, your blog's brand evolves as you become more sophisticated as a writer and experienced as an authority in your field.

Creating a name and brand for your blog shouldn't be a rushed decision. You could build something today that's fun and compelling, only to find that it doesn't really fit with your longer-term goals. This is exactly what happened to me when I first started blogging. Unfortunately, there was really no way for me to foresee how my blogging career would change course so drastically from where I began. But today I know how to build a much stronger brand thanks to the changes I have had to make over the last five years.

Like Lucretia Pruitt of GeekMommy (I tell her story in the previous section), I built a personal brand around the name eMom that stuck to me like glue. It was deeply tied to my blog's brand eMoms at Home, as a blog for moms who wanted to start an Internet business from home. And similarly to Lucretia, I was blogging about marketing, business, and technology for moms. Because I started the blog as a hobby, I didn't really think about the long-term impact of the decision.

Soon thereafter it became clear to me that I had unintentionally boxed myself into a brand that wasn't working. The eMoms at Home name conveyed something quite different from what my blog was really about. Even my readers expressed their discomfort with my blog name. They specifically told me that they had dismissed my site as something they wouldn't be interested in, thinking it was only for at-home moms. They didn't realize that my blog was about the business and marketing topics they were interested in — until they actually read one of my blog posts. I had to wonder, at that point, how many other people weren't reading my blog because they couldn't get past the eMoms at Home name.

After extensive research on business blogging and input from my readers, I changed the name to Sparkplugging in the spring of 2008. It was a difficult transition at first, especially when it came to the technological aspects of moving the old content to a new domain. It took a full six months to get traffic and visibility back to where it was when I first made the switch. But my only regret was that I didn't do it earlier. I should have listened sooner when readers were giving me the feedback that my brand was incongruent with my blog network content. The longer I waited to make the change, the harder it was to get re-established.

So how do you develop a brand for your blog? It covers many aspects of your online presence:

- ✔ **Your blog's name and domain name:** You want the name and domain to be memorable and do one of two things: convey an immediately recognizable image (such as Redneck Mommy, Cool Mom Picks, and TipJunkie), or be so unique that you can associate your brand around your catchy name (such as Chookooloonks, Velveteen Mind, and Tatertots & Jello).

- ✔ **Your blog's tag line:** A *tag line* tells people what to expect from your blog in one short sentence. I love tag lines, because they are a great way to practice getting a big idea into as few words as possible. Plus they can be very helpful for search engine optimization if you use good keywords in them. Here are some great examples:

    - **Run Fat Girl:** From thick to thin — one mile at a time

    - **Starting Fresh at Forty:** The market collapsed and so did I

    - **BlondeMomBlog:** Pontificating about poop and pinot noir since 2005

    - **SportsGirlsPlay:** Raising happy, healthy athletes

    - **The Centsible Life:** Live the life of your dreams on a budget

    As you can tell, all of these blog names and tag lines let potential readers know exactly what to expect if they read that blog. They also let people know that perhaps the blog isn't one they would be interested in reading. This is important, because you don't want just anyone reading your blog. You want that *focused* audience I talk about in Chapter 10.

- ✔ **Your blog's visual design:** In the "Creating a Blog Design with Curb Appeal" section, I give you some tips on how to get a good-looking blog design on a budget. This is an extremely important element that will build trust and credibility with your readers and with potential advertisers. Your blog *must* look professional in order to be taken seriously by advertisers or clients.

✔ **The topics that you write about (and the topics you don't write about):** You want to choose a focused topic with a few related topics (as I describe in Chapter 10). How you inject your personality into your writing also builds your recognizable attributes as someone who is funny, entertaining, informative, or something else. What you *don't* write about also sends brand signals. You may love talking about traditional home life, but you may choose to never talk about politics, family dynamics, or your children.

✔ **How you interact with your readers and the other bloggers in your niche:** This is certainly part of your personal brand as well, but your interactions help to define what your blog is known for. Are you helpful, encouraging, or good for a snarky laugh? These things tell people what to expect when they want to read more about you on your blog.

✔ **How consistent you are with your message:** Consistency doesn't mean never straying off topic, nor does it mean blogging every day. It means setting expectations with your readers and delivering on those expectations. I've even found that my blog readers have unknowingly helped to keep me accountable to my word, because I couldn't face them unless I did what I said I would do. Keeping your actions congruent with your words is also very important.

✔ **The quality of your content:** Quality can be a subjective measure, but it also means writing words that people want to read. Not everyone will think you have a quality blog, but it's important that your readers think so, and continue to think so.

✔ **The business goals of your blog:** Everything you do on your blog should be supporting your chosen business model either directly or indirectly. (I cover blogging business models extensively in Chapter 4.) You could minimize your credibility if the things you write about on your blog conflict with your business goals — such as (for example) being a vocal critic of big businesses if you want to attract big advertising budgets from those businesses. In such a case, you should either focus on a different way of earning revenue or be sure you love big brands.

In an ideal world, you'll know how you want to portray yourself and your blog for all of the above criteria. In reality, you might only have 70–80 percent of these things defined. It's important to not let perfectionism get in the way of action (I'm not so good at that!), but it's important to work on developing your brand with all these things in mind as your blog grows.

 If you're already blogging, you may find that some of your content or image doesn't fit with what you want your brand to be. I suggest making course corrections as soon as you can, because you don't want to end up like I did: spending too much time building a brand that doesn't work for you. Even if that's the case, however, keep in mind that it's never too late to make a change. Both Lucretia and I wouldn't be where we are today if we hadn't started out with strong brands that worked well — and that we later outgrew.

Staying legal if you quote or copy another blog

You may find that another blogger has content you'd like to quote or share. This is perfectly fine if you follow the guidelines of the Fair Use Doctrine. Fair Use does not allow for the copying of entire works and more often refers to written works instead of images. But it does ensure that it's appropriate to quote someone or display images in the context of commentary, criticism, news reporting, research, teaching, library archiving, and scholarship.

The Fair Use rule for blogging is that it's appropriate to copy *partial* text or imagery from another blog if the sole purpose is to direct your own readers to the original source of the information. If you copy so much information that your own readers have no need to visit the source, then you have copied too much. If you do not link directly to the source, then you have also misused another's content.

Writing unique blog content

I frequently hear stories from bloggers who felt like their ideas were stolen. But like the example I shared with Copycat Crafts and Knockoff Decor (see the very beginning of this chapter), many times great ideas come to more than one person at a time. Ideas themselves aren't copyrightable. The only thing that distinguishes your great idea from someone else's great idea is how you put your idea into action.

When it comes to great blog content, having the unique voice and perspective that I talked about in Chapter 3 is your number-one asset. It's your own spin on a topic that creates a connection between you, your readers, and your shared interest in your chosen topics. A great example of this is how Ree Drummond of The Pioneer Woman (http://thepioneerwoman. com) discusses photography and Adobe Photoshop techniques on her blog. There's no shortage of photography tutorials, Photoshop training materials, or photography blogs. Yet Ree combines her passion for country living, family, food, and her reader community into her photography content — and suddenly it becomes difficult to find another blog covering photography and Photoshop techniques the way Ree's does. And her photography content has gotten so incredibly popular that she has a whole group of contributors writing for the section — which is pretty impressive, considering that her primary claim to fame is her cooking-and-recipe content. She frequently holds contests that attract thousands of entries, writes tutorials on how to take better pictures, and offers free downloads of Photoshop actions so her readers can re-create Ree's visual effects in their own photographs.

Ree's photography content would not appeal to photographers interested in the topics she doesn't cover, such as sports, fashion, or photojournalism. She has taken a popular, well-covered topic, injected her unique personality into it, and made it her own. You can do the same for any blog post, even if you're writing about something that seems overdone by other websites. A sewing tutorial, for example, can be made your own by adding your own tips on troubleshooting, or by featuring specialty techniques such as those for upholstery or refashioning old clothes. By adding your own photos or videos, you'll further distinguish yourself from others. Finally, you can share your own projects and patterns based on the things you love to sew, and you'll distinguish yourself from every other sewing blog or website on the Internet.

I do have to admit that ideas and blog content do get copied, which is an unfortunate reality of the Internet. For the professional content thief, there is little you can do to deter them. On this book's online Cheat Sheet (`www. dummies.com/cheatsheet/momblogging`), I have placed a few tools you can use, including how to use the free Copyscape plagiarism checker, how to file a Digital Millenium Copyright Act (DCMA) notice, and how to refute a fraudulent DCMA notice if a competitor files one against you in the hopes of damaging your business. Beyond these tactical efforts, I've found that blogs based on copied content or ideas suffer from several obstacles to success:

- ✔ Search engines are programmed to detect duplicate content and do a fairly good job of identifying the original owner.

- ✔ People with questionable ethics do damage to their reputations when their plagiarism is caught.

- ✔ Bloggers who "borrow" ideas have a difficult time growing a business because they lack the creativity necessary to become successful.

- ✔ And last, but not least, I do strongly believe in good and bad karma. Sometimes it takes a frustratingly long time to kick into action, but no bad deed goes unpunished in the end.

It's my personal philosophy that you should not try to become the punisher if you have been wronged — because by doing so you usually have to stoop to a level that is beneath you. Additionally, time you spend on any form of revenge is time you could have spent making your business stronger and more successful. Ultimately, I have found that the best revenge of all is being totally awesome at what you do best. Anything distracting you from that goal only gives an added advantage to the person who copied you in the first place.

Creating a Blog Design with Curb Appeal

In 2010, I had the opportunity to answer blogging questions on Tori Johnson's Job Club TV show. Her staff asked for my help in identifying up and coming bloggers who could ask their blogging questions for the segment.

I asked around to all my friends for examples of newer bloggers who they noticed were finding success within a year or so of getting started. I was so impressed with the examples they sent my way. These moms were smart, savvy, great writers, and really making waves. They were all different in many ways, but the first thing I noticed that they all had in common was that their blog templates were absolutely beautiful and extremely well designed. See a perfect example of this in Katie Goodman's GoodLife Eats blog (`www.goodlifeeats.com`) in Figure 6-1 — in less than two years' time she was working with brands like Quaker and Dole, and writing for the food section of Paula Deen's (from the Food Network) website.

In fact, a frequently stated working rule of business is that you have 7 seconds to make a good first impression. (For someone like me, with very little patience, I think it's a lot less — but I digress.) In 7 seconds, or even 30 seconds for that matter, new visitors can't get into the depths of your content to decide whether they like you and your blog. You might be the world's most brilliant and engaging writer, but if your blog is difficult to navigate, ugly, and unprofessional-looking, you will (unfortunately) never have a chance to impress people with your wit and intelligence, because they won't even get to the point of reading your content.

Figure 6-1: Part of Katie Goodman's early success came from having a beautifully designed blog.

This doesn't mean you have to spend a fortune on a top-notch graphic designer. One of the best things about the blogging industry as a whole is that there are many ways to get a great-looking website that's very affordable. As I explain in Chapter 2, this is an area where I think WordPress has a definite advantage over using the free Google Blogger. Because most professional bloggers use WordPress, there are simply far more resources available for WordPress blogs. This is especially true when it comes to the availability of high-quality templates that you can get for free or for a very low cost.

Creating a blog logo

If your blog is your name (such as my blog at www.wendypiersall.com), creating a logo isn't as important as when your blog has a name of its own. But when your blog does have its own name, I strongly recommend creating a logo for it. Having a logo creates a level of credibility and professionalism that you can't get with a generic name on a page. When I have launched new blogs over the years, creating a company logo is nearly always my very first step in establishing my blog's brand.

Creative and artistic bloggers may have this part pretty easy, but many of you may be in a panic right now wondering how you'll pull this off. Hiring someone to design a logo for you can be an expensive investment that you may not be ready to make just yet. Thankfully, there are many free and low-cost alternatives to this. A search for *logo makers* turns up hundreds of options.

Customizing your Blogger theme

In Chapter 2, I show you how to choose a theme in Blogger or install a theme on WordPress. Google Blogger has built in customization tools that are incredibly easy to use, which make it simple for you to adjust the design and layout of your blog. Google recently released a very sophisticated template designer tool that virtually needs no instructions to use.

If you want to customize your theme beyond what the template designer is capable of, you can grab a copy of *Google Blogger For Dummies* by Susan Gunelius, or use a site like HTML Goodies (www.htmlgoodies.com) to learn HTML.

Choosing a WordPress theme

When I first started blogging, I chose a free, good-looking theme that I was able to easily customize for my needs. I got compliments on it, and it was very user-friendly. After about a year or so, I decided I wanted to put my old graphic design skills to work and create a custom theme for my blog. I wanted a more unique and professional appearance, and I didn't want other blogs looking too much like my own. So I hired someone to convert my design into a custom WordPress theme, because I didn't know how to use the required PHP and CSS code to make it work properly.

Within a few days of installing my new template, my search engine traffic doubled. I was shocked. I asked my coder if she knew why this had happened, and she said that my old theme was very poorly written and made it very hard for search engines to find and categorize my content. Additionally, because I didn't really know what I was doing, my own adjustments (which I'd made to customize the theme) compounded the problem.

I learned my lesson when it came to using free WordPress themes from unknown sources. But there are even more dangers now, because most new websites today are built using WordPress. The highly respected WordPress developer site WPMU.org (`http://wpmu.org`) published test results regarding the safety and integrity of free themes available online. They tested ten websites that offered these themes that appeared on the first page of a Google search. Thus these would likely be considered the most reputable and high-traffic sites offering themes. Out of the ten, WPMU.org found eight sites offered themes that contained malware or malicious code, one site that automatically added spammy links to the blog in the footer, and only *one* legitimate source for clean, quality, and free WordPress themes. It's not surprising that the only site that stood up to the test was WordPress's own WordPress.org. So if you want to find a safe, *free* theme, it's in your best interests to download one only from WordPress.org at `http://wordpress.org/extend/themes`.

Another kind of WordPress theme falls into the trusted category: premium themes. These themes are put out by professional designers and developers, and I can absolutely make the case that they are worth the price you pay. The prices generally run between $50 and $100 (US dollars), and usually come with plenty of advanced layout options built into the themes themselves. Many of them have an options page or interface that makes it easy, even for beginners, to customize the themes. They also tend to have other great features such as built-in tools for search engine optimization and multiple page and post layout options; they even include the source files from Adobe Photoshop. Having these files makes it easier to edit the theme images without having to change any of the theme code, but does require that you own a copy of Photoshop to use them. If you were to hire someone to do all of this for you, it could cost you five to ten times as much as the theme price. And most of all, premium themes are beautifully created by experienced designers, and you get that great design along with plenty of tools to make your blog both functional and professional-looking. A list of WordPress.org-approved premium theme developers can be found at `http://wordpress.org/extend/themes/commercial`.

Choosing a great template to use is important, but not as important as making it unique to your website. Your blog design is an important aspect of your blog's brand. This is your chance to offer a visual representation of who you are as a blogger and what your blog is about. It's a little bit like choosing the outfit you wear to an important meeting or first date — you want your blog appearance to back up your words and intentions, just as you would when you want to make a great first impression with another person. So you will want to start with a blog template that you really love, and then make it your own by adding your favorite colors and using images that do a good job of illustrating your personality and content visually.

For those of you who consider yourselves very design-challenged, you can easily hire someone to customize a template for both free and premium themes. For those of you who are a little more experienced with design, here are the kinds of things you can do for yourself without having to change your template code very much at all:

- **Change fonts and font colors:** You have a rainbow of colors available to you when it comes to changing them in your theme. For fonts, generally you only have a handful to choose from that are Web-friendly such as Arial, Times New Roman, Trebuchet, and Georgia. For WordPress users, you can also use the All-In-One-Cufon (`www.sramekdesign.com/wordpress/plugins/all-in-one-cufon`) plugin to use a wider range of fonts for more design options.

- **Replace existing image files with your own images:** Just be sure to keep the images at the same dimensions as the previous images, so you don't have to go into the template code to make them fit. You can find the existing dimensions by viewing them in Internet Explorer. Do this by right-clicking on the image, selecting Properties, and reading the dimensions in the dialog box that appears.

- **Change background colors and designs:** Your blog posts and sidebars typically have a white background, which is best for readability. You have the option of changing the appearance of the area behind your main content. You can use a solid color, or a repeating tiled image that looks seamless when it is placed next to itself. You can find a cool seamless background image creator at `http://bgpatterns.com`.

- **Take advantage of thousands of WordPress plugins:** WordPress has such a large developer community that someone has created a plugin for nearly every function you would want on your blog. Plugins can help you create thumbnails, rearrange page elements, and add design features that your theme may not have. I talk about finding and using WordPress plugins in Chapter 2.

Using photography and images in your blog posts

Another interesting thing that successful new bloggers have in common is that they created or used beautiful and compelling images in all their blog posts. Using images within your written text makes your blog more readable and look more professional. Most people will be first drawn to reading your post headline, then scan the text for subheadings, pull quotes, and photographs with captions. These indicators help readers decide whether to stay and read more, or hit the Back button and find content that's more relevant. Walls of unbroken text turn off visitors and are difficult to read.

You need to be very careful when using others' images in your blog posts. You can't assume that just because an image is on the Web that you can use it. Unless you're using purchased stock photography or clearly marked Creative Commons images, you can't be sure you're using the images legally. This is especially true of images you find from search engines, most of which are fully copyrighted. When in doubt, ask for permission before you post someone else's work. If you offer to link back to that person's website, you'll find that many people would be happy to say yes to such a request.

So how do you make sure an image is legal to use in your blog? You have several options for legally obtaining images:

- ✔ **Take and use your own photos:** One of the better investments you can make in your blogging business is to have a good digital camera and use plenty of your own original photographs in your content. You don't need to be a professional photographer, but I have to admit that I think good photographers have an advantage as bloggers. Compelling images create another reason for readers to come back to your blog.

- ✔ **Use stock photographs:** An alternative to taking your own photographs is using stock photography. Stock photography can be expensive, but sometimes can be appropriate. iStockPhoto is a good resource for affordable stock photographs and can be found at www.istockphoto.com.

- ✔ **Search for photos that use the Creative Commons license on Flickr:** *Creative Commons* is an organization that helps copyright owners protect their work in various ways. If you want to find other people's images to use in your blog posts, you need to find works using the Attribution, Attribution-ShareAlike, or Attribution-NoDerivs licenses because you're using these images in a commercial way if you make money from your blog, or plan to in the future. (See the nearby sidebar, "Understanding how Creative Commons affects bloggers" for more about Creative Commons licenses.)

Understanding how Creative Commons affects bloggers

Creative Commons (CC) offers six levels of protections to copyright owners. These are important to understand for two primary reasons. If you ever display the copyrighted work of others on your blog, you need to ensure that each author allows this manner of re-publication. Additionally, if you want to encourage others to use or build upon your own work, you may want to apply a Creative Commons license to your own blog.

The six levels of CC licenses are:

✔ **Attribution:** You can use or alter the works in any commercial or noncommercial manner as long as you give credit to the copyright owner.

✔ **Attribution-ShareAlike:** You can use or alter the works in any commercial or non-commercial manner as long as you give the author credit and allow your own work that uses their material to be licensed under the same criteria.

✔ **Attribution-NoDerivs:** You can use the works in any commercial or noncommercial manner as long as you do not change the author's work and you give credit to the copyright owner.

✔ **Attribution-NonCommercial:** You can use or alter the works in only noncommercial circumstances as long as you give credit to the copyright owner.

✔ **Attribution-NonCommercial-ShareAlike:** You can use or alter the works in only noncommercial circumstances as long as you give credit to the copyright owner and allow your own work that uses their material to be licensed under the same criteria.

✔ **Attribution-NonCommercial-NoDerivs:** You can use the works in only noncommercial circumstances as long as you do not change the author's work and that you give credit to the copyright owner.

For more information on complying with Creative Commons licenses or using a CC license on your own work, go to `http://creativecommons.org/licenses`.

Here's how to find photos with Creative Common licenses on Flickr:

1. **Go to** `www.flickr.com`.

   If you have a Flickr account, sign in. If you don't have a Flickr account, you can still search for photos.

2. **Enter a keyword into the Search field at the top-right of the page and click the Search link.**

   A page appears with thumbnails of photos that match your keyword.

3. **On the search results page, click the Advanced Search link next to the search field.**

   The Advanced Search page appears.

4. **Scroll down and select the Only Search within Creative Commons-Licensed Content and the Find Content to Use Commercially check boxes.**

   You only need to select the Find Content to Modify, Adapt, or Build Upon check box if you plan on altering a photo from its original appearance.

5. **Click the Search button again to show only commercially available images to use.**

   Your search results appear as image thumbnails.

6. **Click a thumbnail to view a larger version of the image.**

   While using Flickr, be sure to follow its terms of service (www.flickr.com/terms.gne) that require you to link back to the photo you use on the Flickr site. This is easily accomplished by simply using Flickr's own HTML code.

7. **Above your chosen image, click the More Ways to Share drop-down list beside the share buttons.**

8. **Click the Grab the HTML/BBCode link.**

   More options appear on the drop-down list, as shown in Figure 6-2.

Figure 6-2:
Click the drop-down list to get the HTML code for an image.

9. **Select your preferred image size from the drop-down list.**

   This drop-down list will only appear if the image owner has multiple sizes available.

10. **Select the HTML radio button.**

    The BBCode is only used for forums.

11. **Select the HTML code (you may need to scroll to select it all), copy it, and paste it into your blog post where you want the image to appear.**

Getting Readers to Come to You

You know the type of person who comes into a room and lights it up just by being there? Even if you don't feel like that describes you, you probably know someone like this — one or more folks who are fun to be around and make you feel good just because they are there. Great bloggers and blogs are a lot like this — they can light up a page just by being themselves. What's cool about this principle is a kind of open secret: Some really successful bloggers who seem to do this light-up thing effortlessly online are not like that in real life, at least not all the time. Somehow blogging allows us to be both more vulnerable and more protected than we are when we interact with the people in our everyday lives. The computer screen is an unintimidating platform that tends to make people braver than they normally are. So even if you don't feel like you can walk into a room and light it up, you may find that this magic trick is easier in the virtual world than you ever imagined.

These kinds of people tend to attract attention by being true to themselves and exuding an easygoing confidence. Yet these people aren't egotistical; they openly share their imperfections, too. This describes most of the successful bloggers I know, *especially* successful mom bloggers.

Networking with other bloggers

While it seems obvious that you would want to know other bloggers, I want to explain some of the reasons why networking with other bloggers is indispensable to building your blog:

- **Finding new readers:** The best way to find new loyal readers is to be introduced to them by another blogger who has a loyal following. Getting links from other bloggers is extremely important on many levels.

- **Cross promotion:** Bloggers frequently promote each other, so you'll want to build relationships with people whom you can help and that can help you.

- **Building links:** Getting links to your blog is extremely important in terms of getting found in the search engines. The more links you get, the higher your blog will appear in the search engine results pages.

- **Finding new opportunities:** Brand representatives and potential advertisers are already aware of many established bloggers. These bloggers are in a great position to recommend others for opportunities that may not be a fit for their blog, or to spread the word about upcoming chances to participate in campaigns or events.

I knew networking was important before I started blogging, but realized early on that I didn't know anything about the etiquette of Internet-based networking. Meeting new people can be challenging on its own, and not knowing the unwritten rules made it even more intimidating. But a few months after I started blogging, I heard about another blogger who was helping to run another blog network. I really wanted to get to know him because he was very knowledgeable and he seemed fairly approachable. I had so many blogging questions I really didn't know who to turn to. I feared it would be insanely inappropriate to just e-mail this stranger out of the blue and ask for his advice. I decided it would be easier to do this if he was aware of who I was, so I linked to one of his blog posts first. Then I swallowed my pride, got way outside of my comfort zone, and sent him a short note introducing myself and asking permission to send him a few questions.

As soon as I hit Send, I started imagining the responses: *Sorry, too busy to talk to you.* Or *No, I don't give out free advice, and how dare you assume that is appropriate?* Or *Well, I think your blog stinks. There's no hope for you in this industry.*

It only took a few hours to get one of the most important e-mails of my blogging career. He wrote me back a warm note welcoming me to blogging, invited my questions, and introduced me to a few of the biggest A-list bloggers. I soon was in contact with them as well, and slowly began building friendships with them. Today it's interesting to look back on it all. One of the people he introduced me to was Liz Strauss, who offered me my very first speaking opportunity at her first annual SOBCon conference. Another person was Darren Rowse of ProBlogger, whose knowledge and advice were absolutely critical to my success in this field. I can trace several of my biggest blogging milestones back to that one e-mail.

I admit that this was back in 2006, and the blogging industry has grown by millions of people since that time. These days it's a little harder to even figure out who to e-mail, let alone hope for those kinds of career-altering introductions. But "harder" doesn't mean "impossible." To this day I still e-mail people out of the blue and receive their messages as well — as recently as yesterday.

In fact, after I sold Sparkplugging and started Woo! Jr., in many ways I had to build a network of blogging friends all over again. I had become a successful, well-known business blogger, but the crafting and education bloggers didn't know who the heck I was at all. In order to gain some exposure for myself in this new niche, I had to get on the radar of the people running successful blogs related to my new topics. Blogs can't get successful without the help of other blogs. It may sound strange, but there are few true competitors in the blogosphere. In fact, we cooperate far more than we compete. The more we help each other, the more we help ourselves.

I didn't realize until recently that I had been using an informal formula as I networked with other bloggers online. It's not an exact science and not everyone responds to my introductions, but most people do. It's based on a simple principle — what goes around, comes around.

Here are the steps I took when I first started networking with other bloggers:

1. Get to know the people in your blogging niche.

   You can find these people by searching on Google Blog Search (http://blogsearch.google.com), Technorati (http://technorati.com), and Twitter (http://twitter.com) for people talking about the topics you blog about. Identify the successful bloggers as well as the ones who are at your level of experience as well. While it's great to get noticed by big-time bloggers, you'll find that the people who are more like you can be far more beneficial and supportive. These are people who have more time and energy to invest in your new friendship.

2. Identify the people you want to get to know better.

   These are the bloggers who you want to emulate or have the most in common with. You can learn a lot about individual bloggers from their About pages, and through the conversations they have with others on social media sites.

3. Start interacting with the bloggers.

   The only way for people to know about you is to let them know you are there. Start commenting on their blogs, following them on Twitter, and becoming their friend or fan on Facebook.

4. Link to their blog posts that you think your readers would enjoy.

   This is a really meaningful step to me on a personal level. I believe it's important to give before you expect to receive. I wouldn't say it's an unwritten rule in blogging, but bloggers really respond to this approach. Don't expect that every time you do this you'll get something in return. But you can expect that the more you link to others, the more they'll want to return the favor somehow.

5. E-mail other bloggers to explore ways of working together.

   I save this step for last, because I know what it's like to get hundreds of e-mails a week about everything from my daughter's weekly class progress report to interview inquiries. As you get to be more established as a blogger, the amount of e-mail you'll have to manage will be enormous. If you want to grab the attention of the person you're writing to, following the steps before this will allow your e-mail to stand out from the crowd, because the recipient will be somewhat familiar with you by now.

   Additionally, you should have a clear purpose for writing (not just to introduce yourself, for example). I always start out these kinds of messages with a few sentences telling the person what he or she would get out of reading the rest of the e-mail. This lets your recipients know that you're making it clear something is in it for them, and that you value their time.

6. I highly recommend getting offline and meeting your online contacts in real life.

The best way to do this is to attend some of the many blogging conferences all over the world. Meeting your blogging friends in real life can transform your online relationships into solid collaborations and partnerships. It's easier to ask for — and give favors to — people you've met in person. Additionally, blogging conferences are the absolutely best place to network with brands, potential advertisers, book publishers, and traditional media journalists. (For more on attracting advertisers, see Chapter 10. I talk about finding book deals and what it takes to get published in Chapter 16. And I also give you some tips on how to speak at some of these conferences and attract media coverage in Chapter 7.)

Using social media to attract new readers

It's astonishing to realize that when I first started blogging, Facebook was only open to college students, and Twitter didn't even publicly exist. Back then, bloggers socialized on each other's blogs and not on social networks, which fostered a community that thrived on linking to each other, commenting, and carrying on conversations via blog posts.

As Twitter and Facebook became more widely adopted, it became much easier for the more personal conversations to move to the social networks. Because so many of us used Facebook and Twitter, they became a common meeting place, much like the office water cooler. This moved the chit-chat off of blogs and into the social media space, and blog posts and comments became more focused conversations. Instead of linking to posts we liked on our blogs, we would share them on the social networks because it was faster and easier to do so.

As early as a year ago, I didn't see the value in spending too much time promoting myself and my sites on Twitter and Facebook. Today I think it's as necessary as having a blog. There are some really important reasons why:

- ✔ **People expect brands and companies to have a presence on social media sites.** If they are looking for you there, you should be able to be found. If you're a professional blogger, you aren't just a mom on the Web anymore. You are *also* a brand.

- ✔ **You can't expect the conversations to come to you.** You have to go out and be a part of the conversations where the people spend their time online.

- ✔ **Social media sites can send a significant amount of traffic back to your blog.** This is especially true of bloggers who have vibrant Facebook pages with thousands of fans.

✔ **Brands that work with bloggers seek out people who are influential across the Web, not just on their blogs.** If they were to choose between a blogger with more traffic or a blogger with less traffic but with a very large following on social sites, they'd most likely choose the latter. This is because they know that they can get their brand message into your community both on your blog and on Facebook and Twitter where there are millions of users.

Setting up a Facebook fan page

I put off setting up a Facebook fan page for far too long, thinking it wasn't a very valuable use of my time. What I have found instead is that Facebook is truly one of the best places to promote yourself as both a brand and a blogger. Women outnumber men on Facebook, and moms are one of the fastest-growing groups of people signing up. If you do no other social media marketing at all, create a Facebook Fan Page.

It's important to note that as soon as you create your Facebook page, it becomes live on Facebook. So it's a good idea to set up your Facebook page all in one sitting. It will take you between 30 and 60 minutes, depending on how much you want to customize the page. You will want to have a copy of your blog logo ready to upload in .jpg, .gif, or .png format. The blog logo image should be 180 pixels wide and no taller than 180 pixels high. This image will also serve as your Profile Image.

Creating your blog's fan page

Follow these steps to create a Facebook fan page:

1. **Go to** http://facebook.com/pages/create.php.

2. **Choose your page category; for a blog fan page, click the Product or Brand icon.**

   This is the section where Facebook categorizes websites.

3. **Choose Website from the drop-down list.**

4. **Type your blog name into the Brand or Product text field.**

5. **Select the I Agree to Facebook Pages Terms check box, and then click the Get Started button.**

6. **Type the characters in the security check image into the text box and click the Submit button.**

   If you don't have a Facebook account, you're prompted to sign in or create one at this point.

7. **Upload a copy of your blog logo by clicking the Upload and Image link.**

8. **In the Upload a Profile Picture dialog box that appears, click the Browse button, select the image you want to upload, and click Open.**

   You will be given the option to crop the image as you wish. To do this, drag the corners of the crop box to the desired position and click the Done Cropping button.

9. **Add your blog information by clicking the Edit Info link at the top of the page.**

10. **In the Name field, confirm that the name of your blog appears as you want it to.**

11. **In the Founded field, enter the month and year that you started your blog.**

12. **Leave the Address, City/Town, and Zip fields empty.**

    Unless you have a specific business reason for sharing this information, it's best to keep this information private. Some examples of when you might want to share your location are if you run local events or if you expect to receive mail. Because Facebook's information-sharing policies are always changing, I prefer to keep private information confidential as much as possible on the site.

13. **In the About field, enter your blog description.**

    This can be your tag line or a short paragraph describing your blog in more detail. This information will appear in the left sidebar of your finished page and viewable to all Facebook visitors. Don't go overboard with lots of information here, because it will overwhelm your readers and clutter up your page.

14. **(Optional) In the Company Overview field, add a longer blog description.**

    I still suggest keeping it to a just a couple of paragraphs or less. You never want to overwhelm people with too much information, because it decreases the chances it will get read at all.

15. **The Mission, Awards, Products, E-mail, and Phone Number fields are optional and may or may not be necessary for your blog.**

16. **In the Website field, enter your blog URL.**

    If you're building a page for related blogs in a blog network, enter each URL on a separate line.

17. **Click the Save Changes button.**

Your new Facebook fan page is done! If you want, you can also upload pictures or videos or add additional links that you think your future Facebook fans would like.

Suggesting your new page to your Facebook friends

When your page is complete, Step 2 is to Invite Your Friends to "Like" the page. It may be tempting to send this out to everyone you know, and that may be appropriate if all your Facebook friends are people who you think would like your page anyway. In most cases, I suggest being more selective and only sending the invitation to Facebook friends that you would feel comfortable asking to "Like" the page if they were in the same room as you. While I don't think that sending out an invitation like this is spam, as social media users get more sophisticated, they also get more sensitive to marketing messages.

As Facebook becomes even more popular with many different generations of people, it's only going to become a more effective marketing tool for your blog in the future. I think it's one of the absolute best ways to build your traffic and brand; I highly recommend it, especially because it's free to use and there are few, if any, other ways to get so much value out of the time you spend on marketing yourself. To get the most out of this valuable resource for bloggers, I strongly recommend reading *Facebook Marketing For Dummies* by Paul Dunay and Richard Krueger.

Marketing on Twitter

As Facebook has evolved, it has become more and more effective as a tool to promote your blog. Twitter, on the other hand, seems to have gotten slightly less effective for blog promotion. Where Twitter excels is as a tool to promote your personal brand. You certainly can promote your blog there, but to be most effective, it should be a smaller, unobtrusive part of your activity on Twitter. Most people don't like to follow folks who are only on Twitter to promote themselves. Yet Twitter's members use their accounts in many different ways, and there are some that prefer to follow their favorite blogs or businesses via tweets instead of RSS feeds or on Facebook.

My personal recommended formula for building your personal brand on Twitter is broken down by the following percentages. This works great for most people using Twitter to promote themselves and their blogs at the same time:

- **10 percent self-promotion:** This would include posting updates about and links to your websites or other projects you're working on.

- **20 percent promoting others:** This would include retweeting friends' tweets, talking about friends' projects, or posting links to content on their websites.

- **30 percent being a resource to the community:** This would include answering questions, offering recommendations, posting links to content that will help your followers in some way and participating in conversations where you could add value.

- ✔ **40 percent conversational interactions that reinforce your personal brand:** This would include talking about subjects and people that you want to be associated with, plus general conversations with friends.

If it's a high priority to you to build your blog's brand separately from your personal brand, then I suggest creating a separate account for promoting just your blog. While you can use this separate account to post links to your blog content, Twitter works best when people feel that they can interact with you a bit more personally. In this circumstance, I would adjust the preceding percentages as follows:

- ✔ **40 percent – 50 percent self-promotion:** This would include posting updates about and links directly to your blog.

- ✔ **30 percent being a resource to the community:** This would include answering questions, offering recommendations, posting links to content that will help your followers in some way and participating in conversations where I could add value.

- ✔ **20 percent – 30 percent conversational interactions that reinforce your personal brand:** This would include responding to comments and starting conversations with your followers on topics related to their interests and your blog.

I have to admit, though, that this is an ideal goal — and a formula I can't always follow. It works best when you can be consistently active on Twitter, and I am not able to do that much of the time. So I've adapted this model to ensure that I maintain both a personal *and* professional presence on Twitter while working to respect the way my followers want to engage with me and my content. I balance the need to keep marketing tweets out of my personal relationships with a commitment to providing consistent links to new blog content for users who want that information. I wish I had time to interact with people on a more personal level on my professional Twitter account, but I don't. I believe it's more important to have an imperfect presence on Twitter than none at all. So my professional account has far fewer followers than my personal account, yet I am able to provide the blog content for the people who want it.

Finding & participating in link parties

A great way to get your best blog posts in front of new readers is to participate in link parties. I have found these to be most commonly found on DIY and how-to blogs, but there are thousands of them all over the Web. A *link party* is when a blog that usually has a good amount of traffic hosts an event in which other bloggers are invited to post a link to a blog post they would like featured. These parties have themes, so they're only appropriate when you've already written a post that fits with the theme of the link party. Such parties can get hundreds of entries, so they are beneficial to both the host blog and those of all bloggers who get featured. The I Am an Organizing Junkie blog (`http://orgjunkie.com`) hosts a weekly Menu Plan Monday link party that's very successful. You can see some of the entries in Figure 6-3.

When a blog hosts a link party, the host blog gets a lot of traffic from all her readers who come to her blog to participate. The bloggers who submit their links get a lot of traffic from the link party because everyone is encouraged to visit each other's blog posts.

You can find new link parties by simply searching for *link parties* on any search engine. First-time participants should be sure to read through the party guidelines, which provide the blogging etiquette tips suggested to all participants. My friend Amanda Formaro has two blogs, Crafts by Amanda (`www.craftsbyamanda.com`) and Amanda's Cookin' (`www.amandascookin.com`). Amanda has a whole system set up to make the most out of participating in link parties. Here are her tips:

- ✔ Bookmark the parties and sort them by day, so that you can sit down for just 10 minutes every morning and submit to the parties available that day.
- ✔ Choose the best photo possible for your thumbnail to encourage people to visit your site.
- ✔ It's common courtesy to link back to the link party, and may even be required for participation.

Amanda gets thousands of visitors to both of her blogs, every month, from her participation in these link parties, so her work pays off. She also says that the visitors who come from them tend to be the very best kind of readers she wants to have: They comment and frequently subscribe to her RSS feed.

Making search engine optimization super-simple

I'll start out by saying I'm a bit of a search engine optimization (SEO) junkie — this is something I truly enjoy working on. Search engines are the biggest source of traffic for all my websites. But SEO doesn't need to be a priority for every single blog. Highly personal blogs that are built around a reader community will likely not do very well getting search engine traffic, just by the nature of the content. Search engine users are seeking answers to questions, to find products to purchase, or want specific information about a topic. So making SEO a priority only makes sense when your blog provides at least some informational content that people would look for on the Web.

Figure 6-3:
OrgJunkie
hosts a
weekly
Menu Plan
Monday
link party to
attract
readers.

When I first started blogging, SEO was incredibly intimidating to learn. I'd heard that blogging was good for SEO, and that was about the extent of my knowledge. There was so much to learn back then, and it was certainly low on my priority list of things to study. I knew I was limiting the amount of traffic I was going to get from search engines until I took the time to learn SEO. But it didn't seem important enough until almost a year later.

Understanding how search engines read websites

When I finally started reading articles about what optimizing for search engines was all about, I felt pretty foolish. The topic seemed so complex and technical, but what I found is that really simple, common-sense writing skills could double my traffic in a fairly short amount of time.

Think of SEO like this: While search engines have very sophisticated technology for sifting through websites and separating the spam from the quality content, they're also kind of like a frazzled mom with too much to do and too little time on her hands. If you were late getting the kids to school, trying to grab a cup of coffee, and had a baby sitting on your hip, but you *had* to classify an article before you could head out the door, you would

- Read the headline
- Read the first few lines of the article
- Read any subheadings
- Try to find a pull quote, photograph, or caption to get an idea of the best information in the piece
- Look at the end of the article to find out what the point of the message was

Search engines treat your blog posts in pretty much the same way. You can write a long blog post with lots of great words that people commonly search for, but ultimately what will define your work is by how it can be scanned and understood in just a few seconds. The good thing about this is when you make your content easy for search engines to scan, it also makes your content much more readable to actual human beings.

SEO jargon

Before I go into how to do this, I want to define a few components of search engine optimization so that it's easier to understand:

- **Keywords:** The word or phrase that people type into a search engine to find what they are looking for. It could be as simple as *summer snacks* or a whole phrase such as *how to get my baby to take her medicine.*

- **Page title:** This is usually (and customarily) the same as the title of your blog post, and should be. A really poorly designed blog template may not handle this matter; if so, you may need the technical expertise to change it manually. It's also called the *title tag.* It appears at the top of your browser window and when you mouse over the top of the window, as shown in Figure 6-4.

- **Heading tags:** These function in the same way as heading tags would in a Word document. Heading 1 tags (or H1 tags as they are commonly referred to) should be only used once and will be your blog title. Heading 2 (H2) and Heading 3 (H3) tags can be used more frequently throughout your posts to group your paragraphs into related subjects.

Figure 6-4:
See how the HTML page title appears on a Web page.

Basic search engine optimization comes down to this: You want to include your chosen keywords in your writing as much as possible without it sounding awkward or unnecessarily repetitive. Keywords are especially important to use in the areas that search engines pay the most attention to: title, introduction, subheadings, quotes, and captions. You don't want to use the same phrase over and over again, but weave the keywords you choose (and related keywords) into your natural written language. Most themes on both Blogger and WordPress will make sure that your page title and heading tags are placed where they should be. It's up to you to write your own subheadings as they relate to your content.

Adding subheading tags

Adding subheading tags to your content is easy. You'll first want to have a blog post written with one or more subheadings included as separate paragraphs. Use Heading 2 sparingly for major sections of your blog posts, and Heading 3 for subsections. Not every blog post will even be long enough to use subheadings — they aren't necessary if your post is short. But they make a big difference in longer posts because they help break up the content into chunks and make it much easier to scan quickly.

Here's how to add subheading tags in Blogger:

1. **Have your blog post open in your blog editor on your Edit Posts page.**

2. **Switch to Edit HTML view.**

3. **Add the h2 tags at the beginning and end of any paragraph you want to format as Heading 2, as follows:**

   ```
   <h2>This is My Heading 2</h2>
   ```

4. **Add the h3 tags at the beginning and end of any paragraph you want to format as Heading 3, as follows:**

   ```
   <h3>This is My Heading 3</h3>
   ```

5. **Click the Publish Post button if the post is finished, or click the Save as Draft button if it requires more editing.**

You can see this process in action in Figure 6-5.

Here's how to add subheading tags in WordPress:

1. **Have your blog post open in your blog editor on your Edit Posts page.**

2. **To add a Heading 2 tag, place your text cursor into any paragraph you want to format as Heading 2, and select Heading 2 from the Format drop-down list.**

Figure 6-5:
Adding
Heading 2
and Heading
3 tags using
Google
Blogger.

3. **To add a Heading 3 tag, place your text cursor into any paragraph you want to format as Heading 3, and select Heading 3 from the Format drop-down list.**

4. **Click the Publish button if the post is finished, or click the Save as Draft button if it requires more editing.**

You can see the result in Figure 6-6.

Figure 6-6:
Adding
Heading 2
and Heading
3 tags using
WordPress.

Figuring out what keywords to use

You may be wondering, at this point, "I get how this works, but how do I know which keywords to use?" I love doing keyword research and knowing what topics people want to know about — or what questions they want answered. Much of the time, their words aren't what I would predict; identifying keywords is a process of discovery. One of my favorite keyword research tools is free, extremely easy to use, and will also give you great blog post ideas to write about. The SEO Book Keyword Suggestion Tool can be found at `http://tools.seobook.com/keyword-tools/seobook` (it requires a free signup).

Here's how to use the SEO Book Keyword Suggestion Tool:

1. **Sign in to the SEO Book website, then go to** `http://tools.seobook.com/keyword-tools/seobook`.

2. **Type a keyword into the text field.**

   Use very simple words here to get the broadest results for your search. Multiple words are always treated as an *And* modifier, not an *Or* modifier. This means that if you type in **holiday ideas**, all of your results will contain both of those words. You will get more general keyword suggestions if you just type in **holiday**.

3. **Click the Submit button.**

See the results for the sample search *holiday* in Figure 6-7.

Figure 6-7: Getting keyword ideas with the SEO Book Keyword Suggestion Tool.

Pay attention to these columns.

As you scroll down to view the results, you'll see a huge amount of data and numbers that are there only for advanced level SEO professionals. The only two columns you need to pay attention to are the WordTracker column with the suggested phrases and the Overall Daily Est column that gives you a ballpark figure for the volume of daily searches for those phrases.

You'll see that there's a very wide range of suggestions, from *Holiday Inn* to *holiday traditions* to *2011 calendar of federal holidays*. If you're a food blogger, you can focus on the highest volume terms that are related to cooking, such as

- ✔ Holiday recipes
- ✔ Holiday appetizers
- ✔ Holiday cookies
- ✔ Holiday diet tips

You can use these keyword phrases as stand-alone blog post titles, or as more general post ideas, such as, "Christmas Tree Sandwich Platter Appetizer Recipe."

The tool pulls information from sources that change all the time, so your results will be different during spring break and in December because of seasonal influences.

Phrases at the top of the SEO Book keyword suggestion list have the highest volume of searches and will — potentially — send your blog more traffic than suggestions lower on the list. I say *potentially,* because if you can rank first on a search engine result page for a suggestion lower on the list, that may send you more traffic than if you rank tenth for one of the phrases at the top of the list.

Don't get too carried away with placing lots of keywords into your content. Write for people first, search engines second. If your writing gets too repetitive or difficult for a normal person to read, search engines might get to the point of penalizing you instead of rewarding you. Extreme use of keywords on a page is called *keyword stuffing,* and it will turn off both your readers *and* the search engines.

Hosting popular giveaways

In 2006 when I first started blogging, I paid a lot of attention to the other bloggers who were finding success. One of those sites was 5MinutesForMom. com (www.5minutesformom.com). Twin sisters Janice Croze and Susan Carraretto seemed to build community and traffic effortlessly from day one. I was incredibly impressed with one of the ways they were doing this: running giveaways on their blog. They were one of the very first mom blogs to use this strategy as a way to build traffic and repeat visitors. Now there are thousands of blogs running giveaways every week.

The premise of running a giveaway is simple — offer a prize to your readers, and they can enter for a chance to win by leaving a comment on your blog post.

The benefits of running giveaways are

- **More visitors:** People like free stuff, so it draws more visitors to your blog.

- **Builds repeat visitors:** If you establish yourself as a frequent destination for giving away freebies, people have an incentive to come back.

- **Builds relationships with brand representatives:** Many times, PR firms will offer free stuff to bloggers for giveaways as a way to build up awareness about new products. This is a good way to build your experience working with brands when you're very new.

- **Incorporate social media campaigns:** You can up the value to sponsors by requiring entrants to visit the sponsor website or by integrating Facebook or Twitter activity into the giveaway entries. If you have a strong social media presence and a large blog that can deliver hundreds of entries, this is extremely valuable to sponsors. When you can add this much value, such an approach can become part of your advertising strategy — and become an additional source of revenue for you.

There are a few drawbacks to running giveaways, too:

- **Poor-quality visitors:** Giveaways tend to draw readers who only care about free stuff, and don't stay long or engage in your content or community.

- **Dealing with cheaters:** I wouldn't have believed this unless I had seen it with my own eyes, but people can and do enter multiple times under different names. You have to police entrants and double-check the IP addresses of commenters to ensure that they aren't scamming you.

- **Time investment:** The time it takes to obtain quality products to give away, write up the posts, manage entries, choose winners, and either ship out prizes or ensure that the PR firm did, can eat up a big chunk of your week. I really recommend carefully watching the time you spend on giveaways versus what you receive in return. Make sure it's a good use of your time.

- **Sponsor follow-up:** Sponsors will want to know the results of the giveaway on your blog, so you need to write up a report letting them know how many visitors and page views your giveaway post received. Additionally, I have had companies promise prizes and then never ship them out to the winners. Chasing after one such sponsor and following up with the four prize winners was enough of a headache to make me consider ending giveaways altogether. Ultimately, in order to make sure I ran the giveaway legally, I had to fork out the money to buy prizes for the winners out of my own pocket.

If your blog content is heavily focused on products and reviews, running give-aways is a great way to build your traffic and increase your advertising revenue. Other kinds of blogs have mixed success with it. The only way to know if they'll work for you is if you test them out with your readers. If you decide to do that, here are suggestions for making it as successful as possible:

- **Only give away valuable prizes:** When giveaways weren't very common, any prize attracted entries. Now that they are so common, your prize really needs to be something that people want in order for them to take the time to visit your site.

- **Make entries easy:** If visitors have to jump through hoops to enter your giveaway, they probably won't. If a sponsor really wants entrants to take an action for a chance to win, consider giving your readers multiple ways to enter. For example, leaving a comment is one entry method, and going to the sponsor's website and doing some virtual window shopping could constitute another entry.

- **Choose winners at random:** This is required by law anyway, but will add integrity to your site if you can prove this is the manner the winner is chosen. You can do this by going to RANDOM.ORG (www.random.org) and taking a screenshot of the number it generates for you, and posting the resulting image with your winner announcement.

I want to point out that I cover *extremely important* legal guidelines on running blog giveaways on your site in Chapter 9. In fact, the actual legal term to use is *sweepstakes,* not giveaways. But since it's more common to call them give-aways, that's what I do in this book. Giveaways can be a legal minefield if you haven't met some highly specific rules and guidelines according to the law. I do not recommend using this technique to attract visitors unless you follow these rules carefully.

Chapter 7

Positioning Yourself as an Expert

*T*he five different blogging business models I present in Chapter 4 make it easy to see that different blogs need very different marketing strategies in order to grow. But to varying degrees, *any* blog will benefit from the material in this chapter. Every blog will be better off with good publicity, media coverage, and a writer who is well known and respected by her peers. That said, you won't automatically have a successful and profitable blog if you're well respected and lots of people are talking about you. In fact, the opposite is true — you can run a very successful blog and remain very much under the radar. But the more credible you are — and the more people are talking about you — the more it will help all your marketing efforts succeed.

The benefits of positioning yourself as an expert really can't be understated. It helps as you are working to establish your brand as I talk about in Chapter 6. It helps when potential clients and customers need the right person for the job or the perfect product to buy. It helps when people are looking on the search engines for someone with your specific experience and background. It helps when advertisers or sponsors are looking for that *perfect blogger* to work with on their next social media campaign. And it helps when reporters, television producers, and the media are looking for a credible expert to feature in a story.

Ultimately, the things you do to position yourself as that expert are only half of the expert equation. You obviously need to be able to communicate your knowledge in a meaningful and helpful way. The other half is making sure that other people hear your message. So how do you publicize your expertise and get people talking about you? The short answer is: Give them something worth talking about. The long answer is the rest of this chapter.

Becoming a Resource to the Blogging Community

In Chapter 6, I explain that the very best way to get yourself established when you first start blogging is by networking with other bloggers. I should say that this isn't just important when you are first starting out, but it's important for your entire blogging career. I also explain in Chapter 6 that networking is best achieved when you take the what-comes-around-goes-around approach. I'm about to take that concept a little further: When you give something to the blogging community as a whole, the community will remember and reward you for it.

What this means is that the more you freely share your expertise and knowledge in a genuinely helpful way, the more you will get known for it. This is easily accomplished by creating informational content such as tutorials, how-tos, and instructional or advice articles. But what if your blog isn't that kind of a teaching blog? You can still give back and be a resource to your peers. Here are some ways I've seen it done:

- Link to newer bloggers.
- Share your latest Etsy find.
- Write guest posts on blogs where an informational blog post would fit in.
- Make yourself available for questions and advice.
- Be a connector and make introductions between people who have common goals.
- Pass along recommendations and praise for people you admire.
- Teach what you have learned about blogging at conferences and events.

A great example of this is Elise Bauer and her insanely successful Simply Recipes blog at `http://simplyrecipes.com`. Her recipes are, of course, a great resource, but that's not the only reason she has such a loyal following. She has also created a valuable tool on her blog: a custom Google search box in which any visitor can search many other food blogs, not just her own. She also is one of the most popular recurring speakers at the BlogHer conference, where she gives workshops on building blog traffic and search engine optimization. And she even created the Food Blog Alliance at `http://foodblogalliance.com`, a community resource blog that shares knowledge, advice, and ideas among food bloggers. With over 1.5 million RSS readers and ranking on page 1 for the highly coveted search term *recipes,* Elise doesn't have to be so generous with her time, talent, and resources. But the fact that she does keeps her as a first thought when the community thinks of successful food bloggers, and has certainly contributed to her overall success. You can see the Food Blog Alliance in Figure 7-1.

Figure 7-1:
Elise Bauer
gives back
to the
blogging
community
with the
Food Blog
Alliance.

Understanding that your competition is really "co-opetition"

Elise Bauer of the Food Blog Alliance absolutely gets that other bloggers in her niche are not competition — they are *co-opetition* (a hybrid of cooperation and competition). Like most of us, Elise realizes that what's good for one blog can be good for the entire blogging community.

I link to other craft blogs frequently from my CraftJr.com blog (www.craftjr.com), even though those links directly help those sites rank well (and sometimes better than mine) in the search engines. I do this for several reasons:

✔ My readers really enjoy seeing a wide range of craft projects, and I can't post new ideas 24 hours a day.

✔ My blog becomes a resource not just for my creative projects, but for many more related projects from around the Web.

✔ Many of these blogs link back to me.

✔ I know that as more craft bloggers succeed, more opportunities will be available to the community as a whole.

In fact, craft bloggers are becoming more successful as a whole — and opportunities *are* flooding in to the writers in this community. My friend and direct "co-opetition" partner Marie LeBaron writes the incredible Make and Take kids' craft and activities blog at `http://makeandtakes.com`. Marie landed a fantastic ad-network partnership last year with Federated Media, who hadn't worked with many craft bloggers before. She also recently landed her own first book deal, and is working on a kids' craft book as I am writing this book. More and more creative- and craft-supply companies and brands are getting involved with social media, sponsoring Marie and several other high-profile craft bloggers. This was evident at the most recent Craft and Hobby Association trade show in which craft bloggers were actually featured as part of the signage at some of the vendor booths. The community is getting so much brand attention, in fact, that BlogHer launched a new event just for craft bloggers in 2011 — BlogHer Handmade. None of this would have been possible if all the craft bloggers only featured their own projects. I really do take that cheesy old adage, "A rising tide raises all ships," to heart. It was our support of each other that created an industry from the seeds planted by a few creative and generous bloggers.

Teaching what you know

If your blog is a teaching or informational kind of blog, I highly encourage you to freely give your advice and expertise away in your blog posts. You may be concerned about giving away expertise for free, but keep in mind that the information is probably available for free already on the Internet elsewhere, and that people who want free information will find it and never pay for it anyway. The value of your expertise is more than just the actual words; it's in how people can apply the information you offer in their own lives. So you can offer the best advice on the planet for free, but the customers who you really want to work with you will still hire you to help them apply that advice to their specific situations. Additionally, it will be *because* of the free resources you provide that these customers find you in the first place. The purpose of informational content is to showcase your expertise, which then proves to your readers that you are the one who can consistently provide the information they want or need. And that's how you start getting known as the go-to gal for whatever you want to be the go-to gal for.

Speaking at Events and Conferences

Nothing boosts your visibility among the blogging community more than when you speak at events attended by your readers and peers. Speaking on a topic gives you instant credibility that can be achieved in only a few other ways, like being quoted in the mainstream media, or by getting a very high profile recommendation. It's really only eclipsed by writing a book on a topic or being on the radio or TV. In the online business world, building trust is extremely important to your success, especially because you usually don't have the benefit of people literally witnessing your real-life actions to back up your words. Speaking experience is a *rock-solid* way of building trust.

When considering speaking at events, you really want to focus on the topics you know like the back of your hand. This is true for a lot of reasons:

- ✔ Your speaking engagements should be supporting your overall business model.

- ✔ Public speaking can be a high-stress situation, and you need a comfortable level of understanding of your subject in order to hold up under the pressure of being in front of a room full of people.

- ✔ When (not if — *when*) you make a mistake or lose your place in presentation, you need to be able to ad-lib good content to get back on track.

- ✔ You will probably be asked questions by the audience, and you need to be able to answer them intelligently.

- ✔ Event leaders want the very best people who can offer the most value to the conference attendees.

For those of you tempted to skip this section, I have a little secret: You can still get all the benefits of public speaking without having to get up alone in front of a crowd. The way to do that is to become a *panelist.* Almost all events and conferences have a combination of workshops and panels led by a moderator. When I have to lead a workshop, I prepare for days and can get so nervous that I literally can't eat. But when I'm a panelist, I sometimes don't have to do any preparation work at all (shhh — don't tell anyone!). The reason is that in a panel format, you share the stage with a group and basically answer questions and have a public conversation together. Getting onto a panel is the absolute best way to get started speaking in front of a crowd.

Applying to speak at events

A few years ago, Liz Strauss gave me my first speaking opportunity at the SOBCon business blogging event in 2007. And for the next few years, I found it was fairly easy to find more opportunities to speak at other conferences after I had established a track record of speaking success. Then, in 2010, I scaled back my speaking engagements to spend more time with my family. As I geared up in 2011 to schedule more speaking events to help promote my book, I realized that the event landscape had changed a lot in the year I had taken off. Turns out that a lot of other men and women had built up their speaking credentials over the years as well, and the pool of speaking talent is growing faster than the number of speaking opportunities available. I used to be able to ask event planners what they wanted me to speak about. I don't have that luxury anymore — I have to be able to submit really compelling speaking proposals in order to prove that I can offer more value to the event attendees than another potential speaker.

Most event planners have their own process for evaluating and selecting the speakers for their event. Some choose the topics they want covered and find speakers who fit the bill. Some allow speakers to submit ideas and then choose the ones they think attendees will like the best. Others will take all ideas submitted and put them to a vote, allowing attendees to decide the topics for the event. This is why it's important to look at each event individually and familiarize yourself with all the factors that will influence selection criteria, such as these:

- ✔ The typical experience level of the event's attendees
- ✔ The kind of topics the event has covered in the past
- ✔ The experience level of the event's current and past speakers
- ✔ The diversity represented in the event's speaker lineup
- ✔ The feedback the event planners received on previous sessions and speakers

For example, earlier I thought I would be a perfect fit for several events, considering the topics covered and interests of their typical attendees. But then I discovered that the past speakers were Fortune 500 CEOs and government leaders. Now, I know I'm good and all, but I'm the first to admit that I am not at that level — yet. As another example, I also checked into speaking at some much smaller local events around the country, but discovered that the event planners were looking for local speakers to avoid paying for out-of-town speakers' travel expenses. So when you are hunting down speaking opportunities, you want to find the events where you can add the most value in relation to the other speakers who will be considered.

When putting together a speaking proposal, first look on the event website to understand the selection process and criteria well. Your main goal is simply this: Give the event's planners what they ask for, plus a little more. Treat it as though you are applying for a job, because that's very much how they will evaluate your proposal. It's perfectly appropriate to e-mail the event planners and ask for any specific guidance on what they are looking for in speaking proposals, but the bigger the event, the less likely they'll have time to respond. I have e-mailed event planners to ask questions like these:

- ✔ Are there any topics that attendees have requested more information about?
- ✔ Are there any holes in the speaker lineup where the planners are having a hard time finding a speaker for a particular topic?
- ✔ (If I know the event planners personally, I ask this one.) Do the planners have any specific topic they would like me to propose speaking about?

After you've done your research, put together your proposal, following their submission format. Many times, the event planners will have a submission form for speakers; you can fill it out to ensure they have all the information they need to make a decision. Because each application process is different, there is no one formula that you can follow that works for all. Instead, you have to tailor each proposal to the event planners' and attendees' needs. But here are a few things you can do to help your proposal stand out from the crowd:

- **Most important: Write an extremely compelling session title:** In fact, I usually spend almost as much time on writing a great title as I do on writing the session outline. If you can't impress the event planners with your title, they won't be convinced you will impress their attendees. You can get ideas by looking at sessions that were held in past events. I also highly recommend reading Brian Clark's 11-part series on Writing Magnetic Headlines. You can find it at `www.copyblogger.com/magnetic-headlines`.

- **Know your audience:** Propose ideas that you know the event attendees will want to learn about. For example, don't propose a basic-skill-level session when the attendees will already be past that level of knowledge.

- **Be specific:** Tailor your session to a specific topic — don't offer a session on Advanced Blog Monetization when that means something very different to many different bloggers. Instead, offer a session on Advanced Advertising Strategies for Low-Traffic Blogs.

- **State attendee takeaways:** This shows that you have specific goals for what you want attendees to get out of coming to your session. It helps the event planners to quickly evaluate whether your session idea will give attendees what they want.

- **Keep it brief:** If it takes you four paragraphs to get your session point across, then you need to clarify your idea better. Conference attendees will be choosing which sessions to attend based on your title and brief summary in the printed event program, so you have to sell the session idea in one paragraph or less.

Choosing which events to attend

Going to conferences can become a pretty expensive habit, especially because many of them don't pay a speaker's fee and may not reimburse you for travel expenses. If you are speaking, you will most likely attend the event for free. Still, you have to choose your events wisely. Many of the biggest events are absolutely worth the time and money investment; others, not so much. But the ones that aren't worth it to me might be invaluable to other bloggers, so I can't really say what is best for you.

The following sections list some of the most prominent and well-attended blogging events geared to moms and women, and they're a great place to start. Remember that there are likely many local events happening in your area, and those may actually be the very best places to get started.

BlogHer

Where: Various locations

What: BlogHer is the largest blogging conference geared to women — with a very large percentage of moms. It's in a different city every year, and it has several smaller conferences geared to specific topics, such as BlogHer Handmade and BlogHer Food. With about 3,000 attendees, this conference attracts the most brands and publicity of all the events mentioned here. The sessions range from beginning- to advanced- level topics, for both personal and professional bloggers. They also offer on-site child care for an additional fee.

Website: www.blogher.com

Blissdom

Where: Nashville, TN and Canada

What: Blissdom hosts a regular conference with three learning tracks: Professional Blogging, Writing, and Brand Sponsorships. They also have an additional day of workshop intensives geared to beginners and bloggers in specific topic niches. Each year this conference attracts about 250 attendees and usually has a few surprise celebrity guests.

Website: www.blissdomconference.com

Type-A Parent

Where: Asheville, NC

What: This event was originally called Type-A Mom and evolved into the Type-A Parent conference. This is the first of the mom-blogging events to specifically welcome dad bloggers. Type-A is an event for bloggers who want to take their business to the next level, so there is a heavy focus on business and marketing topics. Parents with children can also take advantage of Kid Con, which is extremely affordable childcare that is mostly paid for by the event sponsors.

Website: www.typeaparent.com

Mom 2.0

Where: Various locations held annually in the southern states

What: Mom 2.0 focuses specifically on moms and blogging and social media. This annual conference is billed as an open conversation between moms and marketers. Many sessions are led by both established bloggers along with professional brand representatives. Mom 2.0 doesn't offer on-site childcare, but does allow infants 12 months and under into all sessions.

Website: www.mom2summit.com

Bloggy Bootcamp

Where: Six locations in 2011 (San Diego, CA; Boston, MA; Seattle, WA; Chicago, IL; Denver, CO; Atlanta, GA)

What: Bloggy Bootcamp focuses on smaller attendance of 100–125 people to give the attendees a more intimate experience. The founders make an extra effort to offer an inclusive format and plenty of opportunities to easily meet other attendees. If going to conferences is intimidating to you, Bloggy Bootcamp is a great place to start.

Website: www.thesitsgirls.com/bloggy-boot-camp

Evo

Where: Salt Lake City Area, UT

What: Evo is a three-day annual event focusing on the evolution of women in social media.

Website: www.evoconference.com

New and smaller mom blogging conferences

The following events and conferences aren't as well established as the ones I describe in the previous sections. However, they're absolutely worth checking out.

- ✔ **SheCon** (www.sheblogsconference.com)
- ✔ **SheStreams** (www.shestreamsconference.com)
- ✔ **Blogalicious** (http://blogaliciousweekend.beblogalicious.com)
- ✔ **Brands & Bloggers Summit** (www.midwestmomsmedia.com)

General blogging events and conferences

I wouldn't be doing you any favors if I didn't also let you know about the following blogging conferences that are geared toward all blogging and social media professionals. I love the women-only events, but these events tend to offer different and valuable content, and I highly recommend them:

- ✔ **BlogWorld & New Media Expo** (`www.blogworldexpo.com`)
- ✔ **SOBCon** (`www.sobevent.com`)
- ✔ **SXSW Interactive** (`http://sxsw.com/interactive`)

Getting Media Coverage

Getting your name or blog in front of hundreds of thousands (or even millions) of people is a huge achievement; as you might expect, it's not easily accomplished. It takes a lot of time, work, and credibility to get mentioned in the *New York Times* or to appear on the *Today Show*. I've been extremely fortunate to get some amazing opportunities to be mentioned in the media. Sometimes I worked my tail off to get noticed; sometimes these opportunities just fell in my lap. Looking back, it wasn't ever a big windfall of publicity; it was, instead, the culmination of many years of cultivating trust and a good, credible reputation with my peers.

I share more of my own experience with getting media coverage (in particular, by crafting a good media kit) in Chapter 10, and I want to reiterate that I made the mistake of thinking that Internet and blogging fame would *make* me financially successful. What I found out is that in reality, press coverage and a blogging business are like a horse and cart: The press coverage (horse) can pull a blogging business (cart) forward, but you first have to have a cart that works. For more on building a cart that works (building a strong blogging business), check out Chapter 4.

Writing a biography that will impress anyone

Biographies are not the easiest thing to write, even when you've been writing them for your entire career. You want a bio to simply highlight your achievements and allow people to get to know you — in a paragraph. Yes, I know it's a lot to ask of five to eight sentences.

Here are a few things to keep in mind when writing your bio:

- ✔ **Write for the right audience:** Your bio as it exists on your blog's regular About page might not be the same one you submit with a speaker proposal, and you might need still another bio for your advertising page. Highlight the most relevant information for the people you are writing for.

- ✔ **Know when to use first or third person pronouns:** I like to use first person when writing about myself on my About page, because that's where I really want to connect with my readers. But almost everywhere else, I write bios in third person to keep things professional. This is especially true when submitting your bio for publication on any other site than your own, where a first person bio would not make sense.

- ✔ **Let *you* shine through:** You are a blogger, not a government official. Bloggers have personality — usually lots of it. Your bio should have personality, too. That means if you want to add quirky facts about yourself, or talk a little bit about your unconventional background, go for it! Just remember that the purpose of a bio is to convey your strengths in very few words. So keep the tangential information minimal and relevant.

- ✔ **Highlight achievements:** Even if you're a modest person, a bio is a place to showcase your strengths. If you must, you can talk about what you have done in a modest way, but this is usually your *only* chance to showcase your strengths. Don't blow that chance by playing down your accomplishments. A bio is your chance to present (matter-of-factly) your awards, experience, influence, ideas, and everything else that makes you the most awesome you.

When you actually sit down to write a bio, here are my two tips that will help if you get stuck:

- ✔ Find someone else's bio that you like and swap out their information for your own. There's no way you can actually plagiarize someone else's bio unless you're saying you've done something you haven't, so just use it to springboard your ideas.

- ✔ Forget everything I just said and *write*. When I get too hung up on format or specifics, I sometimes just have to write whatever comes to mind and then go back and edit the heck out of it. It's easy to get hung up on writing bios, so this is one of the more frequent ways I write a new bio.

Building your press credentials

For the first year of blogging, I worked 50+-hour weeks cranking out valuable content to try and showcase my expertise and knowledge. That was my number-one goal and my main focus. During that time, I interviewed several bloggers more successful than I was, and tried building relationships with people whom I could look to as role models. I started building a reputation as a blogger whose work may not have been a very big deal (at first), but I knew what I was talking about. After a while, other bloggers started requesting to interview me as well. Speaking at events was a huge boost to my credibility, and also offered more opportunities to be interviewed, especially by event attendees. Those first features were the building blocks I used to build my credibility and experience working as an interviewee. I can say for sure that I flubbed a few questions along the way, and I'm sure my stammering and overuse of the word *uh* caused a few video editors to pull their hair out. Sometimes I totally cringed at seeing myself in video, but I just had to continue to work on improving my communication skills and professional appearance.

Networking with other bloggers was also the key to getting better opportunities to be interviewed. I met several journalists and high-profile bloggers at conferences, or sometimes was just in the right place at the right time. Several years ago, for example, I shared a cab with someone at the BlogWorld Expo who happened to know a newspaper journalist looking for a Chicago-based mom blogger for a feature story. The opportunity may have fallen in my lap, but I can say now that the paper wouldn't have featured me if I hadn't already had an established following, a good reputation, a professional-looking blog, and some success under my belt. And the fact that I was speaking at the conference gave my new friend the confidence that I would be a credible lead to pass on to the journalist in the first place.

Approaching your local media

Although it's probably pretty obvious that nobody is going to get into the paper or on TV after a few weeks of blogging, that's pretty much where the obvious part ends. In fact — even after being on TV several times — in order to write this section, I had to reach out to the people I worked with on those shows to understand exactly what I had done to qualify as TV material. I figured they must have some kind of mental checklist and that I had somehow passed muster. That may be true, but if that's the case, then neither of the people I talked to were aware of it. For them, it was much simpler — they saw a good story to tell and a person who could tell it well. But it wasn't so simple from my point of view. Getting on TV was *years* of taking frustratingly small baby steps from being a blogging nobody to becoming an actual Somebody.

Here's where I sum up some of the things that will help you to get media coverage — but keep in mind that this is not a formula you can follow down to the letter. The following tips are more like general guidelines that will increase your chances of getting media coverage:

✔ **Know what you are talking about:** Journalists or producers aren't going to put you in the spotlight if you aren't knowledgeable in your chosen field. Doing so would make them look bad — it's your job to make them look good.

✔ **Look and act professional:** When they put you and your blog in front of their readers or listeners, they want you to look as credible as you are on the inside. This includes your physical appearance, your blog, and your public interactions in places like Twitter or Facebook.

✔ **Be unique:** It's the media's job to tell a story. If your blog is difficult to distinguish from hundreds of other blogs on the same topic, there's no story to tell.

Interestingly, I learned something else about working with the media while writing this chapter: Journalists, reporters, and television producers come from a traditional media world in which there are strict ethical codes that distinguish between commercial and editorial content. So when I went back to the *Today Show* producer who brought me onto the show in 2009, this is what he had to say:

> "When producing that segment, I was looking for moms who had a unique story and also some visual elements to help tell it. While experience on TV always helps, the most important factor to me was finding women who had a passion about telling their story about connecting with other moms in new ways. It was also key that none of the women be *compromised by any agreements with brands or advertisers.*" [Emphasis mine]
>
> — Ryan Osborn, Director of Social Media, NBC News

I asked Ryan for clarification on that last point, because this is something I hadn't considered before. He didn't mean that the right candidate *couldn't* be working with brands or advertisers. He simply meant that he naturally excludes people from consideration when there is a clear conflict of interest. For example, if I had been a food blogger being considered for a cooking segment, I might have been eliminated if I was also a designated spokesperson for a consumer food brand. This is important to consider as you build your advertising and brand relationships; it gives you one more reason to separate your advertising content from your editorial content, as I discuss in Chapter 9.

Networking with journalists and radio or TV producers

The preceding sections give you an idea of what the media is looking for, so the question that naturally follows is how can you get yourself in front of the media to be considered? The old-fashioned way of doing this is by sending out press releases or calling journalists and pitching story ideas. Today these approaches aren't as effective as they used to be. So I asked local anchor-woman and reporter Nancy Loo, from WGN-TV Chicago, about what works now. Nancy said, "Personally, I am seldom at my desk, so phone calls and voice-mails are least likely to garner a quick response. I prefer e-mail and social media. Pitches should be concise and addressed to the right person who covers your topic area. They should make clear why the subject is news-worthy. For example: 'Mommy blogger hosts massive playdate' will not be as interesting as 'Mommy blogger hosts girls-only playdate: believes boys are not smart enough to keep up'."

She also named the most effective way I have found to get in front of the media: networking. "Networking is key in every business. You can easily get to know your local journalists through social media. We are all encouraged to be on Facebook and Twitter — I have covered quite a few stories that I've spotted first on social media sites." I can attest to that; every time I've been on TV, it has been because of networking, Facebook, or Twitter. This is why it's so critical to establish and nurture your personal brand everywhere you go online. You'll never know when the media is watching you.

Local journalists aren't the only people who you'll want to know — plenty of national publications have writers and producers who are consistently seek-ing sources for stories. In the next set of bullets, I give you some tips on how to meet these people. But it is also important to identify the right people to talk to. Focus your efforts on journalists that are already producing stories on topics similar to your blog topic. Generally speaking, you'll have a much greater chance at getting featured on shows or publications that are targeted to women and moms.

There are a few places you can hang out online to increase your chances of getting noticed. Here are the best resources:

- ✔ **HARO — Help a Reporter Out:** (www.helpareporter.com) Help a Reporter Out was founded by Peter Shankman in 2008 as a way to help reporters, authors, and producers connect with experts via social media. He now gets over 200 media inquiries a day that are sent out to over 100,000 expert sources around the world. I've been interviewed several times by responding to journalist inquiries received via HARO. Plus: It's free and anyone can join. Even if you don't consider yourself an expert yet, HARO e-mails can help you understand the kinds of stories and topics you can contribute to.

   When you're comfortable responding to HARO queries, realize you are dealing with journalists that are almost always on a tight deadline and are probably sifting through hundreds of responses. So that means you have about one paragraph to let the journalist know why you can make a relevant and valuable contribution to his or her story.

It is not appropriate to respond to HARO inquiries with your own story ideas, or to introduce yourself for future consideration. Only respond to inquiries with relevant information on a case-by-case basis.

✔ **Facebook:** (www.facebook.com) As Nancy Loo said, journalists spend a lot of time online looking for story leads. Nancy featured me in a tele-vised special report last year when I reunited with my birth mother on Facebook right before the holidays. How did she hear about my reunion? Through Facebook. Many reporters have public profiles and fan pages; this is a great way to get into conversations with them. This is especially effective with your local media, who are typically much more accessible than national media are.

The simplest way to do this is to comment on their Facebook pages. Again, it is most appropriate to make comments that are relevant and contribute to the overall conversation. If your sole purpose of posting is to ask to be featured in a story, at best you'll get ignored. At worst, your posts may be marked as spam.

✔ **Twitter:** (www.twitter.com) I first met the *Today Show* producer who brought me on the show on Twitter. We had several conversations over four to six months before I got a Direct Message from him asking me to give him a call. After screaming and jumping all over my office, I calmed down and called to talk to him about coming to New York for a segment on Digital Moms. He specifically said that my name had been recom-mended to him, and because he already knew me, I had been the one he called.

So how can you do this yourself? Start engaging in conversations with television personalities, producers, or reporters along with the accounts of television shows and national publications. Give them feedback on what they are currently doing, which shows you are familiar with their respective backgrounds. Suggest ideas for stories and features you would like to see — whether or not you would want to be considered for those stories. My first interaction with the *Today Show* producer was to suggest doing a story on the emerging prominence of Twitter. The producer liked the idea enough to ask me more about what I thought the show's viewers would get out of that segment, and a conversation (and working relationship) followed from there.

✔ **#journchat:** Every Monday from 8–9pm ET, Sarah Evans from http://prsarahevans.com hosts a Twitter get-together called #journchat to discuss the current state of journalism. The umbrella theme for every edition is the changing state of media and new media's impact on what journalists are doing. It's not a place to pitch ideas, but a good conversa-tion to watch and learn from. You can simply follow along every week by searching on Twitter for the hashtag #journchat. Of course, if you meet a journalist during the #journchat that you want to pitch a story to, it is absolutely appropriate to do so privately after the event.

I should say here that just because the media can be easily found online, that doesn't mean that you should be stalking or spamming them trying to get a story written about you. The story they are looking for can only be found by focusing on what you do best — developing your brand and your blog as a valuable resource to your readers.

Creating a press room on your blog

Few things convey professionalism and credibility better than getting mentioned in the media. So if and when that starts happening for you, I highly recommend setting up a special online "press room" — a page on your blog that showcases the stories written about you. A *press room page* is simply a collection of article links, videos, and audio interviews wherever you've been mentioned in the media. You can also include any awards you have received on this page. The more press coverage you get, the more will come your way; it's kind of like a self-fulfilling prophecy. So, to prove to journalists and producers that you are camera-ready or feature-worthy, show off what you've already done.

My Facebook friend Jen Singer created a killer press room page, and has been great about keeping it up to date. You can see it in Figure 7-2 as a great example to strive for when you build your blog's press room.

Figure 7-2: Jen Singer of Momma Said has an excellent press room **page** to **feature** her past press coverage.

Chapter 8

Selling Your Own Products and Services

*B*logging is an extremely effective way to promote your own products or services to sell. Blogs will help you build trust with customers, get found in the search engines, and give your potential customers plenty of reasons to buy from you.

Selling Products or Services

While there are similarities to selling both products and services, they can actually be quite different from each other. In order to persuade your visitors to make an online transaction and buy a product, you need to convince them that their payment method and personal information are safe; they are getting a quality product for the price; you'll send them their purchase as promised, and in the condition described; and that they can't find the same product elsewhere for less money. And these are just the tactical basics; you also need to convince people that your product is something they want or need, which is a more subjective matter.

In contrast, selling services requires a different sales process. In this situation you need to convince people that you are an expert that can deliver results for clients; you have the past experience that demonstrates you can handle the clients' specific project requirements; you are a better person for the job than others who are also qualified to do the same; and they can trust you with their confidential company information.

In both circumstances, the primary goal is to build trust so that clients feel comfortable buying from you. Trust-building is a critical and never-ending process that touches every aspect of your business:

- ✔ **Branding:** Your brand is the first impression you give to everyone, and there's nowhere first impressions count more than in the online world. I talk a lot about branding in Chapter 6.

- ✔ **Site design and functionality:** Your site not only needs to look professional; it needs to act that way, too. Broken links, error pages, and layout problems will immediately send the message that your site can't be trusted to function properly. If your site can't be trusted, people won't trust you, either, especially if you're asking them to enter sensitive financial or personal information. I talk more about professional site design in Chapter 6.

- ✔ **Product development:** Your products need to be what customers want to buy, which might not necessarily be what you want to sell. Even if you're selling services, you need to present your skills in a way that's immediately understandable and meets a clearly defined need.

- ✔ **Writing and content creation:** Your blog is the most effective way to publish your thoughts and ideas that demonstrate your knowledge and expertise. This is even true when it comes to the little details such as word choice, grammar, clarity, and professionalism.

- ✔ **Social conversations:** How you interact with people in your blog comments and on social networks says more about you than your website does. Your personality and actions need to be 100-percent congruent with your professional content and marketing messages. If they aren't, your visitors will tend to believe the worst about you instead of the best.

- ✔ **How you manage disagreements or disputes:** Everyone makes mistakes, and customers know this for the most part. While they like to expect perfection from companies, people are far more forgiving if they see a company correcting mistakes instead of ignoring them. Worse, if a company or a person is defensive or antagonistic, it can lose years of goodwill in a few seconds.

Creating a Line of Products or Services

One of the most important lessons I learned in my first business is that you can't build a business on selling things that you love; you have to sell things people want to buy.

This is why it's essential to do research before you invest in buying, making, or developing products to sell. Market research can be challenging, especially when you may not know what you're looking for. But some really simple tools you're probably already using can help you get a good idea of what people want and need:

✔ **Twitter conversations:** Twitter is a real-time market-research machine, with millions of brand conversations happening every week. If you really want to know what's hot or what irritates people in your industry, just conduct searches on popular words your potential customers would use and talk about.

✔ **Facebook feedback:** I frequently turn to Facebook to ask for my friends' input on trends, news, and purchasing decisions. It's easy to post a quick question to your friends in your Facebook status to ask them what they think about a topic or brand that can give you insights into what your customers might be thinking.

✔ **Google Trends:** As the most used search engine in the world (and with an insatiable appetite for consumer data), Google probably knows more about us as a species than any other company. Google Trends at `www.google.com/trends` can help you mine all sorts of search trends over the course of many years. Google Trends displays hot searches daily, but also allows you to input keywords so you can see the history of how often that keyword has been searched for since 2004. It doesn't give you the specific quantity of searches, but instead simply shows you how the volume of searches varies from average. The 1.00 horizontal line represents the number of *average* searches for that phrase. The 2.00 line represents a number that is *two times higher* than the average. You can see an example of the history of the term *blogging* in Figure 8-1, plus how the number of searches on blogging spikes to more than two times the normal amount in mid 2005 and at the end of 2007.

✔ **Google Insights for Search:** Part of the Google Trends product is a more sophisticated tool called Google Insights for Search at `www.google.com/insights/search`. This tool allows you to dive in deeper and narrow data by location, time range, multiple search phrases, and categories of information, not just individual terms. You can see how the two terms *mom* and *blogging* have been searched over the last few years in Figure 8-2, when the search is limited to the Social Networks & Online Communities category.

Figure 8-1:
Google
Trends
shows the
search vol-
ume history
of "blog-
ging" since
2004.

When you use these tools, here are the kinds of things you want to look for:

- **Conversations around your product category discussing topics like what customers love, hate, can't find, or don't need.** You'll find this kind of information by monitoring conversations on Twitter and Facebook. You can do this by searching for conversations that include words you think your customers would likely use. For example, if you are an eco-conscious blogger, you can use the search feature to find conversations using the words *recycle, global warming,* or *cloth diapers.*

- **Mentions of other blogs, companies, or brands that are getting positive or negative feedback from users.** Again, turn to Twitter and Facebook for this information. You can search for specific brand names, or for URLs of sites that have similar content to yours. You can also watch the conversations of influential people and read what they have to say about the companies they do business with.

- **Growing or waning interest in specific categories on the Google trending tools can predict an increase or decrease in demand for your products or services.** For example, if you are thinking of starting a coupon blog, Google Trends will show you that interest in this subject increased drastically at the end of 2008 when the U.S. was in recession. Alternatively, interest in the subject of real estate dropped around the same time. You can use this as a general indication that the last two years have been great for money-saving websites and harder on sites about real estate.

As you get a better idea of what people want or need, then you can start to develop ideas about what you want to sell that will be useful to your customers. You may think of product development only in terms of actual products. But if you sell your services, I encourage you to think of what you do in terms of packaged service plans, kind of like a cable service provider bundles phone, Internet, and TV packages. I show a great example of this in Chapter 10, from PR and social media consultant Barbara Rozgonyi. Barbara ultimately wants to get hired for a wide variety of projects, but she puts her services into easily understandable and sellable packages to encourage new clients to try out her most popular services. For example, she has put together a starter service package she calls the *Always On PR Strategic Plan Design*. It includes specifics like these:

✔ 90-minute preliminary consulting session

✔ Marketing communications, visibility, and reputation audit

✔ Reports such as website performance and social media mentions

✔ Six-month Accelerated Marketing Plan

✔ 90-minute kick-start strategy session

Figure 8-2:
Google Insights for Search shows trends of searches in specific categories.

The benefits of selling her services in this manner are also listed:

- ✔ **Flat-rate pricing:** New clients can make a purchase knowing exactly what they'll receive and know they won't get charged for unanticipated expenses.

- ✔ **Efficient use of her time:** Barbara puts together a group of services that she knows she can do quickly and efficiently, especially because she'll be doing the same thing for many clients. This way she can create saved reports and document templates that make it easier to produce these service packages in bulk.

- ✔ **Appealing to a range of clients:** Some people only need a little guidance and can do the rest of the work on their own. Others will want to hire Barbara to do everything. Creating package plans like this makes her expertise accessible to clients with small budgets, but doesn't hinder her ability to take on large-scale projects with big budgets.

Choosing an Online Marketplace

For selling physical products, the key to using a blog effectively to send traffic to your online store is to use a soft-sell approach. It's hard to build up a loyal audience if your blog is simply publishing product descriptions and pitches. You want to create content that's useful to the people who are likely to want to buy your products at some point.

A great example of this principle in action is the Sew, Mama, Sew! blog (www. sewmamasew.com), founded in 2002 by Kristin Link. She first started the site as an online store selling specialty fabrics. But her site really took off in late 2007, when she and her writers started a new Handmade Holidays series of tutorials and handmade gift ideas. The blog started becoming extremely popular among craft blogs, and she realized that she needed to be more conscientious about creating useful content that also featured some of her store fabrics and supplies. She now plans out the blog's content on an editorial calendar a month or two in advance — and the Sew, Mama, Sew! blog continues to be one of the most widely read sewing blogs anywhere. You can see her very popular blog in Figure 8-3.

Figure 8-3:
The Sew,
Mama,
Sew! blog
supports an
e-commerce
store for
fabric and
sewing
supplies.

Deciding where to sell your products or services

For those of you selling actual products, you have many choices as to where you can sell online. eBay, Etsy, CafePress, and Amazon are some of the most common marketplaces used by bloggers, and some people venture out to setting up shopping carts on their own websites as well. You don't need to limit yourself to one way of selling online. I've seen bloggers sell products on their own sites, Etsy, *and* eBay simultaneously. This, of course, increases your work load, but it also gets your products in front of the largest number of potential customers. Those who have used this approach have found it's worth the extra time and effort to maintain multiple storefronts. But it is best to get established in one marketplace first before you branch out.

Here's a quick overview of the most popular online store sites to help you determine where you may want to begin. Selling on any of these sites is certainly beyond the scope of this book, but there are extensive training and selling tools available to sellers from each of these marketplaces directly:

✔ **Amazon** (www.amazon.com): No site on the Internet converts visitors into sales better than Amazon. Their site is the one most trusted and most frequently used by shoppers, period. You can sell items for $0.99 per listing, a $0.80 to $1.35 closing fee, plus a varying percentage of the sale price of the item. Some of these fees are waived if you pay a flat rate for their Pro Merchant Subscriber program at $39.99 a month.

To learn more about selling on Amazon, go to: www.amazon.com/gp/seller/sell-your-stuff.html. You can also check out *Amazon.com For Dummies* by Mara Friedman.

✔ **Etsy** (www.etsy.com): For handmade items, nothing beats Etsy. You can also sell craft supplies and vintage items on Etsy as well. Etsy doesn't have the market reach that Amazon does, but on Etsy you'll find buyers more interested in your products because they shop there specifically for handmade items. Etsy charges a $0.20 listing fee plus 3.5 percent of the sale price of your item.

To learn more about selling on Etsy go to: www.etsy.com/how_selling_works.php. You can also check out *Starting an Etsy Business For Dummies* by Allison Strine and Kate Shoup, a new book on the subject coming out in September 2011.

✔ **eBay** (www.ebay.com): It's hard to beat eBay for selling used items and vintage finds. eBay has the volume that Amazon does, but also attracts buyers hunting for a good deal. eBay charges no listing fees for starting prices under $0.99, and then scales the listing fees up based on starting price to a maximum of $2.00 for items with a starting price of $200.00 and up. When an item sells on eBay, you pay eBay 9 percent of the sale price. eBay also has an eBay Stores level that starts at $15.95 per month.

To learn more about selling on eBay go to: http://pages.ebay.com/sellerinformation/howtosell/sellingbasics.html. You can also check out *Starting an eBay Business For Dummies,* 4th Edition, by Marsha Collier.

✔ **CafePress** (www.cafepress.com): CafePress is different from the previously mentioned online marketplaces because it actually manufactures the items sold — you're the one who designs them. The benefit is that you don't have to pay for your inventory before you sell it, and you can sell on CafePress for free. You also control the pricing of your items by choosing your own price markup. In this scenario, CafePress is the one earning the most from each sale, so you need to sell more volume in order to make the kind of profit you could make on your own. The site also has a premium-store feature that starts at $4.99 a month, which pays out a flat 10 percent of the revenue from your store to you.

To learn more about selling on CafePress go to: www.cafepress.com/cp/info/sell/index.aspx.

For those of you selling your services, you may want to consider joining an online service marketplace like Elance (www.elance.com) or Guru.com (www.guru.com). Having done this many years ago, I can say that the main benefit is that you can find a wide range of projects and potential clients who are willing and ready to hire help. The main drawback is that you'll be competing in a global marketplace where your competition may be able to charge a fraction of your normal rates because they live in a country with a lower cost of living. The people that I've seen have the most success with these sites are writers, designers, virtual assistants, Web developers, and marketing consultants.

Elance and Guru work essentially the same way — service providers are charged a small monthly fee, and then also pay a portion of every fee earned from projects gained from the sites. Both also offer a limited option with the monthly fee waived so that you can test the waters and decide if the work you gain is worth the costs.

To learn more about selling your services on Elance go to: www.elance.com/q/find-work/online-work-overview. To learn more about selling your services on Guru go to: www.guru.com/pro/index.aspx.

Setting up a payment system

The great part about working with an established online marketplace is that these sites have a built-in customer base — and they take care of all the sales transactions for you. If you only have a few products to sell, you can also use a service like PayPal to handle your online transactions. For those of you who sell intangible products such as downloads, event tickets, or printables, E-junkie is a great additional service that can manage that process for you.

PayPal (www.paypal.com) has grown to become the largest online payment provider with many different sophisticated products for all kinds of businesses. For bloggers selling a few items, such as e-books or patterns, here's what PayPal can do for you:

- ✔ **One-time payments:** You need only have a PayPal account for a customer to send you money. This is free to set up, and then PayPal charges a $0.30-transaction fee, plus 2.2 to 2.9 percent of the sale, depending on the amount. These payments are handled on the PayPal website. Customers can pay by credit card, bank transfer, or their own PayPal account balance.

- ✔ **Online invoicing:** For the same fees, you can send out invoices to customers and accept credit-card and bank-transfer payments, even when your customers are not PayPal members.

✔ **Accept recurring payments:** You can create subscription-based products and have your customers automatically pay via a PayPal recurring payment. To use this feature, your customers have to be PayPal members, though a professional upgrade is available that eliminates this requirement.

✔ **Add Buy Now buttons:** Give your site a more professional look by adding Buy Now and Add to Cart buttons that allow site visitors to buy immediately from your blog.

Selling downloads

PayPal can handle the payments for your products, but they can't deliver them. That's up to you. If you're selling downloadable products (e-books, music, patterns, printables, software, event tickets, or audio/video content), you can make sure those items are delivered automatically to your customers with a service such as E-junkie (www.e-junkie.com). E-junkie works with a payment provider like PayPal that confirms a purchase, and then sends the downloads to your customers when your transactions are complete.

Here are some business features that E-junkie can manage for you:

✔ **Storage and delivery of all your downloadable files**

✔ **Super-easy-to-use Buy Now or Add to Cart buttons**

✔ **The capability to offer discount codes or multi-product promotion discounts**

✔ **E-mail autoresponders and newsletter management**

Autoresponders are e-mails sent out automatically when a sale is made, so that you don't have to stay next to your computer and watch for transactions.

✔ **Affiliate program management**

If you want to pay other people a commission for sending customers to your site, you can run your own affiliate program and track sales and payments with E-junkie.

Generating Leads for Your Business

The most common way that professional bloggers make a living is by using their blogs to find paid work and sponsorship opportunities. This means that bloggers are finding ways to earn money *because* of their blog, not directly on their blogs. That's why it's vital to be active on sites like Twitter and Facebook, and to be an active networker all the time. Often you'll find new clients from connections you make and the conversations you have with your online friends. Additionally, sometimes you'll need to work with a client and use your connections to help spread the word about the projects you work on.

Most bloggers I know (most *people* for that matter) tend to have an aversion to what would be considered outside sales. Bloggers don't like to think about clients as prospects, about getting sales leads, or about closing deals. It's easier to think about getting your name out there or getting hired. The words are different, but the process is the same. When you're a freelancer, your product is your talent, your leads are your friends, and your closed deals result in getting hired.

Because I've done a little work in outside sales, I can tell you that you'll benefit from borrowing a few tactics from really successful salespeople. I'm not talking about using used-car-salesman-style pitches, but rather about the ways successful salespeople formally gather leads and turn prospects into customers. Salespeople don't throw a bunch of stuff at a wall in hopes it'll stick. They have a formal sales process and consciously move through certain steps from start to finish.

I know that *sales* is a word that can turn people off immediately. But don't worry. This next section isn't really about sales per se, but instead about the sales *process* (big difference!).

Identifying your typical customer

I think I talk about focusing on a niche in nearly every chapter of this book. And here I go again: You need to focus on a niche. Marketing is not just about finding the right clients, but also about avoiding the wrong clients. When you're focusing on a niche, the first step is identifying your typical customer.

The second step goes further than appealing to a group of individuals with a specific need, and encourages you to more clearly define the traits of the kind of client you want to work with.

For example, if you're a coach for women in business, your marketing efforts will focus on finding professional women. But your *typical customer* is a much more specific profile. She may

- ✔ Be self-employed or employed by a company.
- ✔ Be a solo entrepreneur or have a staff of 20+.
- ✔ Work only on nonprofit endeavors, or only on for-profit companies.
- ✔ Be in a certain age range or life stage.
- ✔ Work in a specific industry, such as eco-friendly businesses or food related businesses.
- ✔ Have fewer than 5 years of experience or more than 20.

Getting to a profile of your typical customer involves identifying the kind of client you feel you can help the most, based on your own experiences. Many years ago, when I was a freelance designer, I met and became friends with the now-very-well-known Scott Stratten, who recently wrote *UnMarketing: Stop Marketing. Start Engaging* (Wiley). I was one of his very first coaching clients, and he asked me to identify my perfect client. I was rather surprised that I hadn't really thought about that prior to his asking me. It took me several days to identify my dream client, down to the personality of the client and the exact kind of projects that person would hire me for. It was an extremely valuable exercise, as it helped me to go more consciously after the kinds of clients who'd hire me and the projects I'd most likely be hired for.

You can start to identify your own perfect client by listing the important traits of past clients you have enjoyed working with the most. Then imagine your dream project — and think about the kind of person or company who would hire you for such a project. You can add even more traits to your list as you make guesstimations as to what this client would be like. When I was a graphic designer, my perfect client was another work-at-home mom who was a free-lance writer or marketer. This client would typically work with a wide range of her own clients such as local businesses and area corporations. This perfect client of mine had a steady need for my design services, and was also a mom who understood what it was like to run a business and family from home.

Designing your blog to maximize sales

Liz Strauss of Successful Blog (`www.successful-blog.com`) was the one that first introduced me to this idea — focusing your efforts on one big banana — as found in the book *The Big Red Fez: How to Make Any Web Site Better* by Seth Godin (Free Press). Seth says, "A website visitor is a lot like a monkey looking for one thing: a banana. If that banana isn't easy to see and easy to get, your visitor is gone with a quick click on the Back button." Liz showed me that you need to make perfectly clear what your blog reader can get from being on your site — and the way to do that is to create an impos-sible-to-miss *call to action*. This means, essentially, that you don't make your visitors have to think about what you want them to do. Make it immediately understandable. For instance . . .

- **Buy something:** If you want someone to make a purchase, don't clutter up your sales page with links to your favorite blogs or articles about related topics. Keep it clear — a photograph, a description, and a big Buy Now button.

- **Register:** If your blog has a section that requires people to register, you'll want to explain the benefits of registering at the top of the page, and keep it viewable *without* scrolling.

✔ **Download something:** You might have a free download that either entices people to sign up for your newsletter, or is a case study that shows potential clients what you're capable of. You want to promote this prominently on your pages — and create a separate page free of extraneous information to convince them to download it, functioning much like a sales page.

✔ **Sign up for something:** You may have an event, a newsletter, or a Facebook page that you're promoting. Again, feature this prominently on your blog and minimize distractions.

If you'd like to see a great example of a call to action on a blog, check out Aliza Sherman's newsletter Subscribe button in Figure 8-4. On the site the button is bright red and the most prominent item on the page.

Knowing who your customer is and what you're selling might seem to be basic things, but you might be surprised how few people think through these two steps very clearly. Tailoring your site to attract the right people and sell these things is half the battle.

Figure 8-4:
Aliza Sherman's newsletter-signup call to action.

Developing a Mailing List

I think every single blogger who is selling products or services should have a mailing list. But especially if you're an Etsy seller, please read this section of this book! As a frequent Etsy buyer, I've noticed that sellers do little to no e-mail marketing, and I wish they would. Promoting your new products to your past customers is the number-one way to increase your sales!

Knowing how important and valuable a mailing list is, I'm ashamed to say that I didn't start one until I had been blogging for over four years. I can honestly say that I truly regret not doing it sooner, now that I see how beneficial it has been to my business. You don't have to be selling something to create a good mailing list. My Woo! Jr. weekly newsletter simply features seasonal content and sends traffic to my websites. Having a mailing list has been important in many ways:

- ✔ **It keeps traffic consistent:** Mailing-list subscribers are your readers most interested in your content or products and services. As long as you maintain a regular e-mail schedule, your mailing list will consistently send your most loyal readers and customers back to your sites.

- ✔ **It builds long-term value:** Having a mailing list is important to the long-term value of your site or blog. Consistent e-mail marketing efforts will gradually increase your traffic and profits over time. It's also a great asset to have if you ever want to sell your blog someday because you get to sell both a blog and a built-in client base along with it.

- ✔ **It communicates new content and features:** The fastest way to promote your new projects, products, and site features is through a mailing list. Your subscribers will be the ones most interested in these things, too.

- ✔ **Sells products:** Statistically, e-mail marketing is one of *the* most effective ways to sell products to past customers or people interested in buying from you. Sending a strong call to action with direct links to sales pages directly into customers' inboxes makes it *very* easy for them to make purchases. Plus, your subscribers learn what to expect from your newsletters over time, so if they open them, they have already made a step toward a purchase.

- ✔ **Building loyalty:** Often your visitors may come to your site and love your stuff, but may not be able to buy right at that moment. By signing up for your newsletter, they have given you permission to market to them, and they have expressed an interest in learning more about you. Sometimes, a visitor just needs time to build trust before making a purchase. A regular newsletter is the best way to do that.

Not all blogs need an e-mail newsletter and mailing list. But if you're selling your products and services from your blog, a newsletter will absolutely help you get more sales over time. This is one project I really recommend — and now that I know the consequences of putting it off, I hope you don't make the same mistake I did.

Choosing an easy e-mail marketing provider

E-mail marketing is easy, but it does take some time. You could, of course, send out your own e-mails for free from your own account, but you can quickly run into problems if you don't know what you're doing. The CAN-Spam act was put in place in 2003 to prevent companies from spamming and establish best-practice standards. If you aren't doing everything right, your e-mails could end up in everyone's spam filter — or, worse, get your domain banned from being able to e-mail altogether. Using an e-mail marketing provider will help you ensure that your newsletters are both effective and legal under the CAN-Spam requirements. Another reason to use an e-mail marketing provider is that it has the technology to send out large amounts of e-mails at one time, and is whitelisted by Internet service providers so that you don't have to worry about getting banned.

The two easiest to use e-mail marketing service providers are iContact.com (www.icontact.com) and MailChimp (www.mailchimp.com). Both offer a product that's easy enough for beginners to use at an affordable price. They also have a free option for beginners. iContact.com offers great advanced features plus plenty of tech support. MailChimp has slightly fewer general e-mail marketing features but has a reputation for being extra easy to use. Because these companies are similar and always adding new features, I suggest going to both of their websites, comparing the two, and going with whichever you're most comfortable with.

If you really plan on doing a lot of e-mail marketing in the future, and antici-pate it being a big part of your business, I suggest going with a more sophis-ticated e-mail marketing provider. The one that's most often used is AWeber (www.aweber.com). (I use it, and so do most professional Web marketers.) AWeber isn't quite as easy to use, but it offers options for nearly unlimited custom website integration with its application programming interface (API). Also, at the time of writing, AWeber is more affordable than iContact.com or Constant Contact.

Setting up signup forms on your blog

All e-mail marketing providers give you the ability to add an e-mail signup form to your website. How and where you add it is up to you. Earlier in this chapter, I mention that you want to put your important calls to action at the top of your blog pages. To review: A *call to action* is simply letting your visi-tors know what you want them to do when they visit your website.

I've experimented quite a bit with where to put a newsletter signup form on my sites. When I put it at the top of my blog sidebar, I got a few people to sign up. When I placed it even higher on the page — *and* put it in my blog header — my signup rate more than doubled. I experimented with using one of those annoying pop-up windows in the middle of the screen, and my signup rate tripled. But at that point, I felt that the negative association of the pop-up with intrusion didn't outweigh the benefits I was getting from the additional subscribers. I also felt like it would discourage other bloggers from linking to me (who wants to send their trusting blog readers to a pop-up window?). So I settled on a different kind of pop-up for my sites: It only appears on the bottom of the page and doesn't interfere with viewing the page content. I know that even this kind of pop-up is not perfect and annoys some people — but for my business, it was a good balance between getting a lot more newsletter subscribers and maintaining usability on my blogs. For some people, that kind of pop-up is still too much. For others, it makes more sense to place the pop-up in the middle of the page. You can see the two placements on one of my blogs in Figure 8-5.

The point is that you *have* to test different placements on your blog to see what works for you. Even if you have an aversion to pop-ups, I would encourage you to at least test them out to know for sure that the benefits do or don't outweigh the costs. Over the course of a year, the difference between using a pop-up or not could be tens of thousands of subscribers. For bloggers who are selling products or services, this could translate into several thousands of dollars in additional income. Most e-mail providers have built-in testing tools that will help you with this, along with tutorials to help you apply the tests to your specific blog setup.

Sign up forms

Figure 8-5:
Successfully
tested
placement
of an e-mail
signup form.

Writing effective e-mail campaigns

It's absolutely true that writing effective e-mail marketing campaigns is an art — and a science. Thousands of articles have been written *just* on writing e-mail subject lines. And on top of that, what you write for an informational newsletter is going to be vastly different from if you're writing newsletters for selling things.

As I explain in the previous section, you have to test a lot of different variables to find out what works best for your subscribers. Here are some factors that can influence how many people open, click on, or buy through your e-mails:

- **Day of the week:** I find it fascinating that sending your e-mails on a different day of the week can increase how many people will open your message. I've found that for my kids' activities network, Mondays work best for the most number of opens. But for my craft blog for adults, Wednesdays work best. This is because teachers and caregivers are the main audience of my kids' activities e-mails, and they plan out their weeks every Monday. But crafting women are usually back to their main jobs on Mondays and aren't thinking about craft projects. Wednesday is the day when they start thinking about what they might want to create over the weekend. But I only know this because I tested it by sending out my weekly e-mails at the same time of day on different days of the week for several months, and then went back and looked at which e-mails were opened the most.

- **Time of day:** I know my e-mails get opened the most when I send them in the morning. Unfortunately, I don't always get them out in the morning, and I pay the consequences by getting fewer messages opened! But most e-mail marketing providers will also let you pre-schedule e-mails so that you can get the messages ready prior to when you want to send them.

- **Subject line:** Your subject line is usually the only indication a reader has to determine whether they want to take the time to read your e-mail or not. Subject lines need to be:

  a. Short, so they don't get cut off in e-mail previewers.

  b. Interesting and intriguing, because you want people to want to read your content.

  c. Written without words that frequently get flagged as spam, such as *free, act now, 50 percent off, buy, ad, discount, earn,* and so on. Other typical spam phrases to avoid are *home-based, online degrees, lowest insurance rates, lose weight, eliminate debt,* and similar. (You can tell where I am going with this, yes?)

✔ **Link wording:** A website commits a horrible *faux pas,* in terms of search engine optimization, if it links with the words Click Here — because that offers no clue, to either the vistors or the search engine, about what you've just linked to. The exact opposite is true in an e-mail: There you want to do everything possible to encourage people to click your links. So I suggest using Click Here as your link text very frequently in e-mails.

✔ **Image inclusion:** I have had more than a few people unsubscribe from my newsletters when I didn't include image previews of the website content or products I was featuring. E-mail readers want to be able to determine instantly whether they want to visit your site for more information.

Outside of all these factors, the content of your e-mail needs to be written in a different approach than when you write for your blog. You certainly want to maintain your own personality and voice, but when writing for an e-mail, you'll need to use a lot fewer words than you might be used to. People read e-mails on the fly, and unless they have an immediate reason to read further, they'll quickly hit Delete. This means that what you might normally communicate in a paragraph, you need to convey in a sentence. But remember, the point of an e-mail is not to send out lengthy articles or sales letters. The point is to get people to click and visit your blog or shop. So you need to write just enough for the reader to want to know more.

The reason that this e-mail got a great response was for a number of reasons. I lead the e-mail with three short bullet points to let people know what they will find in the newsletter. It's a visually appealing and simple layout that makes it very easy to scan quickly. The headlines are big and stand out, and are supported with an additional link that says *Click here to read more.* The images let readers know exactly what to expect if they click the links. Lastly, Halloween is one of the busiest holidays for my websites, so my readers are always more engaged at this time of year.

All e-mail marketing providers have excellent training resources for their customers. You can expect to find a support center, FAQ, and even training videos or articles to help you get the most out of your e-mail marketing efforts. You can really rely on whomever you choose to run your e-mail marketing campaigns to help you out. After all, they have a vested interest in your success.

Part III
Working with Advertisers and Brands

The 5th Wave   By Rich Tennant

"Oh, we're doing just great. Philip and I are selling decorative jelly jars on my blog. I run the Web site and Philip sort of controls the inventory."

In this part . . .

This part is the real meat of the book, in which I give you hands-on guidance on ways to attract advertisers and sponsors for your blog.

First, I take you through the important ethics of how working with sponsors may affect your content, and make sure you know the legal FTC guidelines so you can stay out of trouble.

Next, I show you how to pull all your assets together to make sure you look your best when you're ready to pitch yourself to brand representatives. I give you my best advice on how to make sure you get paid what you deserve, and how to price your ad space and blog promotions at an appropriate level.

Lastly, I dedicate three chapters to finding and working with advertisers — by selling ads yourself, by working with a company that will sell ads for you (an ad network), and by selling products on a commissioned basis (also called affiliate marketing).

Chapter 9

Mastering Blogging Ethics

In This Chapter

▶ Understanding how to implement the FTC blogger disclosure guidelines

▶ Ensuring that your advertising sales don't get you banned from search engines

▶ Writing an editorial policy, disclosure policy, and privacy policy

▶ Ensuring that your giveaways are legal

▶ Writing reviews and sponsored content with integrity

This chapter is not only about how you handle potential conflicts of inter-est, but also how these potential conflicts are perceived by your audience. The reason I say this is because on a personal level, you might be (and prob-ably are) completely capable of writing an unbiased compensated blog post. But unless you understand the rules about writing compensated blog posts, you risk getting fined thousands of dollars by the FTC, getting dropped from Google's search engine results, and ruining your reputation, thereby ruining your blogging business. You can still write a compensated blog post and avoid all these consequences — as long as you know how to play by the rules.

The rules, by the way, are not mine. The FTC has its own set of rules, as does Google. The rest are less concrete and open to interpretation by the general public. Your most loyal readers will likely trust your opinion because they know you well. But you also need to be concerned about the readers who don't know you well. Unfortunately, the nature of interactions on the Internet means that most new readers will not trust you right off the bat; they tend to expect the worst. You know how the law says you're not innocent until proven guilty? Same deal with trust: You're not considered trustworthy until you prove you are; you have to earn every bit of trust you receive. So no matter how ethical you are at a personal level, it is your professional level of ethics that will make the most difference in your business and the level of trust it enjoys.

Adapting Journalistic Standards to the Blogging World

The different natures of blogging and journalism have certainly caused friction over the years as blogs have become more influential in the mainstream media. The perceived problem isn't with the fact that bloggers' content and journalists' content are created in such different ways. The problem is that people consume our two different kinds of content in very much the *same* way. People have come to demand a certain level of honesty from the people and organizations that produce the content they read. This is why the FTC stepped into the blogosphere in 2009 and established new guidelines on how testimonials and endorsements must be presented.

While journalistic standards are slightly different for print, broadcast, and online organizations, they share common elements of truthfulness, accuracy, objectivity, impartiality, fairness, and public accountability (that's an adapted quote from Wikipedia). Most of all, journalistic standards establish a separation between the departments that bring in revenue (advertising and sponsorship sales) and the departments that develop content. This creates a natural boundary to prevent many perceived conflicts of interest.

Creating separation between sponsored and editorial content

At the same time, it's next to impossible for most bloggers to operate at the level of journalistic standards that news organizations do. We don't have a sales team to sell advertising and sponsorships for us. We're our own sales team and our own Editor in Chief. We don't have a *perceived* natural boundary between our advertisers' interests and our own business interests, even when one exists internally. So it's wise to follow what's become a best practice in blogging — to create your own separation between content that's sponsored and *editorial content* — your own writing that has no direct ties to outside interests.

Creating separation between your sponsored and editorial content is only necessary when you're writing content that is compensated in any of the following ways:

- When you receive a product/service for free and write a review, testimonial, or endorsement about it.

- When you receive any other form of compensation in exchange for writing a review, testimonial, or endorsement (this includes money, travel expenses, meals or entertainment, or other free products or services).

✔ When you endorse an advertiser or client outside of the context of your blog, as when you're engaged in social media conversations.

✔ When you use an affiliate link in conjunction with a review or recommendation (this doesn't apply to affiliate marketing that is clearly advertising and doesn't include a personal recommendation or endorsement).

There are a few ways to separate these kinds of sponsored content from the rest of the content on your blog:

✔ **Create a separate blog for sponsored content:** Blogger Maggie Mason writes Mighty Girl (`http://mightygirl.net`), a personal blog about her life in San Francisco with her husband and son. She has created three additional blogs that are commercial in nature, the largest being the shopping blog Mighty Goods (`http://mightygoods.com`). By doing this, she is able to easily separate her personal content from her commercial content. See two of Maggie's blogs in Figure 9-1.

✔ **Have sponsored content written by someone else or by the sponsor:** The leading technology blog ReadWriteWeb (`www.readwriteweb.com`) allows its long-term sponsors to write blog posts on the blog. The posts are labeled clearly as "Written by RWW Sponsor." They are also placed in a separate category so that regular visitors know if they are reading editorial or sponsored content. See this method in action in Figure 9-2.

✔ **Write a clear notice at the beginning of a sponsored post, disclosing your relationship to the sponsor:** Amanda Soule's SouleMama blog (`www.soulemama.com`) is one of my favorite examples of sponsored content done well. Each of her advertisers is a perfect match for her audience of creative crafting moms. On any sponsored post on her blog, the post title is prefixed with "SouleMama Sponsor ~" so that blog readers and RSS readers know what to expect from her content. All of her sponsors provide a giveaway, so Amanda's readers love her sponsored content as much as her regular content! See one of these posts in action in Figure 9-3.

Figure 9-1: Maggie Mason created blogs for personal writings and sponsored content.

Figure 9-2:
ReadWrite-
Web
separates
sponsored
content by
having the
sponsors
write it.

Figure 9-3:
The
SouleMama
blog titles
every com-
pensated
post as a
sponsored
post.

Writing an editorial policy

Writing an editorial policy will help you in more ways than guiding your ethics. An *editorial policy* is a short document that clarifies what subjects you will and won't write about on your blog, so it helps to define your niche more clearly than you might otherwise be able to do. In the context of blogging ethics, it's important to have a published editorial policy if you write any posts that are sponsored content, as defined earlier in this chapter. An editorial policy is just as important if you write content that could be *perceived* as sponsored content, even when it isn't. Here's an example: writing reviews only of products that you purchase on your own.

Having a published editorial policy will signal to your readers that you take your content — and their opinion of you — seriously. It will also signal to brand representatives and PR firms that you are a professional and take their marketing objectives seriously, too. All of these things will help you build your reputation and open the doors to bigger sponsorship opportunities down the road.

An editorial policy doesn't have to be long — it can be just a couple of paragraphs. You can place it on your About page, on its own page, or on your Disclosures page (which I cover in the next section). Here are the things you should cover in your editorial policy:

- ✔ How you conduct your product reviews
- ✔ How and when you publish, or might publish, sponsored content
- ✔ The kinds of topics that will and won't be covered in your sponsored content
- ✔ The kind of sponsored opportunities you will or have turned down

Later on in this chapter, I talk about how to create a disclosure policy that covers many of these things. You can combine the documents into one page, or keep them separate if you choose to do so.

Understanding Disclosures and the FTC Guidelines

In 2009, the FTC released updated advertising guidelines that hadn't been revised in nearly 30 years. Most of the media and public attention was focused on the new rules about how blogs must disclose reviews and recommendations. But blogs weren't the only target of the new rules. Guidelines about celebrity endorsements and advertisements that convey a consumer's experience with a product were also changed. In the past, only advertisers were on the hook for any misrepresentations, but the new rules state that *both* advertisers *and* celebrity endorsers may be liable for false or unsubstantiated claims made in an endorsement. Advertisers also used to be able to describe unusual results in a testimonial as long as they included a disclaimer such as "results not typical." But the new guidelines have taken that safe harbor away; now "advertisements that feature a consumer and convey his or her experience with a product or service as typical when that is not the case will be required to clearly disclose the results that consumers can generally expect." For more information, go to www.ftc.gov/opa/2009/10/endortest.shtm.

With these new guidelines, the FTC *had* to include bloggers and word-of-mouth marketers in the update. When a blogger is compensated for a blog post, it then constitutes an advertisement. And there is an increasingly fine line between real celebrities and blogging celebrities. A very well-known blogger can't really say that he or she isn't "enough of a celebrity" to be held to the new FTC standards, especially when a brand is willing to engage in an endorsement relationship with the blogger as it would other celebrity endorsers.

Knowing what you need to disclose

So now the law requires you to disclose any material relationships that you have with brands or advertisers when you write a review or recommend something to your readers. The material relationships you must disclose are the same as the sponsored content criteria I outline at the beginning of this chapter:

- When you receive a product/service for free and write a review, testimonial, or endorsement about it.
- When you receive any other form of compensation in exchange for writing a review, testimonial, or endorsement about it.
- When you endorse an advertiser or client outside of the context of your blog, as when you engage in social media conversations.
- When you use an affiliate link in conjunction with a review or recommendation.

In these circumstances, the FTC specifically states that consumers must be able to see the disclosure when they are viewing the endorsement. So you need to provide your disclosure within your actual blog post — putting a blanket disclosure on a separate page is not adequate.

So how do you write an FTC-compliant disclosure? It's simple — just tell it like it is. Here are some examples:

- ✔ **When you receive a free product to review, include a disclosure like the following example:** "Home Depot provided me with some of the materials I used in this bathroom remodel. I bought the rest of the materials from them with my own money. The opinions I shared about using these materials are my own, and Home Depot did not tell me what to say or how to say it."

- ✔ **When you receive other compensation and you write a review, include a disclosure similar to the following example:** "Disney provided my travel expenses for the trip I just wrote about, and did not provide any additional compensation. They did not require that I write this blog post, nor did they request it. I have written my honest opinion about how much I loved this vacation, and would have been willing to pay for it out of my own pocket."

- ✔ **When you mention a sponsor on Facebook, include a disclosure such as this example:** "My blog sponsor Weight Watchers sent me some of those meal bars and they were awesome. I wish they would send me more!"

- ✔ **When you use an affiliate link in a review, include a disclosure like the following example:** "If you decide to make a purchase through my link, Amazon will pay me a commission for it. This doesn't cost you anything additional. These commissions help to keep the rest of my content free, so thank you!"

Technically, the FTC guidelines do not apply to content that is not considered a review, recommendation, or endorsement. This can be a gray area for bloggers, especially if you simply mention a product or brand you are working with in a blog post or online conversation. Sometimes it would be socially awkward to suddenly throw an FTC disclosure statement into a conversation among friends. Any positive mention of a brand by an influential blogger could be seen as an endorsement, but that wouldn't necessarily fall under these FTC guidelines.

In these circumstances, you must use your best judgment. Know that it is better to over-disclose rather than under-disclose. Several bloggers have added a short disclosure statement to their Facebook or Twitter profiles to ensure that all their conversations are compliant. In cases when your working relationship with the brand is clear to the average person, there is no need to provide an additional disclosure. If it isn't clear, you can preface your statement with a simple, "My client XXX . . ." which leaves no doubt about your working relationship.

Ensuring that your blog discloses to both readers and search engines

Back when I first started blogging in 2006, it was common for advertisers to purchase text-link ads on blogs. These could be in the form of sponsored posts, or they could be simple text links in your sidebar. Advertisers bought text links for two reasons: Links, of course, drove traffic back to their websites, but they also helped the advertisers to get better search engine rankings. In fact, the better your Google Page Rank, the more you could charge for a text link. Google's Page Rank is reflective of the weight that the company places on a website in its search engine results. A higher page rank would mean that you would generally appear higher on the result pages. Links from high-authority sites boost up the page rank of the site being linked to.

In a very controversial 2007 decision, Google took the unprecedented move of dropping the page rank of websites that displayed text-link ads. It didn't just affect bloggers; large news websites such as the Washington Post were affected, too. Google reasoned that it didn't want paid advertisements affecting its organic search engine results, and implied that continued use of text-link advertising would be penalized. It caused a big commotion and a lot of resentment, because if you wanted to maintain your position on Google's search engine result pages, you had to get rid of your text-link advertising. Many people believed that Google was unfairly forcing people to buy Google's ads rather than ads from other publishers.

The affected websites were forced to make a choice — either lose their text-link advertising revenue, or risk keeping it in place and call Google's bluff. I chose the former, and lost a significant source of regular monthly income. The Know More Media blog network chose the latter. The size of their network and amount of text-link advertising they sold would have made it a six-figure loss of *monthly* income. They didn't really think that Google would impose that much of a drastic penalty on their quality, well-established, and trusted network.

Unfortunately, Know More Media lost the gamble. Google dropped all of their blogs from its index, and the network lost millions of page views overnight. Without that high volume of traffic, Know More Media was unable to sell advertising anymore — and went out of business.

The reason this story is so important is because if you write a sponsored post, Google considers that a paid link. Any time you take money from someone and link to that company's website, you run the risk of being dropped from the Google search engine results pages. You can still link to sponsors as long as you use the `NoFollow` tag in your links. (For instructions on using a `NoFollow` tag, see the later section, "Adding the `NoFollow` tag.") Be especially careful about how you sell advertising on your blog — if you specifically state that an advertising package includes a link to the sponsor's website, that is a red flag to Google.

The `NoFollow` tag was created as a way to disclose to the search engines that although your site is adding a link to a certain destination, it is not endorsing the destination site. Initially used for blog comments to combat comment spam, it protected blogs from inadvertently linking to so-called bad neighborhoods on the Web. Linking to known spam or scam sites is against the guidelines of all the major search engines, and will get your site penalized even if you aren't spamming or scamming.

Understanding Google's definition of a paid link

Google's criteria for defining a paid link are different from those that the FTC uses. A paid link, in the eyes of Google, is

- ✔ A text link placed on a blog sidebar, header, or footer that is paid for by an advertiser.

- ✔ A text link within a post that was paid by an advertiser to be placed on your website.

- ✔ A text link within a post in which the content was written at the request of an advertiser or sponsor, and was compensated with money and/or goods and services.

Google has gone so far as to suggest that any and all links within a sponsored post should be treated as sponsored links, even if you are linking to a friend or other reference source not financially connected to the blog post. While I'm not 100-percent certain that this is something Google enforces, if you are particularly concerned about it, it's better to be safe than sorry.

Unfortunately, due to the nature of Google's business, the company is notoriously secretive about any situations that fall into a gray area not mentioned in the preceding list. This is because the Google folks need to keep their full ranking methodology secret so as to keep real spammers from exploiting the system. In the following situations, it may or may not be okay to use regular links without the `NoFollow` tag. Again, if you are concerned, it's better to be safe than sorry (which means: Use the tag):

- ✔ **A blogger gets a free product to give away in a contest and receives no other compensation for mentioning the product.**

- ✔ **A blogger uses an affiliate link that goes directly to the merchant's site (such as Amazon.com).**

  Most affiliate links go through a redirected intermediary domain, making the use of a `NoFollow` tag unnecessary.

- ✔ **A blogger links to a former sponsor just because he or she likes the sponsor's products.**

Google has specifically stated that if a link is paid for, it must not "pass page rank," which means that the link cannot and should not be used to increase the authority of the sponsored site. You have two possible ways to add a link to a sponsor that is compliant with these guidelines:

- ✔ **Add a** `rel="nofollow"` **attribute to the** `<a>` **tag (see the next section).**
- ✔ **Redirect the links to an intermediate page that is blocked from search engines with a** `robots.txt` **file.**

Because the second way is more time-consuming and technical than it's worth, I'm simply going to show you the first way: how to add a `NoFollow` tag to your paid links.

These `NoFollow` tags *must* be added to your links, or you could be banned by the search engines, or displayed lower in the results than you could be. If you don't care about search engine traffic, then okay, this doesn't apply to you. But for professional bloggers, not using the `NoFollow` tag will severely hinder your growth in the long term. Don't settle for short-term gains that will create long-term pains. Adding `NoFollow` tags is easy and completely worth the time and effort.

Adding the NoFollow tag

To add a `NoFollow` tag to a link:

1. **Add a link to your text the way you normally would.**

   The link will look like this:

   ```
   <a href="http://www.SponsorSite.com">My Sponsor Text</a>
   ```

2. **Switch to HTML view.**

3. **Insert the** `NoFollow` **tag by editing the link as follows:**

   ```
   <a rel="nofollow" href="http://www.example.com">My Sponsor Link</a>
   ```

Constructing a disclosure policy

I'm happy to say that creating a disclosure policy is actually the easiest part of this chapter. You can research and write your own disclosure policy, have it checked by a lawyer, and post it on your blog. Or you can use the handy Disclosure Policy Generator at DisclosurePolicy.org. This website walks you through a six-step process as you select the disclosure terms that are specific to your blog, and creates a fully written disclosure policy for you.

Here's how you create a disclosure policy on this site:

1. **Go to** `http://disclosurepolicy.org/generator/generate_policy`.

2. **Select the option button that best describes your type of blog, and then click the Continue button.**

3. **Select the option button with the description that accurately matches what forms of compensation your blog receives, and then click the Continue button.**

4. **Select the option button with the description that accurately describes how your content may or may not be influenced by advertisers, and then click the Continue button.**

5. **Select the option button with the description that accurately describes how any opinions expressed on your blog may or may not be related to sponsored content, and then click the Continue button.**

6. **Select the description that accurately represents how your blog handles potential conflicts of interest.**

   If applicable, fill in the text fields with any current relationships that may present a conflict of interest. These include

   a. Any company or person who is an advertiser or client.

   b. Any corporate or advisory boards you may serve on.

   c. Any political affiliations that would influence your content.

   d. Any related persons who may benefit from your blog.

   e. Any other organizations or people that you have a financial interest in that are relevant to your blog.

7. **Click the Finish button.**

8. **Select and copy the text created for you and paste it into your blog where you want your disclosure policy to appear.**

Crafting a privacy policy

If you aren't selling anything on your blog, you may wonder why you need a privacy policy. Some advertisers and ad networks may require you to have one. Also, because your blog probably accepts comments, you are certainly collecting personally identifiable information. Adding a layer of additional trust to your blog will certainly boost your professional appearance.

Most of us hate privacy policies that are long and written in obscure legalese. But as a general rule, you don't need a lawyer to write an effective privacy policy. All you need to do is tell people what information you are collecting and what you do with it.

Laws about privacy can vary in different states and countries. Check with your local privacy laws to be sure your privacy policy meets any stated requirements. This is far more important if your blog is part of a website that also handles sales transactions.

Here are the things you need to cover in a blog privacy policy:

✓ **Explain what information your blog collects about your readers.**

- Include things like blog comments and any additional information, such as the information you may require if you have visitors who register on your site.

- Mention the analytics software you use, and remind readers that the information that analytics programs collect is not personally identifiable and helps you to improve your blog for your readers.

- If you do any e-mail marketing, explain your opt-in policy, that you send your subscribers the newsletters they requested from you, that they can unsubscribe anytime, and the name of the company that you use for your e-mail marketing program.

✓ **Explain what you do with the information.**

For your blog comments, explain that the information helps to keep out spam, plus allows you to follow up with readers when they seek your input. For your analytics software, explain that the information is used to simply administer and maintain your site.

✓ **If you use affiliate links, explain that a third party tracks sales made through your blog, and that neither that third party nor you will have any access whatsoever to readers' personal information.** All of that information is secured by the merchant who handles your readers' transactions.

✓ **Give readers a link to your contact form or an e-mail address on your Privacy Policy page in case they have any questions.**

Ensuring Your Giveaways and Contests Are Legal

When I first started officially running regular giveaways on one of my Sparkplugging blogs, I was sufficiently paranoid enough to look into contest and sweepstakes laws to make sure I wasn't making any egregious mistakes. But I rationalized that since so many bloggers run giveaways, as long as I ensured prizes were awarded randomly, what could really happen to me?

When it came to writing this section of this book, I knew minimal research and rationalization weren't going to cut it. So I interviewed Christopher J. Borders (`www.hinshawlaw.com/cborders`), a lawyer with a strong background in marketing and promotion law. Suffice it to say that the conversation kind of scared me. I really had no idea that contest and giveaway laws were so complex and varied. Not only do they vary drastically from country to country, they vary just as much from state to state.

The nature of running promotions on the Internet makes things even trickier. You don't have to comply with just your own local laws, but with the laws of where every single one of your participants lives.

I start with some basics first — because mom bloggers most commonly call a giveaway promotion a *contest*. Technically, this is inaccurate because

- ✔ A **Contest** is a promotion in which entrants win a prize based on merit. The prizes are not awarded randomly and are subjectively awarded based on a judging panel or a voting process.

- ✔ A **Sweepstake** is a promotion in which entrants win a prize by random drawing. It is important if you are running a sweepstake and not a contest, that you do not call it a contest.

- ✔ A **Giveaway** is technically not a legal term at all, but can be used interchangeably with the term Sweepstake in blog posts or conversationally. But when you are using legal terms (such as in your rules and regulations), you should use *contest* or *sweepstake*.

For this section of the book, I use the correct terminology, even though bloggers don't commonly use the word *sweepstakes* when referring to their prize giveaways. When I refer to both contests and sweepstakes simultaneously, I use the word *promotion*.

Before I get into the details of what you should be doing to legally run a sweepstake or contest, I outline the big no-no's, the things that are legal requirements pretty much no matter where you live:

- ✔ **You absolutely cannot charge a fee to enter your promotion.** Charging a fee causes your promotion to become a *lottery*, which is a very different (and much more highly regulated) legal entity. You also can't require your winners to pay for shipment of their prizes, though they are responsible for their own taxes.

- ✔ **If you are running a sweepstake, you absolutely must choose your winner randomly.** Additionally, these people are ineligible to enter: your family, anyone who lives at your address, any of your employees or contractors, your sponsor, and your sponsor's employees or contractors.

- ✔ **For U.S.-based bloggers, you cannot run a promotion involving any of the following industries: tobacco, alcohol, gasoline, dairy, insurance, and financial institutes.** Special requirements apply to these industries, and usually the cost of running a promotion won't justify the time you would spend on it.

✔ **You cannot extend an entry deadline.** You must stick to your first stated entry deadline, even if you don't get many entries or you feel the promotion wasn't successful enough. By running your promotion and stating an entry deadline, you have entered into a binding contract with your initial entrants. If you get no entries at all, then you should end the first promotion and start a second one, not continue the first one.

✔ **You must accept all valid entries.** This is stricter than you may think, with the benefit of the doubt going to your participants. For example, your sweepstakes entrants are asked to go to a sponsor's website and name a favorite product in order to be entered into your promotion. They leave a comment that simply says, "I don't know, enter me anyway." That is a valid entry. Conversely, if you state that there is only one entry per person and you find that a person violated that rule, that is *not* a valid entry.

✔ **You must award a prize even if your prize sponsor flakes out on you.** A promotion on your blog is a contract between you and your participants, not your sponsor. If the sponsor doesn't award a prize to your winner, it is *your* responsibility to purchase and award the same prize (or equivalent product if the original prize is unavailable) and send it to the winner. You may think this is improbable, but it has happened to me. Worse, the sponsor promised *four* prizes, so I had to purchase four gift cards, one each for winners who didn't receive their prizes.

You may be thinking that these rules are fairly obvious and easy to adhere to, and you'd be right. But honestly, most bloggers who run sweepstakes do only the above things, because they are the most commonly known laws about promotions.

I must add that these are generally accepted laws in the United States, and that your local laws may be different from these. So take these as a starting point, and please consult a local legal expert to ensure you are in 100-percent compliance with all laws applicable to you.

There are several things all bloggers *should* be doing that you may find quite surprising (especially because I don't see many people doing them currently):

✔ **You must post promotion rules and regulations, and link to them in every sweepstakes or contest announcement, every time.** It's not within the scope of this book to tell you how to write this, but there is a good resource at www.squidoo.com/contest-rules that will help you craft a rules document to post on your site. To be 100-percent safe, you can buy a sample sweepstakes rules form from a site like LeapLaw (www.leaplaw.com) or work with a lawyer to draft one for you.

✔ **You must state the following information in every promotion.** It's safest to spell out these bullet points in each promotion you offer, rather than putting them into your rules and regulations. Your entrants need this information to participate.

- Inform your readers that "No purchase is necessary."

- State that the "Odds of winning are based on number of entries."

- Give a start date and an end date when you will stop receiving entries.

- State how many entries are allowed per person.

- Explain how participants need to enter the promotion (usually by leaving a comment on your blog).

- State the dollar value of the prize being awarded.

- State who is eligible to enter (usually U.S. residents 18 and older — adapt accordingly for your locality).

✔ **You should have a clear policy on how to handle unawarded prizes.** I was surprised how many people never answered prize notification e-mails when we ran them on Sparkplugging. You should state how you will notify winners, how long they have to respond to the notification (30 days is standard), and how you will award the prize to a different winner. While it is not illegal to keep a prize, lawmakers really want prizes awarded. So you should have a standard way of handling this situation and work hard to get the prize into a winner's hands.

Lastly, there are a few things that Mr. Borders mentioned to me that I was not aware of at all. These things are a little quirky because they don't always apply to blogger promotions or are very localized laws. But you should be aware of them to ensure you don't unknowingly break these laws:

✔ If your promotion is giving away a prize or prizes worth more than a combined total of $5,000, then you must post a winner's list, be bonded, and be registered with the states of New York and Florida. This applies if any of your entrants live in either state. You can avoid this by ensuring the combined prize value of all your prizes is less than $5,000.

✔ You must file a 1099 form with the Internal Revenue Service if your prize to any one person is worth more than $600.

After all this, you can perhaps understand why the conversation I had with Mr. Borders about this topic was intimidating. It is my hope that this book can serve as a starting point to ensure bloggers run ethical and legal contests and sweepstakes. It only takes a few people to break the law to attract the attention of an Attorney General, which could change the ability of all people to run promotions on their blogs.

Writing Reviews with Integrity

Bloggers have very diverse opinions about what constitutes a review written with integrity. Some believe that only reviews that are 100- percent uncompensated can be trustworthy. Others believe that one can take free products with no additional compensation and still write an unbiased review. And still others believe that one can accept both free products and additional compensation and write an unbiased review.

Nobody can tell you what is the right formula for you and your blog. I can tell you that the more extreme your opinion is on the subject, the more you will find others who disagree with you. Because blogging was originally a personal medium that became a professional medium, you'll find that those who have blogged the longest tend to feel the strongest about keeping money and business separate. Bloggers who have never known that kind of atmosphere are more accustomed to mixing personal opinions with their business writing.

Two stereotypes are frequently mentioned in this context:

✔ The brand pays a PR firm for blogger outreach, and then the PR firm takes advantage of mom bloggers by getting them to write for free or for very little compensation.

✔ The blogger accepts any and all free products and writes positive reviews no matter what she actually thought.

Sadly, both of these stereotypes actually do exist in real life. But they are the exception and not the norm. I can only tell you what my professional opinion is on the subject, which is in line with the Word of Mouth Marketing Association. Its Ethics Code outlines standards that its members pledge to uphold. They are

✔ Disclosure of your identity.

✔ Disclosure of consideration or compensation received.

✔ Disclosure of relevant professional or personal relationships.

✔ Compliance with the FTC guidelines.

✔ Honesty in all communications.

✔ Honoring the individual rules of other websites, blogs, forums, media outlets, and live settings such as events or company locations.

✔ Refraining from marketing to minors under the age of 13 and complying with all Children's Online Privacy Protection Act (COPPA) regulations.

You can read the entire WOMMA Code of Ethics at `http://womma.org/ethics/code`.

Deciding whether writing reviews fits your business goals

Getting free stuff from brand representatives is something anyone would appreciate. If writing a review blog is your long-term goal and this brings in enough revenue and/or freebies that it makes your blogging time worthwhile, then there is no doubt that writing reviews fits with your business goals.

Writing reviews is also a good way to work toward becoming a spokesblogger, brand evangelist, or brand consultant. The relationships you will form on this path can certainly lead to very lucrative opportunities. Reviews are also an excellent selling tool if you want to be an affiliate marketer.

There are times, though, when writing reviews doesn't make sense for a blog, or can actively hinder your blog's growth. If your blog is meant to be a source of unbiased news and information, I would recommend sticking to more strict journalistic standards. In this circumstance, an advertorial that appears alongside your regular content would be more appropriate. An *advertorial* is a story written to promote an advertiser, usually composed by the advertiser, and clearly labeled as such.

Another instance when it doesn't make sense for you to write reviews on your blog is when you are promoting your own products or services. There may certainly be occasions when this kind of content would be appropriate, such as when the product would be of very high interest to your readers and doesn't compete with your own sales goals. But this would be the exception, not the norm.

I have never found reviews to be very advantageous to my businesses. In my first blog network, we were a resource to the small business community, so there were only a few products that were appropriate to review, and not directly mom-oriented. In my current blog network, writing reviews is something that takes time away from creating our original content and printables. Because adding new content frequently increases my advertising revenue, it makes business sense that I create content that will attract long-term readers to my sites.

I even tried creating a review blog, because I was turning down so many freebies I started feeling like I was leaving too much on the table. While accepting the products was enjoyable, I found that I really didn't enjoy writing reviews. I was not passionate about it in any way, shape, or form. So it made it an easy decision to not include reviews as a major part of my business model. I have only accepted one freebie since I started Woo! Jr., and that was because it was a fantastic opportunity to get exclusive content for my sites. In that circumstance, it made sense, because it fit with my business goals and with my editorial policy.

Your business model and editorial content should be at the very top of your priorities as a blogger. Anything and everything you do should be true to your editorial policy and build your business. If taking freebies and writing reviews contribute to these goals, then you should absolutely pursue them. If not, then you should turn down these opportunities, even though it can be extremely hard to say no.

Preserving honesty while being compensated

Mixing money and opinion can be dangerous. It is generally accepted that money can and will influence your opinion — though it isn't always true. For most bloggers, no amount of money would justify publishing a lie on their blogs. You can say that your opinion's not for sale. But that doesn't change the fact that people who don't know you will assume what is generally accepted: that if you take money for a review, it will influence what you say, even if it doesn't.

Yet, bloggers need to cover their expenses and make a living. If writing paid reviews fits with your business model, then there are ways you can minimize the perception that your blog post presents a conflict of interest:

✔ **Disclose more than you are required to disclose:** If a review is compensated, you must disclose that relationship. But I also recommend disclosing why you chose to write the review in the first place. If you have spent money on the company's products in the past, say so. If you would have written about this product for free anyway, say so.

✔ **Balance all reviews with constructive criticism:** Make a habit of pointing out ways a product could be improved in every review. It's hard for a review to sound credible if all it does is rave about a product. Even the most perfect product in the world can be improved. Balancing every one of your reviews with constructive criticism helps to show that you are willing to be honest, no matter what.

✔ **Be open about the opportunities you turn down:** So much attention is focused on the freebies that mom bloggers receive because that's what the public can see. The public never hears about the opportunities and products you *don't* receive. Okay, I don't suggest writing a list of things you've turned down, but you can be general while still conveying the message that you're picky about what you choose to receive. You can create a simple statement in your sidebar or on your disclosures page saying that you only publish x percentage of the reviews you are offered to write.

✔ **Write about products you know your readers would be interested in:**
Your readers have been attracted to your blog for your voice and the
quality of your content. You can scare them away if you write *any* kind
of irrelevant blog posts, not just irrelevant products. Keeping your blog
on topic also makes you more attractive to advertisers. As I explain
in Chapter 10, advertisers value a focused audience more than large
amounts of traffic.

Avoiding opportunities that risk harming your business or reputation

Not all companies seeking to give you free products are ones you want to
work with. Some are just not a right fit. Others can be slightly deceptive or
even downright manipulative. When you associate your blog and your personal brand with a company product or brand, it is inevitable that you will
both rub off on each other. Like it or not, you can and do become associated
with that brand.

A good example of this is a campaign that occurred recently through a
marketing firm that reached out to mom bloggers. The firm presented the
opportunity to the moms as an outreach to help educate the public about
high-fructose corn syrup. Ultimately, some of the participants didn't realize
that the campaign was being funded by the large lobbying group, the Corn
Refiners Association.

I'm not going to debate the merits of high-fructose corn syrup here — my
point is that some bloggers felt misled by the talking points they were given.
Yet they had already published their posts, and now had to take responsibility for the fact that they had to own words they weren't very happy about
owning. Ultimately, this campaign probably won't permanently harm anyone's blogging business — however, it could have.

It is truly up to you as the blogger to ensure that the sponsors and brands
you choose to work with also represent the values you hold. Here are some
questions you can ask as you evaluate whether a brand is the right fit for you
and your blog:

✔ Is this a company that makes products or services that my readers
would likely be interested in reading about?

✔ Does this brand stand for principles that I agree with?

✔ Does this company have subsidiaries that would present a conflict of
interest for me?

✔ Is this company in an industry that is known for perpetuating scams or
misleading information?

✔ Am I 100-percent sure that this company is a legitimate business?

✔ Does this company sell any products that I would never use in my home, or would never advocate to my readers?

Some very large companies have diverse products they sell and brands they use. You may be thrilled to work with one brand, yet find that its sister company uses child labor in China.

✔ Does this company produce products or services that I feel are immoral, unhealthy, or disagree with?

Even when you have great answers to all these questions, things still can go wrong. For example, one time I was asked to review an online magazine that was just starting up. It was an absolute perfect fit for my readers at the time, and I truly believed that the publication was going to be a great resource for the business-blogging community. I wrote a review, and we were both pleased with the results.

Less than a year later, a new reader came to my blog and read that same review. Upon going to check out the magazine, the reader found the online magazine was gone, and the site had been transformed into a spam domain selling Viagra. The reader left a comment letting me know she would never return to my blog again. I couldn't blame the reader, and I immediately took down the old post.

Thankfully, the consequences of my ill-guided faith in a stranger only resulted in my losing a reader or two. It could have been much worse. As I mention earlier in this chapter, Google's Webmaster Guidelines specifically state that it is unwise to link to what the guidelines call bad neighborhoods. Sites found linking to these kinds of spam sites risk getting treated like a spam site as well. My entire site could have been dropped from Google's index for linking to that spam site — and I never would have known why if I hadn't lost that reader who complained about my review.

Handling the writing of a negative review

There may come a time when you think that you will like a product, take it on for a review, and then find that it is a piece of junk. Suddenly, you will find yourself in a delicate situation, because you don't want to publish a misleading review, nor do you want to alienate a brand you want to work with in the future. Every blogger who has made it big will tell you that if you had to choose between the two, choose to alienate the brand instead of compromising your integrity. But I had this happen to me once, and here is how I was able to maintain a relationship with the brand.

I was offered a camera to review — I needed a camera anyway, so I jumped on the chance. It was adorable — small, pink, and oh-so-pretty. But then I took pictures with it. And they were bad. Terrible, even! I suddenly felt trapped — here was a well-known brand expecting a review from me, and I had nothing nice to say about that piece-of-junk camera. This was a brand that in general I liked and had purchased from in the past. There was also an opportunity to potentially work more with this brand in the future — and I didn't want to burn that bridge by writing a really horrible review.

At the same time, I wasn't about to lie and write a good review, either. So I wrote to the brand representative and informed her of my dilemma. I offered the only two solutions I could think of to the situation:

- ✔ I send back the camera and not write anything.
- ✔ I keep the camera and write a bad review.

I anticipated having to send the camera back. But I was both impressed and happy to hear that the company wanted me to keep the camera and write my honest feedback — even if it didn't like what I had to say. This was a shining example of social media marketing done right, and I was lucky to have been approached by a firm that had as much integrity as I did.

Ultimately, I was able to come up with some nice things to say about the camera. I realized that I was not the right target audience for the company product — but that the camera was perfect for my teenage daughter who didn't care about perfect focus or image noise. And the camera company walked away with valuable feedback. Ironically, because the folks at the company handled my negative feedback so well, I became more loyal to their brand than *before* I had received a camera from them that I hated. And in case you're wondering . . . yes, they did contact me again for projects in the future.

Understanding How Tax Laws Affect Bloggers

While I'm on the subject of reviews, I should point out something that you might not have realized about accepting products to review: Accepting free products constitutes income in terms of how the IRS defines income. I can't speak to other countries' laws, but I suspect that a similar policy is in place elsewhere.

What's even more important is that even if you are just blogging as a hobby, you still must claim the receipt of freebies as income. This stinks, because if you are a hobby blogger, you don't get the benefit of writing off your blogging expenses to offset that income. (Figuring out whether you are a hobby blogger or a blogging business is a whole other issue I've just brought up. I give you some great link resources at the end of this section that will help you address these issues for your own particular situation.)

Bloggers claiming freebies as income doesn't come without precedent: In 2006, the IRS began cracking down on celebrity "goodie bags" handed out at awards shows like the Oscars. These goodie bags typically contained more than $100,000 worth of items. IRS Commissioner Mark W. Everson released a statement that said, "As the world watches the glamour and glitz of the Academy Awards, it's important to keep in mind that movie stars face the same tax obligations as ordinary Americans. We want to make sure the stars 'walk the line' when it comes to these goodie bags."

The tax implications are identical for bloggers. Companies give both celebrities and bloggers free items for one primary purpose: publicity. So the full market value of the freebies you receive must be claimed as Miscellaneous Income on your tax returns. And before you ask, *yes*, this is true even if you do not receive a Form 1099-MISC from the company supplying the free items.

My go-to gal for more in-depth blogging and tax information is the rather brilliant Kelly Phillips Erb, also known as TaxGirl (www.taxgirl.com). Here are some important articles on her site that will help you navigate the issues brought up in this section:

- ✔ **How to determine whether your blog is a hobby or a business:** www.taxgirl.com/ask-the-taxgirl-am-i-blogging-as-a-business-or-a-hobbyist

- ✔ **Expenses that professional bloggers can write off on their taxes:** www.taxgirl.com/ask-the-taxgirl-blogging-related-deductions

- ✔ **Additionally, here are the IRS guidelines on reporting Miscellaneous Income:** www.irs.gov/newsroom/article/0,,id=175963,00.html

Chapter 10

Creating Partnerships with Brand Representatives

*I*n the ongoing conversation between advertisers and bloggers, many brands — and many bloggers — grumble that "the other side doesn't get us." Bloggers complain about being spammed with irrelevant pitches. Brand representatives complain about bloggers' entitlement mentality. Ultimately, I believe these are simply misunderstandings based on two completely different worlds trying to work together.

Mom bloggers interact with their online communities much as they would their offline communities: They share personal stories, give and get advice, and enjoy bringing a sense of authenticity to their online relationships. They live in a world in which encouragement and respect is given and received based on immeasurable personal interactions.

Brand representatives live in a completely different world. They are accountable for sales quotas, results, and have a certain number of mentions they need to deliver to their clients. Encouragement and respect is given and received based on meeting specific goals, and careers are made and broken based on spreadsheets and dollars.

In essence, these two groups speak different languages. This chapter will be your guide to brand-speak. I show you how to identify your assets, understand their brand value, and describe them in a language that brand representatives will appreciate and comprehend. I also explain why some of your greatest mom-blogging achievements don't carry much weight in the world of brands, and how to focus your self-promotional efforts on the things that do matter to them.

Making It Easy for Brands to Want to Work with You

Some of the very best blogging advice I received a few years ago was that I needed to make it brain-dead-easy for brands to work with me. That meant I couldn't sit back and wait for them to create a campaign that I could be a part of; instead, I needed to put all the information they needed right at their fingertips when they came to my site. If I didn't spell out exactly what I could offer to a brand, then its reps didn't have time to figure it out for me. My motto is, "Don't make them think, make them act."

You may already run giveaways, do reviews, and offer your time as a consultant. If that's the case, then a lot more of these opportunities will come your way if you put all the information a brand representative needs in one place.

Building a PR-friendly blog

A great way to lay out the welcome mat for brand representatives is to direct them to a page created just for them. You can call it your Press page or Brand Inquiries page, or whatever works for you. This is like a second About page — but with a bio and information relevant to brand representatives, which is not the same as what your readers are interested in. Brand representatives don't have a lot of time to sift through tons of information to determine whether or not they want to contact you. So put the most important information (from their point of view) first — and keep it short and sweet.

The things you would include on this kind of page are

- ✔ **Professional bio:** Three to five sentences on what makes you different from the other bloggers — and specific past experience that strengthens your street cred.

- ✔ **Blog description:** Three to five sentences on what your blog is about, the kind of readers your blog attracts, and what your blog offers to brands and advertisers.

- ✔ **A media kit:** A simple brochure-style document with information on your traffic, your readers, and specific advertising opportunities. I show you how to write one later in this chapter in the "Building Your Media Kit" section.

- ✔ **How you work with brands:** A list of the ways you are willing to work with brands — this can include anything from reviews, giveaways, product placements, spokesblogger opportunities, advertising, social media promotions, consulting, freelance writing — anything you want to be hired for. I cover this in a little more detail in the next section.

As much as many of us would like to be hired for "all of the above," I caution you to *list only the things you are 100-percent confident that you can do and do well.* For example, if you want to be a spokesblogger but don't know anything about what this kind of commitment entails, I suggest leaving it off your list until you have enough experience to deliver the value you promise.

If you're okay with publishing your phone number, I do recommend putting it on your Press page. Again, this is making it brain-dead easy for brand representatives to contact you. Most will e-mail you, but some prefer to pick up the phone. I got a second phone line just for this purpose.

Make sure you place a link to your Press page in your site navigation or in your sidebar. Also mention it on your regular About and Contact pages so that brand representatives can find the page they want from multiple places on your blog.

Creating specific sponsorship and partnership opportunities

I'll extend my brain-dead easy theme as I talk about the ways you want to work with brands. If you had to go into a restaurant and provide the waitstaff with the recipe of what you wanted to eat because they had no menu, you probably wouldn't dine there very often. Think of your sponsorship opportunities in the same manner. If you give a brand representative a menu of what you offer as a blogger, you have just made it easier to work with you than nearly every other blogger on the planet.

A blogger who has done an excellent job of packaging her professional services is Barbara Rozgonyi on WiredPRWorks. Her two Services pages tell her potential clients exactly what they can hire her to do, while leaving open the option of hiring her for other projects related to her areas of expertise. You can find these pages at `http://wiredprworks.com/social-media-pr-consulting-chicago`, and at `http://wiredprworks.com/social-media-pr-keynotespeaker`.

The following are examples of how you could write up your own sponsorship opportunities for common mom-blogging services — reviews and giveaways:

Review requests

I only write reviews about products that women who are interested in cooking would find valuable. I will only accept a review request in which I am free to give an honest opinion about your product or service. You must provide me with a sample of the product. Please do not send unsolicited samples, as I cannot guarantee that a review will be written under those circumstances. Reviews will be posted within two weeks of receiving your product. I do not charge a fee for reviews, but invite you to look also at my giveaway opportunities to increase your exposure to my audience.

Please submit your review request via my contact form.

Giveaway opportunities

I host weekly giveaways that regularly attract over 500 entries. Giveaway sponsors must be willing to ship prizes directly to giveaway winners. I run contests with several different entry options to help promote your company.

- Giveaways with simple blog-comment entries are $50, and the fee is waived if the giveaway item has a retail value of over $200.

- Giveaways with the entry requirement to visit the sponsor website and browse your product line are $300.

- Giveaways with multiple entry options that include following the sponsor account on Twitter, Liking the sponsor Facebook page, or signing up for the sponsor newsletter are $500.

Please submit your giveaway request via my contact form.

The dollar amounts in the preceding sample may be too low or too high for you; these are fairly average amounts for giveaways. If you don't want to name your rates directly on your website, you can just say something like "Contact me for my 2011 giveaway rates."

Building Your Media Kit

The goal of a well-written media kit is to convince brand representatives and potential advertisers to work with you. The things you want to include are information about you and your blog, your traffic statistics, your social media presence, and your past campaigns and accomplishments as a blogger.

This is where you really want to strut your stuff. But interestingly, many bloggers tell me they have a difficult time with self-promotion; they have a hard time tooting their own horns. And then I hear complaints from brand representatives that other bloggers expect to be treated like royalty when they have nothing to offer in return. I wish all mom bloggers were comfortable talking about their accomplishments — while also being realistic about what that track record entitles them to.

This section of the book may ruffle some feathers, but it can save you some misunderstandings down the line. It's one of the most important things to address when it comes to working with brand representatives. Negative stereotypes of both exploited mommy bloggers and overly entitled mommy bloggers affect all of us, when in reality they are only a small percentage of the mom blogosphere. For what it's worth, I feel I've acted like both kinds of stereotypes in the past, so I write from a place of experience, not judgment.

Getting comfortable with tooting your own horn

If you fall into the camp of underselling yourself as a blogger, then it might help to reframe the thought of what it means to toot your own horn. Self-promotion is not the same as bragging — it's letting potential partners know what you have to offer. Bragging is primarily an ego-booster, all about "me, me, me." Communicating your strengths is more practical and focused: You do it to represent accurately all that you can do for someone you want to work with.

If you have a *really* hard time tooting your horn, it can help to think about yourself in the third person. What would your best friend say about you and all that you've accomplished with your blog? If you're still stuck, go ahead and *ask* your best friend what she would say about you!

You need to be able to showcase your strengths as you write your media kit and your website's Press pages. So the next section walks you through the kinds of things you can say as you craft your pitch. You can also check out a fantastic example of a very well-written horn-tooting profile by Sommer Poquette of Green and Clean Mom at `http://greenandcleanmom.org/advertise`.

Making sure you don't over-toot your own horn

There was an infamous exchange between a mom blogger and a brand representative who was sponsoring a blogging conference a few years ago. The sponsor had been giving away free samples of products, and ran out of them before every attendee could get a sample. One blogger was upset about this, and threatened to write terrible things about the sponsor on her blog if she couldn't get her free samples — implying that her influence as a prominent blogger would harm their brand. It also somewhat implied that giving free samples would "buy" a good review from the blogger, which is not only unethical, but illegal under the FTC guidelines, as I explain in Chapter 9. In a classy move, the brand representative never revealed who the blogger was who threatened him. But he did turn to his friends in the mom-blogging community to help defuse the situation. The interaction has become one of the best-known examples of bloggers acting too entitled and expecting more than they should from a brand rep.

The most objective way to evaluate a situation like this is to consider what you want to get in relation to what you can give. If you want a new stove to review, do you think — realistically — that through your sphere of influence you can deliver three to five actual stove *purchases* because of what you write about the stove? Don't get me wrong; you don't have to track down sales and poll your readers for this kind of information. But when brand representatives choose which bloggers to approach, this is exactly the kind of question they need to answer for their clients. If I run (say) a craft blog with 100,000 monthly readers, I really don't think I could deliver a result of three to five stove sales — because that's not why my readers read my blog. I provide content that my readers are looking for, but I don't have much influence over their stove-purchasing decisions.

Compare the craft-blog example to a hypothetical high-end baking blog with "only" 10,000 monthly readers. The blogger talks about her stove in almost every single post. She posts weekly pictures taken in her kitchen, where her stove is prominently featured. This blog probably *can* influence stove sales, and a brand representative can go back to clients and build the case that this kind of *product placement* offers a big bang for their buck. Even though the second blogger has less overall influence (in terms of readership size), she actually has *more* influence where the brand needs it most.

You always bring value to the table as a blogger. Just keep that value in perspective; balance it realistically against what you are offering in return. The more a product fits in naturally with your blog's purpose, the more you can offer to a brand — and the more you can expect to receive.

Crafting your metrics and other assets into an effective pitch

You can create your media kit in any word-processing or presentation software. The best way to post the kit to your blog, though, is to convert it to the Web-friendly PDF format.

You can download a free PDF maker from CutePDF at `www.cutepdf.com`.

You don't have to be a professional designer to put together a good-looking media kit, but you do want it to look good. (See Figure 10-1 for an example.) Just work with what you have — your head shot, your blog logo, and maybe a few sample photographs that illustrate what your content is about. You can also borrow graphics from your blog template. Create a simple template that will add a touch of your blog design style to every page in your media kit.

Figure 10-1:
A sample media kit from Green and Clean Mom.

I again want to highlight Sommer from Green and Clean Mom, because not only has she written an awesome self-promotional profile, her media kit is great, too. A sample page is shown in Figure 10-1. You can download the entire media kit at

```
http://greenandcleanmom.org/wp-content/uploads/2008/05/2010-and-2011-Green-
and-Clean-Mom-Media-Kit.pdf
```

When you write your media kit, write it in the third person, avoiding using the word *I*. Remember who this kit is for: potential advertisers and brands. They want to know what you can do for them, not what they can do for you.

In Chapter 5, I show you how to mine your blog statistics for information about your traffic, your readers, and your audience demographics as you write your media kit. Be sure to include the following information, organized like this:

✔ **Page one of your media kit — your blog overview:** On the first page of your media kit, place your logo, a head shot, your blog name, your blog tag line, and no more than two short paragraphs of content. Make one paragraph about you, one about your blog. Highlight your accomplishments, however small you think they may be! If you also write for any recognizable publications, mention that here. If you have already worked with any brands on any kinds of events, reviews, or campaigns, mention those as well. Next, state what your blog is known for and who your target audience is. You want to let people know why they should want to work with you. Just keep it brief — you have only one page to convince them to read further, so make it count.

✔ **Page two of your media kit — your blog statistics:** On the second page of your media kit, give highlights of your blog statistics. Mention monthly unique visitors, page views, and brief demographic information. Give a snapshot of your social media presence, too — Twitter followers, Facebook friends, and Facebook fan-page fans. This would be a great place to mention popular posts, how fast your blog is growing, or any press mentions you have received. Make room for a picture here — a popular recipe, your Quantcast traffic graph, anything that gives another visual representation of what your blog is about.

You can certainly stretch this section out over another page or two if you need the room.

✔ **Page three of your media kit — your sponsorship and advertising options:** This is where you use the specific sponsorship opportunity descriptions shown earlier in this chapter. If you sell advertising, outline your available advertising options. I show you how to sell your own ads in Chapter 13, including how to develop an advertising rate card. I recommend including your rate card in your media kit; you don't want to make brand representatives jump through hoops to get the information they need.

You may or may not want your media kit to be on your website. Some bloggers want to make it easily available and simply post it on their About page or Press page. Some prefer to be more private and tell people to write and request the media kit. If you post your media kit on your website, you might not want to include your traffic statistics and rate card for the world to see. So you need to decide how much you want to make public, and how much you want to share only with the people you choose. If you make it public, just remember that anyone can see that information about your blog.

Determining Fair Compensation

Receiving compensation for writing a review or product mention is a controversial subject in the blogosphere — not just with mom bloggers. It's so controversial that the FTC felt they needed to step in to ensure that consumers weren't getting unfairly influenced by advertorials disguised as unbiased reviews. Even traditional publications have had to find ways to ensure that advertising content didn't get mistaken for editorial content.

Bloggers are not journalists. So I do think it is appropriate in some circumstances for bloggers to receive payment for writing reviews as long as they are in compliance with the FTC guidelines and ethical standards I outline in Chapter 9. That doesn't mean it is right for everyone. My personal choice is to not be paid directly for reviews, but I feel comfortable with receiving free products so that I can write an informed recommendation. I know my ethical standards would require that my review be honest in all circumstances. But for my professional career as a whole, I prefer to abide more closely by journalistic standards. This choice would likely be different if my blog was very focused on product reviews.

In the following sections, I give guidelines on fair compensation, specifically as it relates to *writing reviews* or *solicited requests to write about products* from brand representatives. For guidelines on rates for advertising, check out Chapter 13. And for guidelines on fair compensation for consulting fees, see Chapter 8.

Protecting yourself from being taken advantage of

The diversity of the mom blogosphere makes it difficult to give a one-size-fits-all answer to what is too little compensation for a blogger. A new stove may be a *huge* deal to one blogger, while another won't work on the campaign unless that stove also comes with a fat, juicy check. The important part of this equation is not who deserves the stove the most, but who can deliver the most value to the brand.

I give you a very general formula in the next section to help you determine a ballpark value for your work. Yet some bloggers feel that they need to pay their dues and do more for less. Other bloggers may not even be interested in getting paid, and just love writing and getting a free gift card every now and then. Where you draw your line in the sand to ask for compensation or not is a very personal decision.

Most experienced mom bloggers I know didn't initially know where to draw their own lines in the sand, either. They figured it out through experience. Many times, they could only know where to draw the line when they realized they had already crossed it and found they were being taken advantage of.

Conflict can arise when several bloggers vying to work with the same brand have different value structures in place. A hobby blogger may feel that an experienced blogger is acting like a prima donna for expecting so much. The professional blogger may feel that the hobby blogger is undervaluing her work, undermining efforts to raise the bar for all bloggers.

The reality is that some brands will utilize their tiny marketing budget by working with the cheapest labor they can find. And other brands will recognize they get what they pay for, and are willing to pay. It's not up to mom bloggers to change the blogging goals of their peers. You can only control your own actions. That may mean being more selective in the kinds of projects you are willing to work on, and it may mean you will get fewer freebies. Sometimes that means forgoing short-term perks for long-term success.

Blogging about a brand or product always gives value to the brand representative — and whether or not the brand is paying you, the reps are getting paid to work with you. Even when you are a newer blogger, you are providing some publicity, social media exposure, and a blog post that will stay on the Web practically forever.

This is what sets professional bloggers apart from hobby bloggers: Brands will respect your value as much as you respect your own value.

Negotiating a respectable rate for your time and talent

Many people have a difficult time setting a fair price for the services they offer. Mom bloggers are particularly disadvantaged because what they offer isn't a flat product or service. A freelance writer can charge by the article, word count, or by the hour. It is more difficult to put a value on your personality and influence, because this is an intangible thing that varies widely depending on your experience, followers, and even the topic you blog about. Many people find it so difficult to measure their own influence that they give up on trying to put a value on it.

Keep in mind that the reason brands approach you is because *they* value your influence — so you should, too. Ultimately, you are helping them sell their products and services — a fact that you should use to your advantage if you find yourself negotiating with a brand about your compensation.

Any time you communicate with a brand representative, frame your statements in a way that showcases what you bring to the table. Highlight what you are giving to the potential project — your influence, your audience, your voice, your contribution to their bottom line. When you are clear about what you offer, it's much easier to ask for compensation commensurate with your experience.

To help you come to a ballpark valuation of one of your sponsored blog posts, there are a few ways you can calculate a number. The going rate for quality, impression-based online advertising is usually between $1 and $15 per 1,000 impressions. The average is usually between $3 and $10. Only you can decide what rate feels right for your blog.

Say you've been asked to run a contest for your readers, and your sponsor is offering a prize worth $50 — and is also offering you the same prize for running the contest. The following steps calculate the number of impressions you think you can deliver:

1. **Estimate the number of views the contest blog post will likely get.**

   You can do this by looking at past contest post views in your analytics program. This is the number of views just for this one post, not for your entire blog.

2. **Factor in social media mentions.**

   Factor in any tweets or Facebook mentions you may be able to include by adding up your Twitter followers, Facebook friends, or Facebook fan-page fans. Only include the numbers if you will be promoting your contest on the other sites.

3. **Add how many RSS subscribers your blog has.**

4. **Add how many people you have on your mailing list if you have one.**

   Only include this number if you will be promoting your contest to your mailing list.

5. **Take that the total number and divide it by 1000.**

6. **Multiply that number by the dollar rate you want to charge.**

You can use the steps just given to get the formula to calculate fair compensation:

> Page Views + Social Media + RSS Subscribers + Mailing List = Number of Impressions
>
> Number of Impressions ÷ 1000 × Dollar Rate = Fair Compensation

For example, your contest post will get about 3,000 page views, you have 1,500 Twitter followers, 200 Facebook fan-page fans, and 500 RSS subscribers. That's approximately 5,200 impressions, and you feel that charging $10 per 1,000 impressions is fair. So that gives you a dollar amount of around $50 as a baseline to value one of your contest posts.

A different way to value this contest post is to calculate the time it takes you to write the post and administer the contest. Then you can choose an hourly rate for the time involved.

Now factor in what the contest sponsor is offering you:

- ✔ If the free $50 product they offered you is something that you want, then you might decide to do the contest for no extra charge.

- ✔ If the sponsor hadn't offered one of the products to you, you could ask for $50 compensation to run the contest.

✔ Perhaps the brand can offer you a mention on its own Facebook page, and that page has 500,000 fans. Is that worth $50 to you?

✔ Perhaps the brand is willing to feature you on its website, too. Is that worth $50 to you?

The only way you are going to know if what your sponsor is offering is fair is by having a baseline number to compare to.

Knowing when blogging for swag is okay

There are certainly legitimate circumstances when you may feel that working for free is actually worth your time and the publicity you offer to a brand. It can be compared to taking on an unpaid internship. If you intern and get great work experience, then it's a valuable endeavor. If you intern and only pour coffee and deliver mail, then not so much. Here are some of the most common circumstances in which blogging for free could be appropriate:

✔ If the product you receive is something you would have purchased anyway

✔ If the brand is offering publicity for you in return

✔ The brand has invited you to an exclusive event that you want to attend

✔ If you know for certain that working with the brand will help build your sponsorship credentials, leading to future paying opportunities

✔ If the brand rep offers something of great value to you, such as an expensive product or travel expenses

✔ If there is a special charity or cause associated with the opportunity that is especially important to you

Some dear friends would disagree with me about some of these circumstances. But just as there is no-one-size-fits-all policy on receiving compensation, so you should also be choosy about when you accept unpaid opportunities. Take only the ones that will offer value to your readers, bring you closer to your long-term blogging goals, and ones that you will truly enjoy.

An excellent example of a blog post written in exchange for swag is one written by Amy Clark of MomAdvice about an all-expenses-paid trip she and her best friend took to Wilmington, North Carolina. The sponsor asked her to write an honest post about the trip and required no further obligation from her. She wrote a fantastic article about the attractions and accommodations, and because she already writes about family travel on her blog, her readers appreciated the information. See the blog post Amy wrote in Figure 10-2.

The Wilmington/Cape Fear Coast Convention & Visitor's Bureau were so gracious to allow us the opportunity to explore Wilmington's family-friendly offerings. We toured the Battleship North Carolina, The Children's Museum of Wilmington, the Cape Fear Serpentarium, a horse drawn tour of downtown Wilmington, North Carolina Aquarium Fort Fisher, and sampled delicious seafood chowder at Michael's Seafood, took two boat tours of the beautiful beach, downtown shopped, and enjoyed all of the town's offerings.

I can't wait to share with you more as it gets closer to vacation season about my experience in both North Carolina and Orlando for some fun ideas for family travel. I will say that of the places we visited, I loved the Children's Museum of Wilmington and the North Carolina Aquarium Forth Fisher the absolute best and can't wait to revisit them for a trip with my own family. The enthusiasm of the employees was enchanting and I know that we could spend a whole day just visiting these two spots alone.

Figure 10-2:
An example
of a blog
post about
a free trip
received by
Amy Clark of
MomAdvice.

I love featuring this example from Amy, because the company was so impressed with her one blog post that they then hired her to do more free-lance travel writing for them. It demonstrates that when a blogger gives and receives value, more opportunities will come her way.

Turning down a pitch without burning a bridge

I've heard from some mom bloggers that they are concerned about turning away opportunities to work with brands, lest they lose out on future opportunities. Yet there will most definitely be times when a brand or product is really not a good fit with your blog audience or your business goals. If you take every opportunity even if it doesn't fit with your blog topic, you risk alienating readers or becoming too much like a blogging infomercial. Over time, this kind of practice can lead to losses — of traffic, loyal readers, and even your credibility. Those are your biggest assets as a blogger; it pays in the long run to protect them at all costs.

It's not hard to turn down a pitch. In fact, many pitches to bloggers go completely ignored, and yet the pitches show no signs up letting up anytime soon. Of course, you don't want to turn someone down with something like, "I hate your product," because sometimes brand representatives work with several companies. If you are rude to a brand representative, you very well could lose out on future opportunities working with other brands, including some you love.

The most elegant way to turn down a pitch is by saying something like this:

> "I really appreciate you contacting me to work with you regarding your Product X promotion. However, because my blog is mostly about Hobby Z, I don't think I would be effective at giving your product the exposure you are seeking. You might want to contact Anna W. at the XYZ blog, because I think she would be a much better fit. But please keep me in mind for future promotions, especially those related to Hobby Z, because I would love to work with you!"

If you've been blogging for a while, you'll find that you get *lots* of pitches in your inbox, sometimes daily. I'm not suggesting that you respond to every single one of them, because that could become a full-time job in and of itself. When you want to ensure that you preserve the relationship with a particular brand representative for future consideration, use a pitch rejection like the preceding example. Not only will you be building relationships with many different people, but you will be putting you and your blog "top of mind" any time that brand representative needs to pitch anything related to "Hobby Z"!

Chapter 11

Preparing Your Blog for Advertising

. . . .

In This Chapter

▶ Getting hip to Internet advertising terms

▶ Knowing where to place ads on your blog

▶ Putting ads into your blog template

▶ Setting up automatic rotating ads on your blog

. . . .

*I*f you wanted to add advertising to your WordPress blog template back in 2006, you had to figure out what HTML to use — and dig through your template PHP code to insert it. Yes, I messed up a lot of perfectly good blog templates back then! Putting ads in Blogger templates was much easier, but you were also much more limited with what you could do.

These days, hundreds of free resources make it brain-dead easy to include advertising in your blog. And some WordPress blog templates come with advertising sections already built in, making it even easier to put ads where you want to. In this chapter, I show you several easy ways to get ads onto your blog to maximize your ad revenue.

For those of you who are serious about finding advertisers, I also explain the things advertisers expect from bloggers. You may not need this information if you're selling to very small businesses. But if you want to sell to large brands, I explain the advertising standards you need to follow. Additionally, I share some free tools that will make it easy for you to give sophisticated advertising solutions to your advertising clients.

Planning Your Advertising Placements

If you've immediately closed out of an ugly website that's plastered with inappropriate ads, then you probably want to ensure that your readers don't do the same. On the other hand, some people don't want to put ads on their blog at all. I discuss what kinds of blogs are best suited to advertising in Chapter 4.

If advertising is the right choice for you, then the next step is to get your blog ready to display ads. I have to use a lot of Internet advertising jargon to help you do this, so I provide a list of the most important terms you need to know.

Getting hip to Internet advertising terminology

I thought I knew my stuff pretty well when I started selling advertising on my first blog. Then one of my first advertising clients asked me for my *CPM* and monthly *rate card.* They were interested in my *leaderboard* unit *above the fold,* wanted my *ad creative* specs, and could I send them an *IO?* I quickly scrambled onto the Web to find out what they heck they were talking about so that I didn't look like a fool when I responded!

There are hundreds of Internet advertising terms, most of which you don't really need to know. But the ones you do need to know are really important. I would never want you to find yourself in a position of promising something that you can't deliver, or turning down a great opportunity because you didn't realize you had what an advertiser needed.

Above the fold: These are ad placements that a site visitor can see when they view a page without having to scroll down.

Ad creative: The actual ad that will appear on your blog.

Ad creative guidelines: Guidelines that let advertisers know things such as the sizes of ads you offer, whether or not you accept animated ads, how large the ad file sizes can be, and whether or not you accept audio ads.

Ad network: A company that sells ads for a group of websites while keeping a portion of the profits. Ad networks can be very exclusive and difficult to get into, or they can be open to almost any Web publisher. (An example of the latter type is Google AdSense.)

Ad rotation: Running several alternating ads in the same spot on your blog.

Ad server: Software that stores and displays ads for one or more websites. Ad servers are best for blogs that have a large volume of ad spaces to maintain. They also have the more sophisticated tracking tools needed by larger companies or ad agencies.

Banner: A visual picture with text or animated ad. Banners come in standard sizes, the most common of which are

- ✔ **Leaderboard:** A horizontal 728 x 90-pixel ad usually appearing at the top of a page.

- ✔ **Medium Rectangle:** An almost-square 300 x 250-pixel ad that fits well into most blog sidebars.

- ✔ **Wide Skyscraper:** A tall (vertical) 160 x 600-pixel ad that also frequently appears in blog sidebars.

- ✔ **Square Button:** A small 125 x 125-pixel ad that generally appears with several more ads in a group. This size is frequently used by small businesses, but has been eliminated as a standard size for large scale advertisers.

Call to action: This is when you make a specific request of a site visitor to take an action on your site. Examples would be, "Click Here," "Sign up for my newsletter," or "Add item to cart."

Click fraud: The false inflation of clicks by manual or automated means. This is meant to either fraudulently increase earnings when a publisher earns revenue on each click, or give a misleading impression that an ad is performing better than it actually is.

Click through: This is the action of a Web visitor clicking an ad and viewing the next page on the advertiser's website.

comScore rankings: comScore is the industry leader for measuring Web traffic, used by large advertising agencies to plan how they purchase their ads. comScore ranks websites and groups of websites so media buyers can plan effective advertising campaigns. Most blogs aren't large enough to get listed on comScore, but many get listed through its larger ad network. Related to comScore is the TAL (Traffic Assignment Letter), described later in this list.

Contextual ads: The process of displaying ads based on relevance to the content on a Web page.

CPA (Cost Per Acquisition): The amount an advertiser will pay for each new customer or sales lead.

CPC (Cost Per Click): The amount an advertiser will pay for each click on an ad.

CPM (Cost Per Thousand): The amount an advertiser will pay for each 1,000 views of an ad. (Remember Roman numerals? The *M* stands for a thousand.)

Frequency cap: The act of limiting the views of an ad to a certain number per visit or length of time. This could be anywhere from one hour to one month.

Geotargeting: The act of limiting the views of an ad to a certain geographical area.

House ads: The ads you run when you have no paying ads to run. House ads promote your own website or services.

Impression: A single instance of an ad appearing on a page.

Inventory: The number of ads you can run per day, week, or month. You can calculate this number by multiplying the number of ads you have on each page by the number of page views in a given time period.

IO (Insertion Order): Kind of like an invoice or purchase order that you provide to your advertisers before they run your ads. It typically includes the dates the ad will run, the banner sizes and placements, and your ad creative guidelines. There's no specific format for an IO; this is something you can simply type up in a word processor and send to your advertising clients.

Landing page: The page that an ad is linked to and is viewed when a user clicks on an ad.

Rate card: Your price list of available ads on your blog. Generally bloggers charge by number of impressions or a flat monthly rate.

ROI (Return on Investment): The amount of money an advertiser earns compared to how much it spends on advertising. Generally, advertisers want to spend less than what they earn, but sometimes very large brands are unable to track direct sales from their ads.

ROS (Run of Site): Giving an advertiser the exclusive right to be the only advertiser on your blog, usually at a premium rate.

TAL (Traffic Assignment Letter): An agreement that's required by members of some ad networks. The letter assigns your comScore traffic ranking to be part of a larger ad network, rather than ranking your site individually.

Text ad: An ad that's purely text and no graphics. (Make sure you read Chapter 9 about selling text links to ensure your blog doesn't get a search engine penalty.)

Tracking link or referral link: A special URL that an ad is linked to so advertisers can track the results of their advertising purchases. Advertisers generally provide their own tracking links to publishers. But if you need to create one yourself, you can use a free service like Bitly (`http://bit.ly`) to create tracking links.

User-initiated: Playing audio or video only when a user clicks a clear Start or Play button. The alternative is an audio or video ad that starts automatically when the page appears, which is generally considered very intrusive.

Choosing the best sizes and placements for your ads

I wish I could tell you that there's a standard content-to-advertising ratio, but there really isn't one. Every Web page is different; what works for some will not work for others. The most important general rule to follow is that your blog readers are there — first and foremost — to read your content. So make that content easy to find.

Generally speaking, you don't want more than four to six banner ads on any one page. For blogs that tend to have shorter blog posts, I recommend sticking with four ads. Longer pages that require scrolling can get away with adding more ad units without distracting from the content.

Above-the-fold ad placements

Companies such as Google have invested much time and energy to determine where ads perform best on a page by getting the most click throughs. It uses tools that create a *heat map* to show what parts of a page are *hot* (with the highest number of clicks). You can learn more about Google's ad placement recommendations at `www.google.com/adsense/support/bin/answer. py?answer=17954`. See Figure 11-1 to view Google's heat map and recommendations for ad placement.

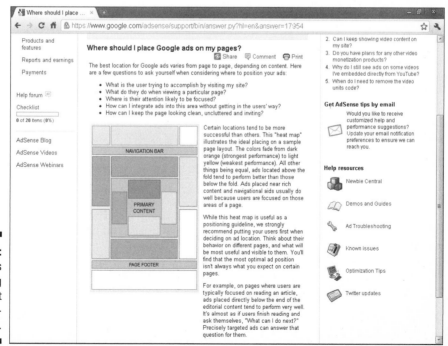

Figure 11-1: Google's advertising placement recommendations.

As you can see, both Google and others have found that ads perform best when they are at the top of the page above the fold or placed within your content area. Above-the-fold ads are the most desirable for advertisers, and usually cost more than ads below the fold. But you can't squeeze more than two ads at the top of the page, because you only have a limited number of pixels to make a great impression on a new reader. Whether you place one or two ads above the fold is a personal preference. Following are two great examples of above-the-fold ad placements that don't intrude on the blogger's content. Laurie Turk from TipJunkie uses a leaderboard ad above her content and a medium rectangle ad at the top of her sidebar, as shown in Figure 11-2. Amy Clark from MomAdvice has a narrower content area and uses a wide skyscraper ad to the right of her content (see Figure 11-3).

Below-the-fold ad placements

Depending on the type of ad, sometimes below-the-fold placements can actually perform better than above-the-fold ads. A great example of this is using an ad placement within your content or right at the end of a post.

Figure 11-2:
TipJunkie has two above-the-fold ad placements.

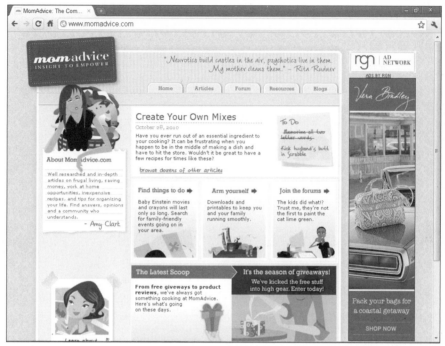

Figure 11-3:
MomAdvice
has one
above-
the-fold ad
placement.

The end of a blog post is a great place to put a *call to action* — inviting your readers to do something next after reading your post. Choose your call to action carefully. An ad that pays by the click (such as Google AdSense) is a better choice for this position than an ad that just pays by the impression. Alternatively, you may want to reserve this area for suggestions to read related blog posts, to subscribe to your feed or newsletter, or to comment on your blog. See Figure 11-4 for an example of a blog that effectively combines several calls to action at the bottom of a blog post.

Cindy from SkipToMyLou makes the most of the end of her blog posts by placing a below-the-fold ad, RSS and social media sharing buttons, and three related post suggestions.

Figure 11-4:
SkipToMy-
Lou
below-the-
fold ad
placement.

Putting Ads into Your Blog Template

The physical process of placing ads in your blog will vary based on the blogging platform you use and your blog template. Blogger blogs make it very easy to include advertising in their gadgets, but you have less control over the overall functionality of your blog. You can similarly add advertising to WordPress blogs in widgets, which are similar to gadgets, plus have more sophisticated advertising management tools available to you via WordPress plugins.

Here I'm specifically referring to the self-hosted WordPress.*org* blogs that I showed you how to set up in Chapter 2. WordPress.*com* does not allow its users to place advertising on its blogs.

The basic process of placing an advertisement in your blog is to copy your ad HTML and paste it into your template. Your ad HTML is generally provided by your advertisers, so the addition is an easy process. The following sections show the easiest ways to place advertisements in Blogger and WordPress.

Putting ad HTML in a WordPress widget

To place an ad in your WordPress blog, you add the HTML to your
WordPress widget as follows:

1. **Create a new text widget by selecting Appearance⇨Widgets from your
   WordPress Dashboard.**

2. **Drag the Text Widget over onto your sidebar to activate it.**

3. **Enter your ad HTML or JavaScript code.**

   When the widget opens automatically, paste your ad's HTML code in
   the text area below the title. If you want to add a title such as "Our
   Sponsors," you can do that, too.

4. **Click the Save button, and then click Close.**

5. **Click and drag the widget to move the ad widget to where you want
   the ad to appear.**

   No further saving is necessary.

Check out Figure 11-5 to see these steps in action.

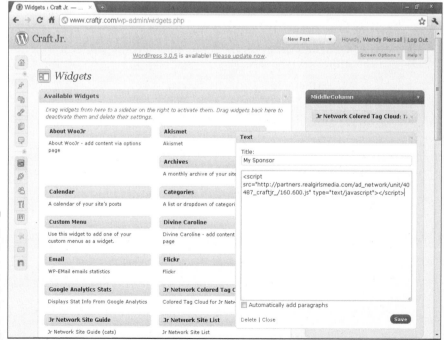

Figure 11-5:
Adding an
advertise-
ment to a
WordPress
blog in a
text widget.

WordPress widgets can be used anywhere in your template, not just in your sidebar. They are particularly useful in your header, where you can have easy access to the most prominent part of your template design. To find out more about creating customized widgets, check out *WordPress For Dummies,* 3rd Edition, by Lisa Sabin-Wilson.

Putting ad HTML in a Blogger gadget

To place an ad in a Blogger gadget, follow these steps:

1. **Add a new gadget by clicking the Design tab on your Blogger Dashboard.**

2. **Click Add a Gadget in the place on-screen where you want your ad to appear.**

   Doing so places the ad.

3. **Click the plus sign next to the HTML/JavaScript option.**

4. **Enter your ad HTML or JavaScript code and a title.**

   When the gadget opens automatically, paste your HTML code in the text area below the title. Add a title that will help you remember what's in this gadget — this title will also be visible on your blog template.

5. **Click Save.**

6. **Click and drag the gadget to move the ad gadget where the ad should appear.**

   No further saving is necessary.

Check out Figure 11-6 to see these steps in action.

Figure 11-6:
Adding an advertise-ment to a Blogger blog in an HTML/JavaScript gadget.

Selecting Appropriate Backup Ads

After you know how and where you want to place ads on your blog, you need advertisers! I've seen newer bloggers make up their own "This ad space is available" ads, which I think are okay if they're used sparingly. I recommend not using them in every ad spot you have available, because that sends the glaring signal that nobody is advertising with you. You want to send the message that your ad spots are valuable, and announcing your full vacancy undermines that goal.

At the same time, in order to attract advertisers, you don't want to have zero ads on your blog, either. Potential advertisers need to know that advertising is available on your blog. So there are a few things you can do to fill up your ad inventory while you're waiting for paying advertisers to show up. These ads can also serve as backup ads.

Having backup ads in place is an important part of your advertising strategy. There may come a time when an advertiser has to abruptly pull its ads from publishers' websites, and you don't want to waste your page impressions and lose out on revenue. One of the harder lessons I've learned as a blogger is to resist the temptation to put all the eggs in one basket. Even the most consis-tent ad revenue can disappear in an instant in the online marketing world.

House ads

House ads are simply banner ads that you use to promote yourself on your blog. The point of house ads is to get your users to engage with more of your content. If you have a few popular posts that got lost in your blog archives, this is the perfect way to highlight the content and introduce it to newer readers. Other things you can promote are your RSS feed, your mailing list, a current contest you're running, or simply a blog category page. Blogger Jennifer Wilson runs ads for her own Biz Bootcamp on her separate Simple Scrapper blog (http://simplescrapper.com) that you can see in Figure 11-7.

To make your own house ads, you need a photo-editing program and some simple design skills. You want to make the house ads look like part of your site, so you can borrow graphics and text from your blog template design. Or for as little as $20 (U.S. dollars), you can use an easy banner-ad-making tool such as www.bannersnack.com.

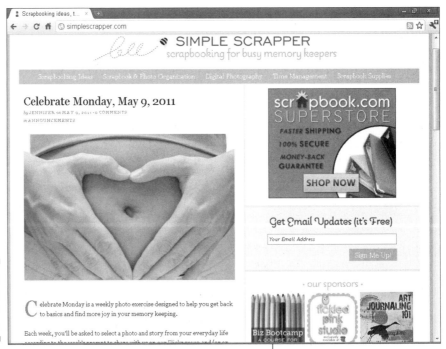

Figure 11-7: House ads on Simple Scrapper.

A house ad

Charity ads

If you have a favorite charity or cause, you can run ads to help promote it. Larger charities such as the Red Cross will have a Public Service Advertising section on their websites that have Web banners you can use. For smaller charities, you can simply ask them for a banner to put on your site, or make one for them. Depending on your state tax laws, you may even be able to write this off on your taxes! Check with a local accountant to find out if this is an option available to you.

Ads from other bloggers

I love the idea of helping out fellow bloggers, so swapping ads with other bloggers is one of my favorite options. The best approach for swapping ads is to find a website that is somewhat similar in size as yours. If you swap with a blog that is much bigger or smaller than yours, the disparity may cause unnecessary resentments — unless the other blogger is a very good friend, of course. If you don't have any blogging friends you can swap ads with, check out the MomBloggersClub.com forums, where ad-swapping requests are posted periodically.

Affiliate banner ads

I cover affiliate ads in depth in Chapter 14, but they are worth a mention here because adding affiliate banners is super-easy. The added bonus is that they give a good impression because they demonstrate that larger companies want to work with you. Affiliate ads only pay revenue when you refer a sale to the merchant advertiser. And I'll be honest; affiliate banners aren't as effective at driving sales as in-post text links are. But if you have no advertisers at all, adding affiliate banners is a great place to start.

Using Helpful Advertising Tools

When you're first getting started, placing ads in your blog in the manner I explain earlier in this chapter is the easiest way to get up and running. But as you get more established, you may find that running all your ads starts getting harder to manage. You could have several advertisers whose ads have different start and end dates. You could have other advertisers that want to stop running ads at exactly 20,000 impressions. And you could also be running backup ads in your rotation to fill in the gaps. And yes, managing all these details can get time-consuming very quickly.

That's when you need ad management software to help you automate many of these tasks. In the following sections, I show you two of my favorite ad management tools for bloggers.

Using the Advertising Manager plugin for WordPress

The Advertising Manager by Scott Switzer is one of the most popular and recommended ad management plugins for WordPress. The software is built to work automatically with over ten common ad networks — plus you can add your own ads as well. The plugin lets you manage all your ad placements in one place, with simple settings that allow you to dictate how and where ads appear on your blog. You can place ads in your blog template as well as in individual blog posts or pages. It also lets you rotate several ads in one ad unit, allowing you to assign a weight to each ad so it automatically shows your higher paying ads more frequently than the lower paying ones. It also integrates with OpenX, an even more powerful ad management tool I explain in the later section, "Using the OpenX OnRamp ad server."

Setting up a new ad in the Advertising Manager plugin

Follow these steps to set up a new ad in the WordPress Advertising Manager plugin:

1. **Download, install, and activate the Advertising Manager plugin.**

   If you don't already know how to add a WordPress plugin to your blog, I explain it in Chapter 2.

2. **From your WordPress Dashboard, choose Ads⇨Create New.**

3. **Paste your ad code into the text field and click Import.**

4. **In the Name text box, enter a name according to where the ad unit appears on your blog, such as Leaderboard or Under Post Medium Rectangle.**

   If you want to be able to rotate ads in the same ad unit, you need to name all the ads that will appear in the same position with the same name. So all ads named "Sidebar" will rotate in the spot where you place your *Sidebar* ad tags as shown later in Steps 11 and 12. The name you choose won't be publicly displayed.

   The Name field may auto-populate for you. You can still name it however you see fit.

5. **The Account Details fields will be automatically populated for you. If not, you can leave them blank.**

6. **Under Ad Format, choose the ad size, or enter your own if the ad has nonstandard dimensions.**

7. **Under Website Display Options, select where you want the ads to appear.**

   You still need to place the ads into your blog posts or blog template. But if you have specific pages or sections of your site where you don't want ads to appear, these options allow you to block ads by criteria such as categories or author. Select the check boxes for where you want the ads to appear, and deselect the check boxes for where you don't want the ads to appear.

8. **Under Advanced Options, give your ad a weight if you're rotating more than one ad in an ad unit.**

   A weight of 1 is the lowest, and a weight of 2 means that the ad will appear twice as much as a weight of 1. A weight of 0 will stop the ad from running altogether.

   See the last section of this chapter for an explanation of the OpenX Market option in this step — you can leave it deselected for now. By selecting this check box, you can easily run ads from the OpenX Market as long as you are signed up for its service.

9. **On the right sidebar in the Notes section, be sure to enter identifying information such as Molly's Etsy Shop Ad.**

   That will be the only way you'll be able to tell ads apart in the Advertising Manager Dashboard.

10. **Click Save.**

    The rest of the settings can be safely left at their defaults.

11. **To place the ad unit into a blog post, switch to HTML view and place your cursor where you want the ad to appear. Then select the appropriate ad unit name from the Insert Ad drop-down list.**

12. **To place the ad unit into your blog sidebar, go to the WordPress Widgets page by clicking on the Widgets link under the Appearance menu.**

    A new widget appears as an option for you to place on your sidebar labeled _Advertisement._

13. **Click and drag that widget onto your sidebar where you want your ad to appear.**

    The widget immediately expands and offers easy configuration options. You can give the ad a title in the Title text box (such as Our Sponsors) or leave the title blank.

14. **Select the ad you want to appear from the drop-down list.**

15. (Optional) If you want your ad to appear with no widget formatting, select the Hide Widget Formatting check box.

Some themes have a separator or special header for each widget, and selecting this will hide your theme-specific formatting. You can test the appearance with and without the formatting to see which one you prefer.

16. Click the Save button to apply the advertisement widget changes.

For intermediate users who want to position the ads in other places on a blog template, you can do so by adding a bit of code to your template file. Type '**[ad#name]**' (where *name* is the Name of your ad) into your template file through the Template Editor (found under Appearance⇨Editor) where you want the ad to appear. If you don't know where to add this information to your template, this tutorial on Tamba2.org will help you find it at `www.tamba2.org.uk/wordpress/adsense`.

Using the OpenX OnRamp ad server

Earlier in this chapter, I mention that there are easy ways to provide sophisti-cated advertising solutions to your ad clients. This is not something a beginner needs to worry about, but I do think it is important to explain for the intermedi-ate and advanced level readers of this book. If you're selling ads to advertising agencies or larger companies that do a lot of online advertising, typically they need special information from you to help them determine whether their ads are working. Most of all, they need to know exactly how many ad impressions you deliver and how many clicks each ad receives. Sometimes they may also require more sophisticated targeting (called *geotargeting*) that you can't do on your own. For example, the advertiser might only want its ad shown to visitors in the United States and Canada, but nowhere else.

An ad server can do this for you. An *ad server* is software that will allow you to manage all your ads from one place, even if you have more than one blog. It displays the ads, rotates them, targets them, and provides performance reports for your advertising clients as well. OpenX (`http://openx.org`) has a product called OpenX OnRamp that is a free ad server I recommend when you get to the point that manually managing your advertising doesn't cut it anymore.

Here's when an ad server will be a benefit to you:

✔ When you have multiple blogs with many ad placements, and it becomes difficult to update all of them manually.

✔ When you need to track advertising revenue in specific ad placements. For example, I needed an ad server to track this when I was paying my blog writers a portion of the advertising revenue that only their blogs earned, even though I ran the same ads across my entire site.

✔ When you have an advertising client that requires performance reports, geotargeting, or frequency capping.

✔ When your advertiser wants to be able to change out the ads that appear on your site on its own. Ad servers can give you the ability to provide your clients with their own logins and upload new ads on their own schedules.

✔ If you happen to have one advertiser who pays per impression and another that pays per click, an ad server will help you to track both, even if you rotate them in the same position.

The reason I like to suggest OpenX is because it is an extremely powerful and sophisticated tool — it probably has more features than you will ever need. But another important benefit of using OpenX is that it has an option called the *OpenX Market*. The OpenX Market is similar to an ad network, as I explain in Chapter 12. You can use this service as a way to find lower paying ads as backfill when you don't have higher paying ads to display. (*Backfill ads* are ads to run so that you can at least make some money off of your ad inventory when you can't find a premium advertiser.)

For more information on how to use and sign up for the OpenX OnRamp Ad Server, go to `http://openx.org/publishers/community-ad-server`.

For more information on how to use and sign up for the OpenX Market, go to `http://openx.org/publisher/ad-marketplace`.

Chapter 12

Finding and Joining an Ad Network

. . . .

. . . .

I'm a big fan of ad networks — that's because my main source of income is from them. Ad networks aren't for everyone, but they can be a great addition to many different kinds of blogs. For some bloggers, it will add just a few dollars to your earnings every month. For some, it can be thousands or tens of thousands of dollars. It all depends on how much traffic you have.

The premise of an ad network is simple — a company sells ads for a group of websites and splits the revenue with the bloggers or Web publishers. Three or four years ago, not many ad networks worked with bloggers, but today hundreds do. The best ad networks are picky about the sites they represent — and they focus on small niche audiences, which means they can charge premium advertising rates. The least-desirable ad networks take almost any website and run ads you would probably be very embarrassed to display on your blog. In this chapter, I show you how to find the great ad networks, avoid the bad ones, and I help you choose the right one for you and your blog.

Unlike other sources of income, there are only two ways to grow your income with an ad network: hope the network can get higher ad rates, or increase your traffic. That means you don't have as much control over your earnings with an ad network as you do with any other way of monetizing your blog. The biggest complaint from bloggers who work with ad networks is that they rarely have enough *inventory* for all their publishers. That means the ad networks haven't sold enough ads to fill all the ad spots and page views that all their publishers have available. Sometimes this happens from seasonal changes; for example, January is typically a bad month for advertising in general because it's right after the holiday season when most consumers aren't making many purchases. Other times, it's a problem with the network — it may have a poor sales team, have taken on too many publishers, or is too narrowly focused on a target audience and can't bring in enough advertisers to work with.

But when an ad network is successful, and when a blogger has enough traffic to show lots of ads every month, there really isn't an easier way to make money from your blog. Ad networks almost always pay based on how many ads are shown, not based on clicks or on eventual sales. So as long as you have people visiting your blog, you earn revenue. You don't have to sell or maintain anything, and that frees up your time to focus on what you're great at — blogging.

Deciding Whether an Ad Network Is Right for You

As I outline in Chapter 10, only a few blogging business models conflict running ads with your best interests. This is when you're blogging to sell your own products or to promote your professional services. Even then, running ads on these blogs can still work, especially if the ads are promoting complementary and not competing products and services. But if you're really focused on getting a sale or client, ads can definitely distract your readers from that goal. Or (worse) your readers can click an ad and buy from a competitor rather than from you.

If you choose to run ads in these circumstances, be sure to keep the ads off the pages from which you want your visitors to make an actual purchase — in particular, keep your product-description pages and your shopping cart clear of ads.

Making money with an ad network is a pure numbers game. More traffic means more money. If you have a blog with a good amount of traffic, or even the potential for a good amount of traffic, then I think working with an ad network is a very effective way to monetize your blog.

Two of your biggest concerns about working with an ad network should be

- ✔ What happens if you don't like a displayed ad?
- ✔ Can you work with other ad networks or sell your own ads?

These two questions have the biggest influence on your overall success and bottom line. If your ad network suddenly starts displaying flashing green banners that audibly say "You have WON!!", you'll most likely lose a chunk of your blog readers' respect and trust. And if you're locked into using only one ad network that suddenly has inventory issues, well, your paycheck can be cut in half or more.

Most ad networks that I've worked with and that are used frequently by mom bloggers have addressed both of these concerns well. They care very deeply about making sure only quality advertisements are displayed and will let you work with other advertisers in certain circumstances. I explain those circumstances in more detail later in this chapter — usually it's just a matter of ensuring you comply with your ad network's reasonable guidelines.

Determining whether your blog is ready to be accepted into an ad network

Most — but definitely not all — ad networks have a minimum level of traffic that your blog must have before you can apply to join. It might be a number of page views or number of unique visitors. Sometimes the threshold is low enough that most established bloggers can qualify. Some require half a million monthly unique visitors or more — these ad networks don't work with many mom bloggers!

Even if your prospective ad network doesn't have a minimum traffic requirement, most require that your blog topic and audience fit a certain target audience. There are ad networks for food bloggers, craft bloggers, home décor bloggers, political bloggers, technology bloggers, and even pet-loving bloggers. Of course, several large, established ad networks target a more general audience of women or moms. While these aren't so narrowly focused, they're considered some of the biggest powerhouses in the industry, so they attract very large brands and good advertising rates.

The last thing that most ad networks will require is that you display at least one of their ads *above the fold.* That means the ad is at the top of your blog pages and is visible without the user having to scroll down. This is considered your premium real estate in regards to ad placements, and the most likely place for your readers to click the ad. You really can't have more than one or two ads above the fold without cluttering up your blog design and turning off readers. So you'll need to ensure that your blog template can accommodate an ad placement in your blog header and/or at the very top of your blog sidebar. For more about placing ads in your blog template, see Chapter 11.

It's important to note that your choice of blogging platform can influence your ability to get into an ad network and how much you can earn from advertising. WordPress.com users are not allowed to display advertising at all. Certain levels of LiveJournal accounts require that you display their ads on your blog, which will prevent you from displaying your own ads or those from your ad network. And while you can display ads on Blogger.com blogs, you'll never have the kind of control over placement and functionality that you can get with a self-hosted WordPress.org blog. For bloggers who are serious about making money on their blogs from advertising, using a professional content management system is a real must.

Understanding the pros and cons of ad networks

I mention earlier that the most common complaint you hear from bloggers using ad networks is that they usually don't have enough inventory to fill all the available ad views that your blog generates. Each ad network handles this situation differently. Some will allow you to put your own backup ads into place so that you can run self-promotional ads or use Google AdSense when there are no paying ads to display. Other ad networks require that only their ads can be shown in the spots where their ad networks appear on your blog. In these circumstances, the ad networks generally display their own house ads, and sometimes they'll pay you a tiny amount for these impressions, which is (of course) better than nothing.

In a bad economy, inventory issues can be a real problem for ad networks. Sometimes it means they can't take any new publishers, and applicants are put on a waiting list. For bloggers, it can mean a huge cut in revenue. There have been months where I've earned more total revenue with less than half the amount of traffic of my busiest months of the year. It certainly makes it frustrating to do all the work to generate lots of traffic only to find that you haven't earned anything more than any other month of the year.

Sometimes switching to a different ad network can earn you more money — but for the most part, if one ad network is having a hard time selling ads, then all of them are. If you really do want to switch to a different ad network, I highly recommend contacting one of the bloggers in the networks you want to join and asking what the experience has been like. Every time I've gotten frustrated with my own ad network, by asking around, I've found that the grass is never greener on the other side of the fence. But if you're trying to get into a big ad network and are currently working with a small one, then switching could give you an instant pay raise.

None of these things are going to be too much of an issue for you if you don't have a lot of traffic to begin with. Until you get into hundreds of thousands of page views a month, ad network earnings are pretty meager. Some blogs and blog topics will simply never get huge amounts of traffic, especially those that attract a small niche audience. In these circumstances, it makes more sense to use ad networks as a backup — and focus instead on other ways to generate revenue. Affiliate marketing might be a better bet if you can promote the right products to your unique group of blog readers.

Applying to join ad networks

In the later section, "Comparing Ad Networks for Parenting Blogs," I outline some of the most popular ad networks with mom bloggers. Each has unique criteria that it requires of the publishers it works with. Each of them has a website with an application page that you can fill out to apply to join its ad networks. Here they'll ask you general questions about your blog and how much traffic you have. If you have more than one website that you want considered, be sure to include all your URLs in the application.

Almost all the applications will request your current traffic levels. Don't be tempted to fudge your numbers here, because when you start running its ads, it will know exactly how much traffic you actually do have. It's appropriate, though, to combine the traffic from multiple websites you own — as long as you're applying for all of them to join the ad network together.

Sometimes filling out an application isn't enough to get a response. It sounds strange, but I've had more than a few applications ignored by ad networks. When this happens, I've tracked down other bloggers in the network's program and have asked them for a specific person that I could contact. This has helped in several ways. Sometimes getting the referral of a friend is enough to push your application to the front of the line. Other times, you'll get the exact reason why they ignored you. The ad network may not be taking new applications at this time. Occasionally ad networks have private selection criteria that you didn't meet, and at least you can get a personal response letting you know what you have to do to get approved in the future.

Asking Questions before Signing Your Ad Network Deal

After you submit your ad network application, it can take a few days or a few weeks to get a response. If you're approved, you'll be asked to sign an agreement and perhaps several other forms.

It's *really important* to read through the agreement and any forms carefully, even if you hate legal mumbo jumbo. When you become a part of an ad network, you aren't just agreeing to take its advertising revenue. You're also agreeing to deliver very specific things to the ad network's advertisers, and you need to make very sure you know what you're getting into. Some ad networks have control over what appears on your blog, and even what you write about. You need to be 100-percent clear on what you can and can't do to run the ad network's ads on your blog.

If you read nothing else in this chapter, please read this section. I know that getting into these kinds of legal details can be tedious, so I've come up with a list of questions for you to ask. Some of these questions are obvious, some not so obvious. Some I learned to ask only after it was too late to ask them, ending up costing money out of my own pocket.

✔ **Where do the ads need to be placed on my site?** Most ad networks require that the ads need to be placed above the fold. And if so, your blog template needs to accommodate this requirement.

✔ **What ad sizes does the network use?** Expect to run the most common sizes, which are 728 x 90, 300 x 250, and 160 x 600. Again, make sure that your blog template can run these sizes; not all templates can handle these sizes and still look good.

✔ **What other ads can I have on my site?** Some networks require the exclusive right to all your ad spaces. Some require exclusivity only on the portion of your pages above the fold. Some require that their ads occupy the highest ad spot on the page. And still others require that they be the only banner ads, but you can sell text ads. Be very clear about what the network requires, because it could drop you if you don't comply with the agreement on ad placement.

✔ **Can I still sell my own ads?** Some networks require that you work only with them or specify that you can't join any other ad networks, but will still allow you to sell your own ads to advertisers. You probably won't be able to sell your own ads in the same placements where the ad network ads appear, so you'll need to create separate placements for the ads you sell that are in compliance with the rest of the terms of your agreement.

✔ **What else do I need to place on my site besides the ads to be a part of the network?** Many networks also require that you include some kind of badge or a widget that promotes the rest of the network. Usually it's not a big deal, but you do need to take that factor into consideration because it will take up space on your pages.

✔ **What is the *range* of rates I can expect to earn from running the network's ads?** I made the mistake once of asking this question differently, and ended up getting an answer that referred only to the very top rates the ad network charged. In reality, I earned far less, because not all my inventory was filled and because the ads I displayed were all sold at different rates. So be sure to ask what to expect in a good month and in a not-so-good month.

✔ **What is the revenue split? Is there an administration fee?** Ad networks keep a portion of the revenue your blog earns in exchange for selling the ads for you. While it seems like a lot, the percentage split isn't too different from what you would have to pay in commissions if you hired someone to sell ads for you. 50-50 is the most common split, but this can vary. It's important to know also whether you'll be splitting the full revenue or whether there's an administration fee taken off the top before the split. It may not be a big amount for now, but 10 percent off the top of three million page views can *really* add up.

✔ **What are the ad network's payment terms?** You want to find out whether the network pays you monthly or quarterly. Also find out how long it typically takes to receive payment — whether it's 15 days, 60 days, or 120 days. Some networks will pay you through PayPal, while others cut checks and send them in the mail. Some networks will pay you no matter what; with others, payment is contingent upon the advertiser paying the network (which means you have to wait for its billing cycle to finish before you'll get your money). If the payment to you is contingent on the advertiser making payment, you'll want to find out what happens in the unlikely event that the advertiser doesn't pay.

✔ **What happens when the network doesn't have any ads to run?** This is especially important if the ad network requires some level of exclusivity. If it has no ads, and you can't run anyone else's ads, you have a problem on your hands. Many ad networks have their own backup ads to run, which are also called *backfill* ads. These ads don't pay very much, but at they least pay something. Several ad networks will let you run your own Google AdSense ads as backfill, but not all of them will.

✔ **What kind of advertisers does the network normally work with?** While this may not be in the contract, you do want to ask this question, or look at the network's existing ads to determine what kinds of ads you can expect to run on your site. If it has existing relationships with large, well-established brands, this is a good sign. If you have concerns about the quality of ads it's running currently, then I wouldn't apply to that ad network in the first place.

✔ **Can I control which ads are shown on my site?** Some networks allow you to accept or reject every ad that comes through their networks. Others will simply give you what they have and you have to run them, no matter what. I've never had a true problem with this, because the ad networks I've worked with are just as picky as I am about working with quality advertisers. Sometimes you'll want to keep an ad off your blog — an obvious no-no (for example) is an ad for alcoholic drinks on a kids-oriented site. If you do want to limit where the ad shows up, and you don't have direct control over your ad approvals, usually you can just e-mail the network and ask it to remove your site from the campaign. Not all ad networks are set up with that level of control, so be sure to know what you can and can't do.

✔ **What is the term of the contract?** I've heard of contracts with no set term, and some that require you to be bound to an ad network for up to three years. This may be a point to negotiate if you're concerned about getting into something too long-term.

✔ **Who will take credit for your comScore ranking?** *comScore* is a service that is the industry standard for measuring the amount of traffic on large websites. Media buyers rely on comScore to find the websites they want to advertise on. Ad networks place a high value on increasing their existing comScore rankings, because the larger their reach, the more desirable they are to advertisers. Many networks require that bloggers *assign their traffic* so that the network achieves a higher comScore rating. That means your traffic becomes part of the ad network's overall rank, rather than being an individual site. While this isn't a bad thing, you do need to make sure that you can get your comScore rank back when the contract ends.

Also, you can assign your traffic to only one ad network at a time. If the ad network requires that you assign your comScore rank to it, you can't work with another ad network that requires this, too. Plenty of ad networks don't require this, so if you're looking to work with a second ad network, you'll have to make sure that only one gets your comScore traffic assignment.

Comparing Ad Networks for Parenting Blogs

In the following sections, I highlight some of the top ad networks for mom bloggers. However, don't feel just because you're a mom who blogs that you should automatically join an ad network targeted at mom bloggers. If your blog is on a more focused topic such as food, fashion, or technology, there might be a better-fitting ad network for your content. Please refer to the online Cheat Sheet (at www.dummies.com/cheatsheet/momblogging) where I list a wider range of ad networks — and be sure to contact several networks to ensure that you're getting the best possible match for you and your blog.

The BlogHer Publishing Network

The BlogHer Publishing Network was one of the first ad networks to focus on moms, and the very first to focus on mom bloggers. BlogHer now works with a far larger audience of both moms and women, and is still a pioneer leading the efforts to help mom bloggers earn an income from their work. Figure 12-1 shows the BlogHer advertising network home page (www.blogherads.com).

The BlogHer ad network has the following requirements and benefits:

- ✔ **Minimum traffic requirement:** None as long as your blog is at least 90 days old and updated weekly.

- ✔ **Target audience requirement:** Blogs must be written by women or have a large percentage of female readers.

- ✔ **Revenue Split:** 50 percent / 50 percent after an administration fee. The percentage improves for bloggers generating over a million ad impressions in a month.

✔ **Editorial requirements:** You can't display BlogHer ads on pages that contain editorial content that has been commissioned and paid for by a third party. This includes paid advertising links and reviews if the product was received for free and worth more than $40 U.S. If you're using a self-hosted WordPress blog, The BlogHer Publishing Network technical team can help you set up your blog to easily comply with these guidelines automatically.

✔ **Other benefits:** In addition to banner ad campaigns, BlogHer has other revenue-generating opportunities for bloggers in the ad network: review programs, sponsored conversation programs, Twitter posse programs, and brand ambassador programs. They've worked hard to create opportunities for bloggers whose traffic alone might not generate adequate advertising income.

✔ **Extra benefits for mom bloggers who don't belong to their ad network:** BlogHer is unique because of its size and influence in the blogging community. Even if you don't belong to this ad network, you can still participate in its content-syndication program and earn revenue on your existing blog content. See www.blogher.com/what-syndication-blogher for more information on this uncommon opportunity.

Figure 12-1:
The BlogHer ad network home page.

Moms Media

Moms Media is a specialty division of ValueClick, one of the largest ad networks reaching nearly 80 percent of all Internet users. Moms Media is an ad network that's focused more on quality rather than size. It works very closely with publishers to offer the best possible revenue and fill rate.

Figure 12-2 shows the Moms Media advertising network home page (www.momsmedia.com).

The Moms Media ad network has the following requirements and benefits:

- ✔ **Minimum traffic requirement:** None; it evaluates each application on a case-by-case basis with a focus on quality content.

- ✔ **Target audience requirement:** Moms, of course, but also prefer to work with blogs that attract moms at very specific stages, from the first trimester to moms with kids age 13–18.

- ✔ **Revenue Split:** Varies according to campaign, and the publishers have influence over setting ad rates.

Figure 12-2:
The Moms
Media ad
network
home page.

✔ **Editorial requirements:** There are no specific editorial guidelines, but there are more opportunities for bloggers who can segment their own content.

✔ **Other benefits:** Moms Media offers highly relevant advertising, and has the ability to use the parent company ValueClick for backfill ads. Because ValueClick is so well established, Moms Media will almost always have paying ads to display on your blog.

Burst Moms Network

Burst Moms Network is a specialty division of Burst Media, one of the oldest established online ad networks. While Burst has a minimum traffic requirement, it does not have set terms and conditions for all the publishers that join the network. Burst works to build a custom advertising agreement with each of its publishers to meet the different needs of each website.

Figure 12-3 shows the Burst Moms Network home page (`www.burstmedia.com/landing_page/moms/index.htm`).

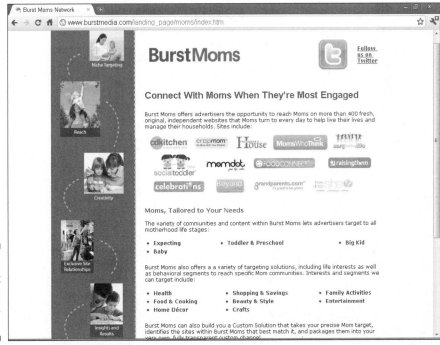

Figure 12-3: The Burst Moms Network home page.

The Burst Moms Network has the following requirements and benefits:

- ✔ **Minimum traffic requirement:** 10,000 monthly unique visitors.

- ✔ **Target audience requirement:** Moms who can be categorized by either life stages or lifestyles and interests.

- ✔ **Revenue Split:** Varies.

- ✔ **Editorial requirements:** Burst states that it looks, first and foremost, for a blog with a professional design and logo with uncluttered sidebars. Burst prefers working with bloggers who have media kits ready and are aware of their statistics via Quantcast or comScore; those indicators convey that the blogger is in tune with her business.

- ✔ **Other benefits:** Burst Moms Network has several different advertising options beyond standard banner ads, including home page takeovers and social media campaigns. Because the terms are flexible, you can work with the network in a range of ways, from being a backup network to exclusively representing your site.

IZEA: SocialSpark and SponsoredTweets

IZEA is a company that has two primary programs that match up bloggers and social media users with advertisers. While it's not a mom-specific network, mom bloggers do make up the largest segment of users — and its advertising clients are most interested in moms who blog as well. These sites don't work like a traditional ad network (as outlined in this chapter). Instead, they act like a marketplace in which bloggers can find advertisers to work with, and advertisers can find bloggers willing to write about their products.

The other difference with IZEA's sites is that they don't help you sell banner or text advertising. Instead, they offer opportunities to write about topics or take actions that advertisers are willing to pay for. They have two programs with which you can earn money that are relevant to bloggers and people who use Twitter: SocialSpark and SponsoredTweets. I have served on the advisory board of IZEA since 2008, helping make product changes to benefit its bloggers as the company grows.

SocialSpark

SocialSpark is a platform that makes it very easy to write sponsored blog posts that comply 100 percent with the standards from the FTC, WOMMA, and Google (which I explain in Chapter 9). It has also built tools that automate the measurement of your traffic and following on social media sites. Result: Bloggers with more influence and visitors can charge higher rates, commensurate with the higher value they can offer to advertisers. But even newer bloggers can find opportunities in its marketplace.

SocialSpark has a simple system in which you set up a profile, browse opportunities in its marketplace, submit the blog post to ensure it complies with all regulatory guidelines, and get paid. You can find out more and join its program at www.socialspark.com.

SponsoredTweets

Just as the name suggests, SponsoredTweets is similar to SocialSpark, but pays its publishers for sending out tweets instead of blog posts. It also has an automatic system in place to ensure you disclose that your tweet is an ad, plus measurement tools to give the advertisers insights as to how many people saw or clicked your tweet. You can find out more and join this program at www.sponsoredtweets.com.

Google AdSense

Google AdSense isn't a mom-oriented ad network, nor is it the best advertising option for most mom blogs in the first place. There are certainly exceptions to this, especially if you blog about products or brands. I include it in this section because I believe that all bloggers who display advertising should have a backup ad provider — and AdSense is a great solution for this need. AdSense approves almost all applications, especially those from legitimate sites. It works to keep spammers out of its program, but welcomes all publishers of quality content. Plus, almost all ad networks will allow you to simultaneously display AdSense ads, so it can be a good supplemental income, too.

In the past, AdSense had a bad reputation for displaying irrelevant or inappropriate ads, and for being a very poor revenue source. In the last year or so, I've been quite impressed with the improvements on all fronts, and it has become the second largest source of income on my blog network. AdSense has made a successful effort to attract more *display advertisers,* which are regular banner ads instead of just text ads. It's also much better at displaying ads that are very relevant to the content on your page. And AdSense has just rolled out a much more advanced ad-blocking feature that virtually eliminates the worry of inappropriate ads showing up on your blog. You can even block ads from nearly any category you don't like, even if a particular ad (or category) wouldn't normally be considered inappropriate.

Some website owners make six and seven figures a year from their AdSense earnings. To learn more about how AdSense works best, check out *Google AdSense For Dummies* by Jerri L. Ledford.

Chapter 13

Selling Your Own Advertising

● ●

In This Chapter

▶ Selling advertising to small businesses and large brands

▶ Understanding how to choose the right advertisers to partner with

▶ Finding advertisers for your blog

▶ Understanding what turns off potential advertisers

▶ Developing your own custom social media campaigns

▶ Finding ways to participate in existing brand campaigns

● ●

I honestly think that selling your own advertising is one of the most intimidating parts of being a professional blogger. It isn't just slapping up a
button in your sidebar — suddenly you need to have a way to take payments,
track results, and hardest of all, figure out what the heck to charge.

If you're feeling overwhelmed, don't worry; I didn't know any of this stuff
when I first started, either. I figured it out as I went along. I found some great
advertisers that were both other bloggers and huge corporations. I also left
a good deal of money on the table. Sometimes that was okay; sometimes I
kicked myself in the butt for it.

Thankfully, blogging offers so many ways of selling advertising to brands that
you can dig through this chapter and very likely find one that works for you
and your blog.

Understanding Your Options for Selling Ads

You basically have two ways to sells ads on your blog: selling the ads yourself or using an ad network.

In Chapter 12, I talk a lot about working with ad networks, in which they sell
the ads for your blog in exchange for a portion of the revenue. While at first
blush, it seems better to get 100 percent of your advertising revenue than 40

percent to 60 percent of it, you may find that the ad network will earn you more money. For example, selling your own ads, you'll get 100 percent of an ad's $500 revenue, but that doesn't come close to getting 60 percent of the $5,000 revenue (that's $3,000) from the ad network. While you do have to share ad revenue when working with an ad network, that's not always a bad thing. Not only can it usually sell more ads than you can, but it also takes care of all the administrative work that comes with dealing with advertisers.

That administrative work can be significant. Large brands expect to be able to have sophisticated ad-serving technology, which means that they want a lot of control over how and when their ads are viewed. They may want to only show an ad once per visit, or only to people in southern California. To be able to sell to large brands, you need an ad server that allows you to give your advertisers that kind of control.

On the flip side, it may seem easier to work with small companies instead. Often, small companies don't have the experience to run a successful advertising campaign, so may need more hand-holding on your part. Or they may have set up a very ineffective campaign and hold you accountable for results that are outside your control. A great example: A woman bought an ad from me once to promote a contest she was having. She first sent me a banner that was over 500MB, which would have slowed down my entire website. Then she sent me a corrected banner ad, but had me link it to a page that was so confusing that you couldn't even tell there was a contest running. When she received no contest entries, she was upset with me, although the problem was on her site, and not in her ad. So I ended up spending a good deal of time giving her free consulting on how to create a better *landing page* (the page an ad is linked to). And then I ran ads for her for free for several more months. It was a mess that cost me a good deal of time and money — but you have to "take care of business" when you are selling your own advertising.

Yet there are several bloggers who only sell their own advertising and do so very well. Many of these people tend to want to be extremely selective about the advertising they display on their blogs. I think all bloggers should be selective about which advertisers they choose to work with, because the ads will reflect positively or poorly on you. But if your blog is in a highly specialized niche in which there are fewer advertisers to be found, or if you want to be highly specific about the kinds of companies that advertise on your blog, then your best option is to sell the ads yourself.

Selling Banner and Text Advertising

Selling banner and text ads may be the most common ways to sell advertising on your blog, but they're not the only ways. I cover those in the next section, but I wanted to mention them now so you know an essential point right away: Banners and text links are only a part of what you can offer to sponsors. The smaller you are as a blogger, the more creative you can get with creating custom campaigns to really maximize everything you have to offer.

But even with highly specialized advertising packages, it's very common to include banner and text advertising into your proposals. So here's a list of the basic ways you can present banners and text advertising:

✔ **Banner ads:** These are image-based ads displayed in your blog's header and/or your sidebar. They can also be animated or video ads. They come in standard sizes (as I explain in Chapter 11). The most common sizes you'll see on blogs are 300 x 250 pixels, called the Medium Rectangle; 728 x 90 pixels, called a Leaderboard; 160 x 600 pixels, called the Wide Skyscraper; or 125 x 125 pixels, called the Square Button.

The Square Button is not a standard size for large advertisers anymore as of February 2011. But it's commonly used among smaller advertisers, many of whom work with bloggers.

See banner ads in action in Figure 13-1 on Randa Clay's FreeStuff4Kids blog (`http://freestuff4kids.net`).

Figure 13-1:
Banner ads appear at the top and in a sidebar.

- **Text-link ads:** When an advertiser pays you to link to its website in a blog post or in your sidebar, that is considered a text link. Google's AdSense ads are also considered text ads. This form of advertising is a little controversial because text links can sometimes affect the search engine rankings of those you link to. Be sure to read Chapter 9 — especially the section on adding `NoFollow` to your text links — to make sure your site doesn't get penalized for this practice.

  See text-link ads in action in Figure 13-2 on Elizabeth Edwards' Table for Five blog (`http://table4five.net`).

- **Sponsored posts:** A blog post written at the request of an advertiser, also called an *advertorial.* It could be a review, a giveaway, an informational piece, or what would be considered a product placement post. An example: Tabasco paid bloggers to create a recipe that included Tabasco sauce and post it to their blogs. (I talk a lot more about developing sponsored posts in Chapter 9.)

  See a great example of a sponsored post in Figure 13-3, in which blogger Katja Presnal of Skimbaco Lifestyle & Home (`www.skimbacolifestyle.com`) reviews a complimentary Whirlpool washer and dryer set.

Figure 13-2:
Text-link ads appear in the Shopping section of the sidebar.

Figure 13-3:
A sponsored
post.

The FTC regulates how some sponsored posts appear on blogs and often requires a specifically formatted disclosure. Chapter 9 briefs you on disclosures and the FTC guidelines for selling sponsored posts.

Delivering value to your advertisers

Just putting an advertisement in front of your readers doesn't mean that you're offering your advertisers the best value for their dollars. You must have a good alignment between your advertisers and the interests of your readers. If you have a blog about your adventures with newborn twins, it's likely that most of your readers are in an age range and phase of life similar to yours. So ads targeted at moms who are empty-nesters won't get the same sort of response as they would on a blog such as The Roaming Boomers (www.theroamingboomers.com), a travel blog by and for retired couples.

You're probably tired of hearing me mention this, but here we have one more big reason to *focus your blog on a niche*. Doing so not only enables you to sell advertising more effectively to sponsors, but also makes it easy for you to deliver value to your advertisers. My friend Lisa Sabin-Wilson (author of *WordPress For Dummies*) is launching Allure Themes, which is a line of premium WordPress themes for women's blogs. She asked me which mom blogs she should advertise on, not knowing which of them had more traffic or influence. I told her that as long as she found a blog that was dedicated to helping mom bloggers, it didn't really matter how big or small they were. She could be pretty much guaranteed that nearly all the readers of those blogs would be interested in her themes. The same can't be said for advertising on blogs that are targeted at all bloggers, or even at tech-savvy moms.

To put this in context, the size of the blogs Lisa is targeting is irrelevant as she puts together her advertising plan. This is because any blog that is so tightly focused on her niche (women bloggers) is going to give her a good return on her investment. As you focus on your own specific niche, you become an increasingly valuable place for companies to advertise, even when you don't think your blog is big enough yet. I discuss this in more detail in the next section, "Finding advertisers for your blog."

Ultimately, you want your advertisers to be happy, so anything you can do to help their ads get better results will encourage them to stick with you. Here are some of the ways you can do that and increase the value of the advertising you sell:

- ✔ **Mention your advertisers in a periodic *Thank You to Our Sponsors* post.** Just be careful to follow the same `NoFollow` guidelines as you would when selling regular text links (see Chapter 9).

- ✔ **Rotate ad placements.** If you have several advertisers and the older ads are pushing the newer ads lower on the page, you can rotate the ads that appear at the top of your pages — and have a sequence of whose ads get to be there. This gives all your advertisers equal access to the prime real estate in your sidebar. You can do this with the Advertising Manager WordPress plugin and OpenX OnRamp, as discussed in Chapter 11.

- ✔ **Offer to let advertisers run different versions of their ads.** This is a more sophisticated solution that you can offer if you are using an ad server (as discussed at the end of Chapter 11). Ad servers allow your advertisers to display multiple versions of their ads, and they will even give automatic preference to the ads that get the most clicks.

For even more ways to add value to your advertisers, read through the section "Creating Customized Sponsorships for Brands and Advertisers" later in this chapter. You can do some handy things — for openers, you can include social media promotion, create custom content, or participate in other campaigns that the advertiser is working on.

Finding advertisers for your blog

One of the more common questions I get about working with advertisers is "How do I find advertisers for my blog?" The answer is: It isn't easy. Even with 300,000+ visitors a month on my Woo! Jr. blog network, I don't get many legitimate inquiries about advertising on my sites. So don't assume that once you build it, the advertisers will come. Instead, you really have to go out and find advertisers and sell them on working with you. The more traffic and influence you have, the easier it is to do this, but don't be fooled. It isn't ever easy.

You'll first want to create a page on your website with advertising information for potential customers. Almost every major website has an advertising page; studying these can be a great way to get a feel for what you can put on your advertising page. One of the best is the advertising site set up to support BabyCenter (`www.babycenter.com`) at `www.babycentersolutions.com`. This site is very comprehensive and details such things as mom-market statistics, various advertising options, and specifications for the types of advertising it accepts. BabyCenter has also conducted several surveys of its site users and moms in general, and has great facts backed up by data that show why advertising with it can deliver results to clients. When you can state facts such as, "60 percent of BabyCenter moms will see your ad and nearly half of them will click it," it's pretty easy to get people interested in working with you. You can see what I mean in Figure 13-4.

Of course, most of us — myself included — don't have these kinds of results to stand on. So your advertising page will probably look different, but should still contain information on who reads your blog and the things you've accomplished that advertisers would want to know about. You don't need to put it all on this page: just an overview of the advertising options

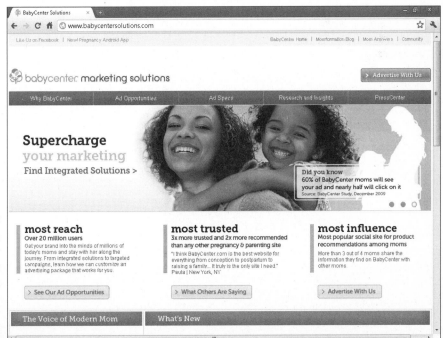

Figure 13-4: BabyCenter serves as inspiration on how to sell ads professionally.

you offer, highlights of why people would want to advertise with you, and ways to get more information, such as a phone number or contact form. You want to put all the details of what you offer into your media kit, which is usually a downloadable PDF file that showcases all your strengths. I show you how to write one in Chapter 10, and can also steer you to an excellent example from Janice Croze and Susan Carraretto from 5MinutesforMom. com (`www.5minutesformom.com`). You can see it for yourself at `www.5minutesformom.com/mediakit.pdf`, and also see some of it in Figure 13-5.

When you have an advertising page set up, you want to start going after advertisers on your own. So you want to identify the kinds of companies you would want to promote on your site and compile a list of your target companies. At this point, don't worry about how realistic or unrealistic it is to actually get these advertisers to work with you. It is more important that you create a comprehensive list of leads to pursue. And by comprehensive, I mean both large and small companies, because you'll have more luck with the small ones, especially if you're first starting out.

Figure 13-5:
The
5Minutes-
for-
Mom.com
media
kit that
promotes
its
advertising
and
sponsorship
options.

Here's how to find companies that could become potential advertisers:

✔ **The companies behind the products and brands you already use and love:** Remember that these companies still need to be relevant to your blog's content. You may be a huge fan of Firestone tires, but it won't advertise on a blog dedicated to homeschooling.

✔ **Companies that create products you know your readers would use and love:** If you have an organic-cooking blog, there are plenty of quality products that you've probably never tried — yet. You can find this kind of potential advertiser through search engines or by looking through the product catalogs of larger websites that carry similar items.

✔ **Companies advertising on blogs that are similar to yours:** You may be concerned that this appears as though you're trying to steal your competitor's advertisers. In fact, most blogs don't have a super-large readership, so advertisers are always looking for ways to reach more people who are interested in their products.

When you have a list of potential advertisers, start contacting the ones you think would be the most likely to say yes to your inquiry. These would be the companies that are the best possible match to your existing blog readers, and those that are already involved with other blogs or in social media marketing on Facebook and Twitter.

Admittedly, this whole hunt for advertisers takes a little bravery, and it definitely takes developing a thick skin to handle some initial rejections. There are a ton of factors that affect why potential advertisers would say no to you — nearly all of which have nothing to do with you or your blog. Budgets may be tight, timing may be off, and/or they may have very strict criteria governing the kinds of websites they can work with. But if you're really having a hard time getting a response from companies, you may want to ask a friend to give you some feedback about your blog. Not just any friend, but the friend who would dare to say an honest-but-supportive yes to the question, "Does this dress make my butt look big?"

The following list shows things that are common turn-offs to potential advertisers (and so things you want to avoid):

✔ **Strong use of controversial language or profanity:** Sad but true, the effects of freedom of speech can certainly limit your revenue. This isn't true all the time, but happens far more often than not.

✔ **Poor site design or navigation:** If your site is confusing, or your sidebar is so bloated with buttons and widgets that it's many pages long, advertisers will fear that their messages may never get noticed in the clutter of your template.

✔ **Lack of focus:** Again, the niche thing, I know. Yet, even if you're fairly well focused on a niche, many other blogs may be more focused than you are. Advertisers are always interested in the highest possible percentage of relevant potential customers.

✔ **Competitor ads:** Having a competitor's ads already in place can work either for or against you. Sometimes advertisers want to be seen where the competition is, in the same way you always seem to find a McDonald's next to a Burger King. But if you're clearly loyal to a company's competitor, it will probably take a pass on advertising with you.

Determining what rate to charge

Another question I get all the time is "How do I determine what rate to charge an advertiser?" The answer is always: It depends. Not all blogs or ads are created equal. My biggest struggle was how to price my ads appropriately so as to not undervalue what I offered while also keeping the ad affordable to my small-business clients. I finally had an *aha* moment a few years ago when I realized I could create two different advertising programs — one for big budgets and one for small budgets.

The key to creating effective different advertising options is to remember that it's important to make one option clearly more valuable than the other option. It isn't very fair to charge one advertiser $100 for the exact same ad another pays $500 for. So here are some ways you can differentiate your advertising packages and justify charging more to the clients who can afford it:

✔ **Position of ads on the page:** All advertisers will pay more for ads *above the fold* (those that are visible to readers without scrolling down). Reserve these spots for your highest paying advertisers.

✔ **Size of ads:** Bigger is indeed better when it comes to banner ads. Large advertisers particularly prefer the leaderboard and medium rectangle sizes. You can reserve these ads only for your higher rates, and sell smaller square buttons at a lower rate.

✔ **More or less views:** You can guarantee that your premium advertisers get the majority of your ad impressions, and limit the impressions of smaller advertisers. Again, you can do this with the tools mentioned in Chapter 11.

✔ **Offer additional exposure to larger advertisers:** Perhaps your premium advertisers also get a mention on Facebook, a sponsored blog post, or you create a special video for them. The more options you have to promote your advertisers, the more effective the advertising will be.

So, did I just make it even more complicated to figure out what to charge? I hope not — because it's a common stumbling block to identify a one-size-fits-all fee to charge. First, focus on the easiest fee to determine: What you would charge other bloggers and small business owners. You're probably not selling this kind of advertising to get rich, but more to help out other small businesses like yours. This number can be pretty arbitrary, and you can charge whatever amount you feel you would pay to another blogger running a similar ad such as this. Anecdotal evidence suggests this number is between $5 and $50 a month, based on what I've seen other bloggers charge. If you're still struggling with identifying a number, here's what I recommend:

- ✔ **Start high:** It's *much* easier to have a higher advertising rate and offer discounts than it is to raise existing rates. Like, a gazillion times easier.

- ✔ **Offer package deals:** By offering a discount for three or six months, you're killing two birds with one stone: You're giving people a choice of different price levels, and you're getting a longer-term client in the process.

- ✔ **Offer barter opportunities:** Moms are masters at bartering. This makes it easy for you to get cool stuff, while making advertising on your blog even more accessible to other small businesses.

Now for the hard part: determining a rate for real advertisers that have a real budget. If you're just talking about banner advertising, then the going rate is anywhere between $5 and $25 per 1,000 ad impressions (see Chapter 11 for my ad terminology guide). Text links and sponsored posts can go for $5 to $500 dollars or more. A lot of factors affect these ranges:

- ✔ **Seasonality and economic environment:** This is the law of supply and demand that affects the advertising industry as a whole. You'll get the best rates during the back-to-school season and the holidays, because they're the most important shopping periods of the year. And likewise, ad rates are better when the economy is good and worse when the economy is bad. This is also true of industry-specific seasons — for example, summer is the most important season for a travel blog.

- ✔ **Traffic volume:** Many very large advertisers just won't mess with advertising on smaller blogs, because it's not cost-effective for them. There are too many variables to manage, and not enough ad impressions to justify the time spent on managing them. The more traffic you have, the more appealing you'll be to large advertisers. You can also band together with other blogs in your niche and sell advertising together, which I talk about in Chapter 16.

- ✔ **Focused niche:** Sorry to bring it up again, but the more focused you are, the more dollars you can command with relevant advertisers. They have set profiles of the kinds of people most likely to buy their products or services. If your blog readers fit the bill, those advertisers will want to get in front of them and will pay well for it. If not, they'll go to another blog or site that can give them the potential customers they're looking for.

> ✔ **Your overall online influence:** The more established and well-known you are as a mom blogger, the more that advertisers will want to align themselves with you. Remember, you may not be a household name, but in your niche, you might be pretty darn well known and respected. Again, it's the law of supply and demand.

When you're trying to decide what rate you want to charge, keep in mind the considerations I talk about earlier in this chapter — especially the part about delivering value to your advertisers. If you're very close to your readers and you have a close-knit community, then it's more likely that your readers will patronize the advertisers you choose to work with. You may want to ask your blogging friends what they charge if they're selling advertising, and use what they tell you as a guide. Ultimately you'll just have to pick a number that you can live with — hopefully one that doesn't overcharge your advertisers or undersell you. That number may only become clear with time and experience, and that's okay. It's more important that you move forward and start getting advertisers, rather than worrying beforehand about whether the rate you've chosen is right.

All that being said, sometimes advertisers will come to you with a fixed budget and name their price. In such a case, you don't have to come up with your own rate — but often the rate they want to pay is far lower than what you would normally charge.

While it may be tempting to take a low rate to get your foot in the door, remember: Once you've sold ads at a certain price point, it's going to be difficult to raise that price later. So it's up to you to either negotiate a better rate, or at least make it clear that you're only willing to take that rate for this one project to establish a working relationship. If that is the case, make your standard rate clear, and state that you hope this initial advertising campaign will prove your value to this advertiser. This gives you negotiating room in the future — after you can show you can deliver results.

Turning down an advertiser or firing a client

As a blogger, your personal brand and blog's brand are your biggest assets and should be protected as though they're gold, because they are. So it's quite important for you to choose what advertisers you work with carefully. This isn't such a big concern with big brands, because it's going to be clearer to determine who you want to associate yourself with. Sometimes it's harder to determine whether a small business is a good match for you, because it may not have built up a reputation that you can evaluate. I told the story in

Chapter 9 about an advertiser I worked with and wrote a blog post for very early in my blogging career. Six months later, that advertiser was out of business — and my old blog post was linked to a page that now redirected the visitor to a spam Viagra site. It certainly wasn't an advertiser I was happy to be associated with, and it definitely reflected poorly on me and my business.

The best way to gauge whether an advertiser is a good fit for your business is to review the following questions:

- ✔ **Would I take on this advertiser if money wasn't an option?** If your blog was financially successful and you had the luxury of turning this advertiser down, would you? If the answer is yes, then you should probably turn down that advertiser now.

- ✔ **Would other sponsors feel comfortable being associated with this advertiser?** If this is a company that could be perceived as untrustworthy, or in an industry associated with scams, then you could potentially scare away other more appropriate advertising partners.

- ✔ **Can I really deliver results for this advertiser?** I've had advertisers approach me in the past with products that were great items, but in light of what I knew about my readers, they just wouldn't be interested. It is best to work with advertisers when you have a win/win/win scenario: Your readers win because they like the product, you win because you have advertising revenue, and your advertiser wins because it has actually gained new customers from working with you.

- ✔ **Would my readers really want to buy this product or service?** I've turned down more advertisers than I've taken on, because so many of them have (quite frankly) poor-quality products that I would never buy. I won't promote anything I wouldn't be willing to buy myself, because I would never want to lose my readers' trust. Maintaining trust with your audience is more important than any advertiser on the planet.

- ✔ **Does this product or service fit with my niche?** If you're blogging about raising ADHD children, you probably won't offer a lot of value to an advertiser like Home Depot.

Okay, here's another squirmy question: When would you want to fire an advertiser? Well, it's mostly when you find that a company is (or has become) one you no longer want to be associated with, for whatever reason. You might also find that the marketing/advertising rep is demanding or difficult to work with, or starts to fit into some of the negative categories described in the preceding questions. Whatever you do, don't burn a bridge. The blogging and online advertising community is a small world, and you may find that burning one bridge has also burned several more without your realizing it. You can check out Chapter 15 for more tips on firing people, where I talk about what you may need to do if you find you need to fire a writer.

Creating Customized Sponsorships for Brands and Advertisers

Back before Twitter and Facebook were such an integral part of our lives, the conversations that happen on these sites were happening on blogs and in forums. So, even though you can sell advertising on your blog as I outlined earlier in this chapter, it's becoming more and more important that advertising programs become integrated social media marketing campaigns. Traditional banner advertising doesn't get a great return on investment in the first place. The average click-through rate on a banner ad is only 3–10 clicks per 1,000 views — kind of horrible by any measurement of advertising success. Advertisers are moving away from doing simple banner advertising and putting together entire campaigns that tie banner ads into a Facebook outreach program — with a Twitter campaign that may even be supported by television, radio, or magazine advertising. Companies are finding that the more they can truly engage potential customers in real conversations and actions, the more likely the marketing campaigns will turn out successfully.

As a mom blogger, you'll find that your best opportunities won't be limited to things you can do on your blog. Building up your community on Facebook and Twitter will open the doors to more ways that advertisers can work with you — and sometimes may be the deciding factor as to whether they work with you or with someone else. In fact, I did see a complaint just this week from someone who resented the fact that she didn't get chosen to work on a project because she didn't have a big Facebook following. The reality is that people are chosen to be a part of large campaigns for many reasons. The people who were chosen for this particular project had all the qualifications the producers were looking for — one of which was that participants be active on Facebook. That, unfortunately, ruled out many other highly qualified participants.

But creating customized campaigns for advertisers isn't just limited to social media outreach. I've seen several excellent campaigns developed around creating special content for a particular advertiser. This can include tutorial projects, videoblogging, helpful articles, giveaways, or any other kind of content that incorporates the advertiser's products or services into quality blog posts that readers enjoy — even if the posts originated in response to a sponsor's request. There are also many opportunities to have sponsors foot the bill to send you to an event or conference, as long as you work with them to promote their products or services to your readers and while you're at the event.

Custom campaigns are just that: custom. That means there's no way I can tell you exactly how to put together a custom campaign. But examples help, so I can tell you about a campaign I put together with Epson in late 2009.

Epson custom campaign — a case study

Back when I was still running Sparkplugging, I decided I wanted to find a sponsor to bring my entire team of bloggers to the BlogWorld Expo conference in Las Vegas. Because we were a team of nearly 15 people spread out all over the country, this was no small feat. Soon thereafter, I met Barbara Jones of One2One Marketing, who was working with Epson printers to do some social media marketing targeted at work at home moms. To put together a proposal, I had some solid assets to work with:

✔ Sparkplugging's 15 blogs, 14 writers, and a sizable monthly audience in Epson's target demographic: women business owners.

✔ A strong presence on Twitter, with six writers being active, regular — sometimes fanatical — users.

✔ The honor of being a featured speaker at the BlogWorld Expo.

✔ An established audience interested in contests, kids' printables, and home office solutions.

✔ An established local presence with other bloggers in a major metropolitan area.

✔ An online reputation as a highly trusted person and company with a focus on supporting the online small business community.

What Barbara and I developed was the following campaign:

✔ Epson sent my team to the BlogWorld Conference.

✔ We set up a separate blog on our network to share video coverage and interviews of speakers for the entire show. That meant 14 people were creating valuable content on topics our readers loved, with occasional mentions of Epson. We also set up a channel on YouTube that was branded with the Sparkplugging and Epson logos.

✔ We gave away a new Epson printer at the show in a fun contest, and also gave away a printer to a randomly selected blog reader who could not attend the show. This further engaged our regular audience with the campaign at the event.

✔ I was already booked to speak at the BlogWorld Expo on selling advertising and sponsorship packages directly to advertisers. I spoke briefly about the experience of bringing my team to the event at which I was speaking — which spread the awareness of Epson's sponsorship among the attendees of the event.

The trip was a huge success — we built significant buzz at the BlogWorld event, with coverage of the sponsorship also being mentioned on the BlogWorld site. Epson was thrilled with the increased conversation we created on Twitter around its brand. Our YouTube videos got thousands of views, as did the special BlogWorld/Epson blog on Sparkplugging.

Barbara and I also hosted a small dinner party with local Chicago mom bloggers as a social gathering. Barbara hired a professional photographer to take pictures at the event, and we printed them out continuously at the party on the Epson printer, giving them to our guests as fun souvenirs of the evening. We never pitched the printer at all, but instead let the quality of the photographic prints speak for itself.

At the end of the campaign, we obtained a special discount code just for our readers to purchase the Epson printer at a discount, soon before the holidays. While I was never privy to actual sales results of the campaign, I was able to monitor our traffic as measured by Quantcast, which can also track the affinity of our visitors and the other sites they visit. The Epson website (http://epson.com) was in the top ten most likely sites to be visited by Sparkplugging visitors, as you can see in Figure 13-6.

Figure 13-6: Sparkplugging visitors were 3.3 times more likely to visit Epson.com after our ad campaign.

As you can see, I took what I had to work with, and went after a sponsor who had much to benefit from being a part of the campaign I wanted to put together. Here are some thoughts on how you can do the same:

✔ **Know what you have to offer.** List the things you can do for a company and the assets you have to work with. These things would include your social media presence on Facebook and Twitter, the number of readers you have, your popular content, your insights into what your readers love and want to purchase, whatever advertising you can offer, your personal brand and reputation, and the friends who could help you promote whatever campaign you can create.

✔ **Brainstorm ideas on what you can propose to a company.** This is going to be very specific to your blog topic, but think about what you know your readers would get excited about. If you're a craft blogger, you can approach the maker of a craft material and create a campaign around what you can do with its products. If you're a home décor blogger, you can find a paint brand or home improvement company that can sponsor a contest using its products. If you're a small-business blogger, you can find products that appeal to solopreneur business owners and write helpful business articles that are brought to your readers by your sponsor for the month.

✔ **Put together a plan with your readers' best interests in mind.** Any large-scale project like this can fail quickly if it's too focused on promotion and less on the people you're promoting to. So be absolutely sure that whatever you plan will ultimately create a great experience for your readers, however that may work. Their enthusiasm for your campaign will make or break the eventual outcome, so make sure that there is something big in it for your readers so that they can get invested in the process with you.

✔ **Put together a professional pitch.** To go after big dollars, you'll need to prove you can deliver on a big scale. You'll need plenty of data to back up your proposal, because corporations live in a spreadsheet-driven world. It will also help if you have any other case studies of smaller marketing campaigns to showcase that you have the experience to pull off what you're promising to do.

Ultimately, you may or may not be able to get a company to buy in to your sponsorship idea. The benefits of thinking big like this far outweigh the costs of the time it takes to plan and work on selling the idea. Even if you aren't successful this time around, it will raise your credibility and visibility — drastically — with companies who now know they probably want to get in front of your readers. That may also mean that if they do their own social media campaigns in the future, you'll be the first person they think of when planning their own blogger-outreach campaigns.

Participating in social media marketing campaigns

By and large, you're more likely to have an opportunity to participate in an existing social media campaign than you are to sell your own right off the bat. The best thing you can do for yourself to gain access to these gigs is to raise your visibility as a blogger and social media mom. By *visibility,* I mean that you'll need to actively socialize and promote yourself pretty much all over the Web, as well as attend live conferences and events where you get to meet other bloggers and brand representatives in person. This process entails everything that I talk about in Chapter 6 about building your personal brand — especially regarding what you're known for and what people say about you. This is important because it's not very likely that you (or most of us) will be at the table while a big company is planning its next big campaign. What you can do is establish your reputation so well that someone who *is* at that table thinks of you when it's time to find a blogger to bring on board.

A great example of this approach is how Esther Crawford used videoblogging to build her following — and to establish herself as a mom with social media savvy. When Esther decided she wanted to lose the baby weight from her recent pregnancy, she chose Weight Watchers and videoblogged the process of losing over 20 pounds. Weight Watchers noticed. And it ended up hiring her as an ongoing social media consultant and to be a part of its recent television advertising campaign, with Jennifer Hudson as the spokesperson. You can see one of the images from the campaign in Figure 13-7.

While this strategy may seem relatively passive, building your personal brand is critical if this is the route you want your blogging career to follow. Brands and companies look for a certain type of mom when they want to plan a new social media project. Such a mom has

- ✔ A strong personal brand that is recognized and respected by her peers.
- ✔ A large following on Twitter and Facebook.
- ✔ A prominent voice in her respective niche, and is usually one of the more recognized names on that topic.
- ✔ A blog with strong, unique, and high-caliber content.
- ✔ The skill to promote herself without spamming friends or being overly pushy.

✔ The ability to elicit a response from her community, through blog comments, tweets, and Facebook conversations.

✔ The attention of the traditional media and journalists through coverage in newspapers, magazines, radio, and TV appearances.

In short, companies look for a mom who can be a true ambassador for their brands and have the social clout to spread the word for them. The more you can accomplish these things, the more your name will come up as a blogger associated with your chosen field.

Here are some ways to be proactive about finding opportunities in existing social media campaigns:

✔ **Active networking:** This is a situation where in-person networking is most important, especially at blogging and social media conferences. Hundreds of brand representatives go to these conferences to get to know the blogging community better — and to scout out bloggers they can work with in the future.

✔ **Build your credibility:** None of us who have taken part in big social media campaigns got here easily. We all had to prove our worth and work our tails off to build up enough credibility to get hired. You may need to start small, but everything you can do to prove you know how to spread the word about something is one more step closer to the bigger opportunities. You can also create your own campaigns promoting things you love to buy as a consumer, but make it clear that you're doing it of your own accord. It's not ethical to imply that a client hired you for work they didn't hire you for.

✔ **Ask for it:** Your blog should make it clear that you're interested in working with brands on campaigns and marketing projects. Mention that availability on your About page and your advertising page — and be sure to include it in your media kit as well.

✔ **Research social media agencies:** Most of these kinds of campaigns aren't put together by the companies themselves; their marketing agencies handle that job. When you see a new campaign involving social media moms, find out which ad agency is behind the campaign. That's usually pretty easy to do by interacting with the campaign participants (such as the person who's running the Facebook page or Twitter account). You can also simply ask the bloggers involved in the campaign. Introduce yourself to these agencies and let them know you would like to be considered for future promotions in your area of expertise.

✔ **Create campaigns to promote yourself:** If you can't find a campaign to be a part of, create your own — and promote yourself in a creative and fun way. The more you can prove that you can deliver more awareness and results, the more value you have to brands and companies.

✔ **Build on your successes:** Any time you can add an accomplishment to your blogging résumé, use it as a step toward your next opportunity. Publish mini-case studies of things you work on, create a portfolio of past projects you've worked on, and keep your media kit and advertising information up to date. Every time you gain more experience, it's one more thing you can use as a reference to get in on the next opportunity that comes your way.

Chapter 14

The Basics of Affiliate Marketing

*A*ffiliate marketing holds a special place in my heart because it got me blogging. Back in 2005, when I first learned what it was, I was so excited about it that I quit my job to start a social networking site that made money from affiliate marketing. I heard that blogging would help my affiliate marketing site do well in the search engines, so I started a blog, too.

Little did I realize at the time that I would soon give up my social networking site idea to blog full time. I found that blogging opened up a lot more doors than running a straight affiliate site did. But I also found that what I had learned hadn't gone to waste — bloggers can make great money with affiliate marketing.

In this chapter, I share my hard-learned lessons with affiliate marketing — including best practices that work well for bloggers. I also share a few of my favorite successful affiliate marketing sites so that you can see these tips in action. Plus I give you a quick and easy way to start adding affiliate links to your blog to see whether it's right for you.

Understanding How Affiliate Marketing Is Different than Straight Advertising

Affiliate marketing is very similar to finding regular advertisers for your blog. The key difference is that with affiliate marketing, you get paid only when you refer a sale or lead to a merchant. Multimillion-dollar companies such as CouponCabin.

com and BradsDeals.com started with humble roots in affiliate marketing. That being said, not every blog can create a large income from affiliate marketing.

Affiliate links are HTML or JavaScript links that work pretty much like a regular link. They can be either banners or text links and send your visitors to the sales page of the product or service you're recommending. These links are more sophisticated than a regular link because they track the referral from your blog so the advertiser can pay you the commission should a sale be made.

Determining whether your blog would be a good candidate for affiliate marketing

When I started with affiliate marketing, I put up my first affiliate link in a post that talked about a product I liked, and then I sat back and anxiously waited for the commissions to start rolling in. And I waited . . . and waited. Five months later, I finally referred my first sale. It didn't take long to realize that this was going to be harder than I thought.

My biggest obstacle at the time wasn't that I was using the wrong technique — in fact, I can say confidently that I was definitely on the right track. My problem was that I didn't have enough visitors to my blog. An important part of affiliate marketing is your *click-through rate* (the percentage of visitors who click that affiliate link) and your *conversion rate* (the percentage of people who click your affiliate link versus the percentage of people who actually buy something from the advertiser after clicking your affiliate link).

Say an average click-through rate is 1.5 percent, and a good conversion rate is around 2 percent. So if you have 100,000 visitors, 1,500 (1.5 percent) are likely to click the affiliate link, and of those 1,500 clicks, only 30 (2 percent) are likely to buy the product and earn you a commission. In other words, your blog traffic has to be fairly substantial if it's going to be a good candidate for affiliate marketing.

The other important criterion for a blog to be a good candidate for affiliate marketing is that the topic needs to be related to specific products or services. Many blogs, especially more personal mom blogs, don't often talk about products on a regular basis. The most successful affiliate blogs tend to focus on product reviews or product information. Even though affiliate marketers don't sell products directly, in a sense they pre-sell products to readers. Here's a good way to think about affiliate marketing: Think of it as a personal recommendation to a friend.

Blogs that don't do well with affiliate marketing tend to be those that don't have content that relates to products or services sold through affiliate programs. Personal blogs or news and commentary blogs are examples. Even some product blogs might not do well if their content attracts an audience that's heavily focused on finding freebies instead of paying for things. It's not that these readers don't make purchases; it's just that they aren't looking to make a purchase when they come to this kind of site.

An exception to this would be if you could find an affiliate program that offers coupons or pays for leads. A *lead* is defined differently by each merchant, but can include things such as a site registration, a newsletter signup, or a formal request for information from the merchant. Specific actions have to take place in order for the lead to qualify for a commission, and usually payment for a lead is quite low, on the order of $3 or less. The good side of this is that because the user doesn't need to make a purchase, it's more likely that you can get a qualified lead commission. Don't let the low amount of payment deter you from promoting lead-based affiliate offers. The amounts add up — I've earned hundreds of dollars from leads over the years.

The last criterion that will help you determine if your blog is a good candidate for affiliate marketing ironically has nothing to do with your blog. Instead, it depends on what state you live in. In the course of writing this book, an important development occurred: My home state of Illinois passed a new *Affiliate Nexus Tax* law. The simplified explanation of this law is that it requires all U.S.-based online retailers (like Amazon.com) to collect sales tax from Illinois customers if an Illinois-based affiliate (like me) refers the sale to Amazon.com. The unfortunate side effect of this law is that online companies would rather stop working with Illinois-based affiliates than collect the tax. So overnight, more than half of my affiliate income vanished as hundreds of online retailers ended their affiliate agreements with Illinois residents. Note, though, that sales tax is not levied on all online purchases. Most downloads, services, and lead-generation transactions are immune to the new tax policy. So this law doesn't completely eliminate all affiliate marketing efforts in my state, just most of them.

It's wisest to ensure you don't have too many eggs in one basket. Build your blogging business carefully so that a sudden new development such as this new tax law won't put you out of business.

This is a rapidly changing policy initiative that is affecting more and more states recently. To find out if your state laws may impact your affiliate marketing efforts, check out the Nexus Tax section of the Performance Marketing Association website at www.performancemarketingassociation.com/nexus-tax.

Understanding what it takes to be successful at affiliate marketing

Say you have a blog with good traffic, and you have a blog on which talking about products is a fit with your content. Writing authentic, truthful product reviews and recommendations is the most important talent a blog-ging affiliate marketer can have. Tiffany Washko has been blogging since 2005 and earns a living from affiliate links on her NatureMoms.com blog. Tiffany's advice is dead-on accurate for bloggers new to affiliate marketing. She says

> [You need to build] a truly GREAT blog with useful content that people WANT to read. While you do need to be a salesperson to make affiliate sales, you shouldn't be obvious about it or make every post about trying to sell something. A balance is needed. If your readers enjoy reading what you write and they trust you as a source of information, they're more likely to click your affiliate links and buy.

Striking that balance between selling and creating compelling content isn't for everyone. Additionally, the FTC guidelines I talk about in Chapter 9 do also apply to affiliate links. I also cover review ethics in that chapter, which apply whether you're compensated for the review financially, by receiving free products, or by affiliate links.

Even Tiffany found that it took time to build her site to the point that she could earn a living from it. Money trickled in slowly, at first just enough to cover her hosting and site-maintenance fees. It wasn't until two years later that she earned enough revenue from her blog to make her friends and family sit up and take notice.

Her personal story is also compelling — she was diagnosed with colon cancer at the age of 28. She told me

> That experience reinforced my desire to blog because the community I had created online was so supportive. It also helped me to see how important it was to keep on writing and blogging about natural health and wellness because if I could get cancer at 28 years old, then anyone could.

NatureMoms now keeps growing every year, and her persistence has paid off. You can see an example of one of her most financially successful blog posts at www.naturemoms.com/blog/2008/12/28/vita-mix-5200-bpa-free-blender, which is also shown below in Figure 14-1.

Although reviews are both compelling and effective, they aren't the only way to create a successful affiliate blog. Char Polanosky created DollDiaries.com in late 2006 as a way to share her and her daughters' passion for American Girl dolls — and sharing information she got about upcoming doll releases and news. It took her a while to figure out how to actually make money from this blog. Her turning point came in May 2007, when she posted about a rumor of a new historical doll that was scheduled to come out in September 2007. Her traf-fic boomed — and the site was established as a favorite for doll fans.

It wasn't long before the big doll makers started to take notice. Because her blog was so focused on a tight niche, it was the ideal place for several big-name advertisers to promote their newest dolls. She began supplementing her affiliate-marketing income with advertising income in 2009.

Char has expanded her content to talk about all things related to dolls — accessories, doll-themed birthday parties, free doll printables, reviews, coupons, and especially collectable dolls. She credits her success to her passion for dolls, focusing on a narrow topic and audience, and her ability to get creative and look beyond a typical "mommy blog" format.

You can see Char's Doll Diaries blog in Figure 14-2. You can also see an example of one of her financially successful blog posts at `http://dolldiaries. com/camp-rock-mitchie-and-shane-dolls`.

Figure 14-1: Successful affiliate marketing-based mom blog NatureMoms. com.

Figure 14-2: DollDiaries. com earns revenue from a combination of advertising and affiliate marketing.

Getting Started with Affiliate Marketing

One of the things I love about affiliate marketing is that not many bloggers will be big enough to get a large company such as Amazon or CafeMom to pay up front for traditional banner advertising, but both these companies accept most applicants into their affiliate programs. I truly believe that banner ads lend a sense of credibility to a website, especially if the ads are appropriate, well-designed, and matched to the interests of the site audience.

Honestly, getting started with affiliate marketing is remarkably easy. The basic process is to apply to join programs and post banners and text links after you've been accepted.

The most important thing is to work with merchants you like and trust, because you wouldn't want to risk sending your visitors into a scam or bad experience. As with all advertising, the brands you choose to work with will always reflect on you.

Joining affiliate networks and programs

An *affiliate network* is somewhat similar to an ad network. Almost all large e-commerce sites work with an affiliate network. Affiliate networks provide the online software to track all the traffic and sales for both the merchants and the publishers. They then earn a percentage of the sale on top of what e-commerce merchants pay to affiliates. All reputable affiliate networks are free to join as a publisher — you should *never* pay for the opportunity to help someone sell products. Two notable large online retailers also run their own independent affiliate programs: Amazon and eBay.

The three largest affiliate networks are

✔ Commission Junction (CJ) at www.cj.com

✔ LinkShare at www.linkshare.com

✔ Google Affiliate Network (GAN) at www.google.com/ads/affiliatenetwork

These three affiliate networks represent many large online retailers such as Overstock.com, Disney.com, Target.com, and BestBuy.com, as well as thousands of small online retailers.

Out of the three largest affiliate networks, I personally feel that Commission Junction is the easiest to use, so I walk you through applying to their program. I recommend joining all three for the most access to a variety of merchants. I also highly recommend joining Amazon's affiliate program, which is one of the most respected affiliate programs in the industry. The application process to join the networks or Amazon program is similar across the board.

Applying to the Commission Junction affiliate network

If you haven't yet started your blog, or if there's very little content on your blog, any affiliate program manager will have a difficult time determining whether your application is appropriate or even legitimate. Don't apply to any affiliate program until you're established with at least eight to ten blog posts so that you can get the best possible chance of getting approved.

When your blog is ready for affiliate network ads, follow these steps to apply with Commission Junction:

1. **Go to** www.cj.com **and click the Publishers tab.**

2. **From the Publishers page, click the Join Now button.**

3. **Select the radio button for your language preference, select your country from the Country of Residence drop-down list, and select a currency from the Functional Currency drop-down list, and then click the Next button.**

4. **On page 2 of the application, scroll to the bottom of the Service Agreement list box and click the Accept button. Select the radio buttons for the Code of Conduct, Privacy Policy, Age Certification, and Certification of Authority policies.**

Read through the information carefully — always know what you're agreeing to!

The rest of the page is a long form requesting information about you and your blog.

5. **In the Site Information section, enter the name of your blog in the Web Site or Newsletter Name field, and enter your blog URL in the Web Site URL field.**

6. **In the Website Description box, give a brief overview of your blog, putting an emphasis on the aspects of your content that are most relevant to your affiliate network application.**

For example, "[Your Blog Name] is a mom blog that discusses health and green-living ideas for other moms and families. Topics include product recommendations, healthy cooking, giveaways, and daily tips for greener family living."

7. **Select your general topic from the Category drop-down list.**

Just get as close as you can to the best match for your blog; you can change this later if necessary.

8. **Select the range of visitors you have from the Current Monthly Unique Visitors drop-down list.**

(CJ abbreviates *unique visitors* as UVs.) You can find this information from your analytics program, as explained in Chapter 5.

9. **Select the appropriate check box(es) in the Define Your Promotional Methods section.**

For a blog, you'll mostly likely select the Web Site / Content option. Select the other check boxes if appropriate: Search Engine Marketing refers to paying for traffic from search engine ads, E-mail Marketing refers to using affiliate links in e-mail newsletters, and Software refers to adding affiliate links within a software program you create.

10. **Disclose whether your site gives specific incentives to its visitors; if so, describe your blog's incentives in the text box.**

An *incentive* is a reward to offer — such as discounts (or other price-oriented rewards), points, or other direct compensation in return for making a purchase through your affiliate links.

11. **Fill in the information in the Contact Information and Company Information sections, and select the method of payment in the Payment Information section.**

    These sections are pretty self-explanatory.

12. **Enter what you see under the Please Enter the Characters into the Box Below into the text box, and then click the Accept Terms button.**

After you complete and submit your application, you can expect to wait 24–48 hours before your application is reviewed and either approved or rejected. Nearly all applications to affiliate networks are approved unless they suspect that your site is engaging in illegal or unethical activities.

Applying to merchant programs

After you're approved to become a publisher in an affiliate network, you need to apply to specific merchant programs in order to start adding links to your blog. While getting accepted into the affiliate network is relatively easy, that isn't always the case with getting accepted into merchant programs.

Some merchants are especially particular about the kinds of websites they're willing to let their ads appear on, even when they don't have to pay unless a sale is made. There are a handful of merchants I've wanted to work with over the years; I've applied to their programs multiple times only to get rejected (again). Hey, it happens. If you don't get accepted into the merchant programs of your choice, don't take it personally. Merchants can be rather secretive about their evaluation criteria — and a rejection does *not* necessarily equate to a disapproval of your site or content.

Most merchants on the whole will accept a publisher application as long as they think that your blog will attract people who would be their potential customers. For example, an online shoe retailer will certainly accept a fashion blog into its program, but very likely won't accept a blog that discusses politics or cooking. So be picky about the programs you apply to — start with a few that you think are the best possible fit for your content.

Again, using Commission Junction as an example, here's how to apply to a merchant program. The process is very similar in the other affiliate networks, too.

1. **Log in to your Commission Junction account.**

2. **From your Dashboard, click the Get Links link.**

3. **Search through the Advertiser Categories to find merchants you're interested in promoting.**

There are a lot of categories, so start with the category closest to the topic of your blog. You can also do a keyword search to look for a specific merchant.

If you can't find a specific merchant, that company may be using a different affiliate network or perhaps isn't running an affiliate program at all. The best way to find out whether a favorite retailer has an affiliate program is to go directly to its website. Usually a footer on the home page will have a small link called Affiliates or Referral Program. If you can't find a link there, and you're pretty sure those folks run an affiliate program, contact them directly to ask how you can become one of their affiliate publishers.

4. **When you find a merchant that you're interested in, click the company name or logo to read more about its program.**

   The company's Details page will display the available links, the commission structure, and how commissions are earned through its programs.

   These details can vary widely from one merchant to another; evaluate them carefully to make sure you think you can be successful promoting the company's products.

In some cases, only certain products or actions will qualify for a commission — don't assume that you can earn compensation from promoting a particular product just because you've seen it on the company website.

5. **When you find a merchant you want to work with, you can apply to the company program by clicking the Apply to Program button at the bottom of the website's Details page.**

   Sometimes you may have to agree to additional terms to submit your application. A few merchants have extra guidelines for their affiliates on top of the standard Commission Junction agreement. These usually have to do with rules about prohibited marketing practices, so read through them carefully.

Just as there's great variance in merchant programs, there is just as much variance in the time it takes to be approved or rejected from a program. Some will automatically approve new applications. Most respond within five business days. The longest I've waited for an application review was well over two months.

If you get approved, you should get an e-mail from the merchant via Commission Junction welcoming you to the program. If you're not approved, you'll get a message from the merchant within your CJ account, not via e-mail. To find the account message center, from the CJ Dashboard, click the Mail link.

Understanding the different ways of adding affiliate links to your blog

Generally speaking, text links in your blog posts perform better than banner ads. People are simply more likely to click a link as they're reading (versus clicking a banner ad next to the content). As you can see from the two sites mentioned earlier in this chapter, both have had the most financial success using text links in posts. Affiliate banners are appropriate when you don't already have paying advertisers, or if you want to add them to a blog post in addition to a text link.

It's very easy to add affiliate links to your blog; it isn't much different from adding any other text link or image to a blog post. All you have to do is use the URL or code the affiliate network provides you and copy and paste it where you want it to go in your blog post.

Always use the text link in a natural way so as to not distract the reader. You want to add the links using the communication style you normally write in for your blog. Suddenly putting a text link for a blender in the middle of a post about gardening isn't going to do very well!

Adding a product catalog link to your blog post

Many merchants have what's called a *product catalog.* This is a selection of some or all of the products that they sell on the company website, with a direct link to each and every one; these links are the most effective at generating sales. Product catalog links work best when you're talking about a specific product, and you want to send your readers directly to it rather than to the merchant's home page. The disadvantage to this kind of link is that almost all product catalog links change over time — and the link might not point to the right page after (say) six months to a year. The link will still refer a sale if readers can find what they're looking for on their own.

I recommend you check your old product catalog affiliate links and update them every six months to ensure that they still work. To help with this task, I also recommend a great plugin for WordPress users at the end of this chapter called *Pretty Links.*

Here's how to create a product catalog text link in Commission Junction. Note that this option will only be available to you if you have been accepted into at least one merchant program, as explained in the previous section:

1. **From your CJ Dashboard, scroll to the bottom of the page and select the merchant you want to link to from the My Advertisers drop-down list. Then click the Go button.**

2. **Under the Get Links box on the upper-right of the page, click Product under the By Type heading.**

   If that option is grayed out, then this merchant doesn't offer product catalog links. Skip to the next section of this chapter to add a non-product catalog link instead if you wish.

3. **Find the product you want to link to by scrolling through the product list or searching by keyword.**

   If this merchant has fewer than 1,000 products in its catalog, a list will appear with all the available products in its catalog. If this merchant has over 1,000 products in its catalog, then you can only search by keyword for the product you're looking for.

4. **Click Get HTML under the Get Links heading in the last column.**

   The following link options in Step 5 get a little techy and may make things more confusing for you than they need to be. Unless you know what these options mean and what to do with them, you really don't need to change them from the defaults. You can just skip to Step 6 if that's the case.

5. **Set your link options as shown in Figure 14-3.**

BabyEarth Detail » Product Search Results » Product Detail » Get HTML

The tracking code is for	Craft Jr.
Set link to open a new browser window?	☐ Yes
Hide tracking code in link?	☐ Yes
Encrypt link?	☐ Yes
PID	3427989
AID	10398035
SID	
Image URL	http://www.babyearth.com/images/images_big/11-0660-03.jpg

Update Link Code

Copy and paste the following HTML code into your web pages. You must include all the above html in your links. Any missing html, including the image source, will prevent the link from tracking properly and result in a loss of commissions.

```
<form method="get" action="http://www.dpbolvw.net/interactive" target="_top">
<table border="0" width="600" cellpadding="5" cellspacing="0">
<tr>
<td valign="top" width="10%"><img
```

Highlight V Copy Code

Eco-Friendly Ribbon - Hot Stripe

Copy and paste the following HTML code into

```
<a href="http://www.anrdoezrs.net/click-3427989-10398035?
url=http%3A%2F%2Fwww.babyearth.com%2Fearth-love-n-paper-eco-friendly-
```

Figure 14-3:
Setting up optional link options for a Commission Junction text link.

a. If you have multiple websites, use the The Tracking Code Is For drop-down list to select the site that you're going to place the text link on.

b. Select the Yes check box beside Set Link to Open a New Window if you want the link to open in a new window.

c. I always select the Yes check box beside Hide Tracking Code in Link. Hiding the tracking code displays the final destination URL rather than an unreadable tracking URL, which can be confusing to readers. The tracking URL sends the reader to the right destination; it just does it by first linking through one of CJ's domain names. This option doesn't work in all browsers, by the way, so if you test it when you're done and it doesn't seem to work, try a different browser to view your page.

d. I always select the Yes check box beside Encrypt Link. Encrypting a link disguises your standard affiliate number in the link URL. This prevents other people from putting their own affiliate numbers in place of yours and stealing your commission.

e. The SID field is a place you can put your own additional tracking ID into the link. You may want to do this if you want to track more specifically where the final sale came from. I've done this when I wanted to see whether a certain blog post sent more sales than another post using the same link. I explain SIDs in more detail in the later section, "Tracking your affiliate links to improve your sales."

f. Set your Destination URL if you want to change the default page that you're linking to. Not all affiliate links have this option, nor do I recommend changing it for a product catalog link. The option won't be visible if it isn't available.

g. Enter a URL in the Image URL field if you want to use a different image from the one that's offered. Again, not all affiliate links have this option, nor do I recommend changing it for a product catalog link.

h. Click the Update Link Code button if you've made any changes.

6. **Choose an option for copying the link code as follows; place your cursor in the appropriate link code box, click the Highlight Code button, and copy it by pressing Ctrl+C or ⌘+C.**

   • The first box of link code actually creates a full product feature link, including a photo and description. You can preview this at the bottom of the page (pretty confusing, I know).

   • The second box of link code creates a plain text link.

   • The third box of link code creates a plain product image link without text.

7. **Go to your blog post, place your cursor where you want the link to go, and paste the code into your post by pressing Ctrl+P or ⌘+P.**

   Make sure you're viewing the post in HTML mode and not the WYSIWYG mode.

8. **Test your link by clicking on it and ensuring it directs your browser to the intended page.**

I *always* test my links to make sure they send my readers to the intended destination. I especially do this if I made any changes in Step 5 or edited the HTML manually to ensure I didn't somehow break the link in the process.

Adding a standard text-ad link to your blog post

Another kind of text link is one that's a standardized written ad created by the merchant. These links generally point to the merchant's home page or a category page. They aren't quite as effective as the product catalog links, but still perform better than banner ads do. Because these links tend to be written in sales speak, you can't use your own natural voice when you post them. Nothing is stopping you from changing the ad's words, though you should read through the merchant's program terms to ensure that it allows its affiliates to change its pre-determined text links. If you change it and the merchant has a rule against this, it could void the commission, though this is rare.

Here's how to create a standardized text link in Commission Junction.

1. **From your CJ Publisher Home page, scroll to the bottom of the page and select the merchant you want to link to under the My Advertisers drop-down list, and then click the Go button.**

2. **Under the Get Links box on the upper right of the page, click Text Link under the By Type heading.**

   If that option is grayed out, then this merchant doesn't offer standardized text links.

3. **Choose the text ad you want to use.**

   I always test the link to see the page I am sending my readers to. If I think the page looks bad or is confusing to the reader, I won't use it; I'll select a different one instead.

4. **Click Get HTML under the Get Links heading in the last column.**

As with the previous set of steps, the following link options in Step 5 get a little techy; they may be more confusing than they need to be. Unless you know what these options mean and what to do with them, you really don't need to change them from the defaults. You can just skip to Step 6 if that's the case.

5. **Set your link options as shown in Figure 14-4.**

   a. If you have multiple websites, use the Web Site drop-down list to select the site that you're going to place the text link on.

   b. I always select the Yes check box next to Encrypt Link. Encrypting a link disguises your standard affiliate number in the link URL. This prevents other people from putting their own affiliate numbers in place of yours and stealing your commission.

c. If you want the link to open in a new window, select the Yes check box beside Set Link to Open a New Browser Window.

d. I always select the Yes check box beside Hide Tracking Code in Link. Hiding the tracking code displays the final destination URL rather than the unreadable tracking URL, which can be confusing to readers. The tracking URL sends the reader to the right destination; it just does it by first linking through one of CJ's domain names. This doesn't work in all browsers, by the way, so if you test it when you're done and it doesn't seem to work, try using a different browser to view your page.

e. The SID field is a place you can put your own additional tracking ID into the link. You may want to do this if you want to track more specifically where the final sale came from. I've done this when I wanted to see whether a certain blog post sent more sales than another post using the same link. I explain SIDs in more detail in the later section, "Tracking your affiliate links to improve your sales."

f. Enter a URL in the Destination URL field if you want to change the default page that you're linking to. Not all links have this option.

g. Click the Update Link Code if you've made any changes.

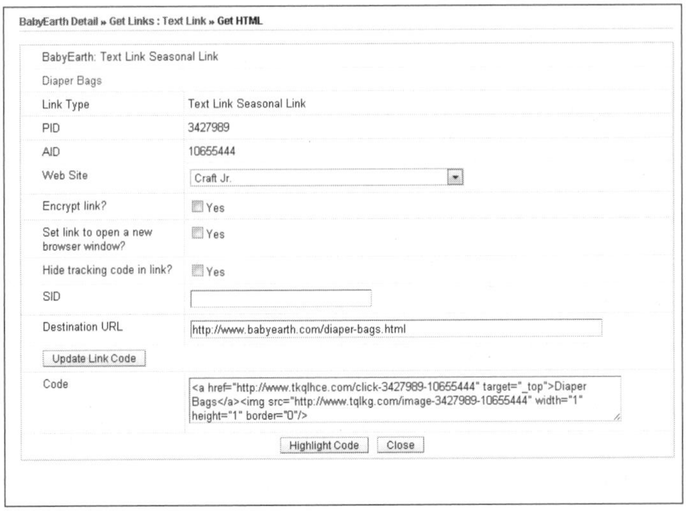

Figure 14-4:
Setting up optional link options for a Commission Junction text link.

6. **Place your cursor in the link code box, click the Highlight Code button, and copy it by pressing Ctrl+C or ⌘+C.**

7. **Go to your blog post, place your cursor where you want the link to go, and paste the code into your post by pressing Ctrl+P or ⌘+P.**

Make sure you're viewing the post in HTML mode and not the WYSIWYG mode.

8. **Test your link by clicking on it and ensuring it directs your browser to the intended page.**

I *always* test my links to make sure they send my readers to the intended destination. I take special care to do so if I made any changes in Step 5 or edited the HTML manually. I recommend you do the same. The idea is to ensure that you haven't somehow broken the link in the process.

Adding affiliate banner links to your blog

Affiliate banner ads have never worked well for me on any blog whenever I've used them. That's because banners generally get a 0.10-percent click through, as compared to a 1–5-percent click through for text links.

As I mention in Chapter 11 about using backup ads, I think that using affiliate banners while you're trying to get paying advertisers is the most appropriate use of these low-performing banners. I've had luck when a banner includes a coupon code, but only when I place that ad into a blog post and put the merchant's offer into context. In five years' time, I've earned less than $10 dollars from an affiliate banner ad in a sidebar.

For the few times an affiliate banner is appropriate, here's how to create a banner link in Commission Junction:

1. **From your CJ Publisher Home page, scroll to the bottom of the page and select the merchant you want to link to from the My Advertisers drop-down list, and then click the Go button.**

2. **Under the Get Links box on the upper-right of the page, click Banner under the By Type heading.**

3. **Choose the banner ad you want to use; base your choice on the size dimensions you need.**

   Notice, as shown in the EPC (earnings-per-click) columns, that some banners earn more than others. This isn't a guarantee that this particular ad will work better than another one on your blog. But if you can't decide between several ads, go with the one with the highest EPC.

   I always test the link to see the page I am sending my readers to. If I think the page looks bad or is confusing to the reader, I won't use it and will select a different one.

   If you don't see a banner in the size you need, go ahead and ask the merchant's affiliate manager to create one for you. As long as it's a standard ad size, your advertiser will usually be happy to accommodate your request.

4. Click Get HTML under the Get Links heading in the last column.

Yep, if you've been following the earlier sets of steps, you'll find this note familiar: The following link options in Step 5 get a little techy and may make things a tad confusing. Unless you know what these options mean and what to do with them, you really don't need to change them from the defaults. You can just skip to Step 6 if that's the case.

5. Set your link options as shown in Figure 14-5.

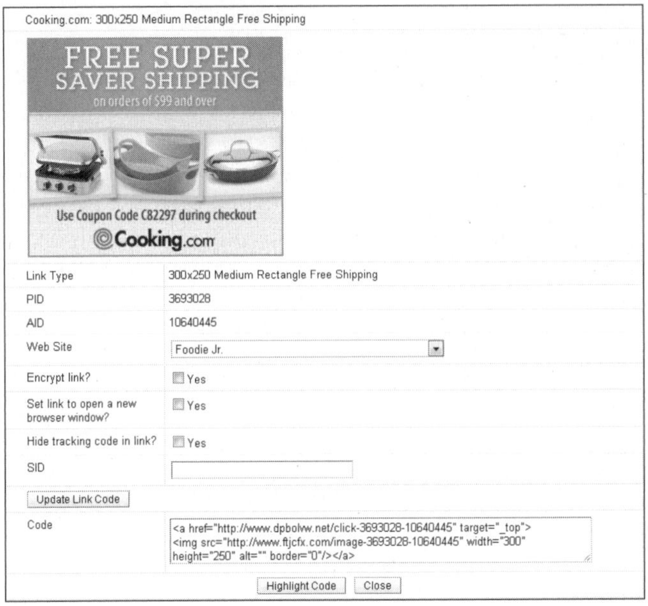

Figure 14-5:
Setting up optional link options for a Commission Junction banner link.

a. If you have multiple websites, use the Web Site drop-down list to select the site that you're going to place the text link on.

b. I always select the Yes check box next to Encrypt Link. Encrypting a link disguises your standard affiliate number in the link URL. This prevents other people from putting their own affiliate numbers in place of yours and stealing your commission.

c. Select the Yes check box next to SetLink to Open in a New Browser Window if you want the link to open in a new window.

d. I always select the Yes check box beside Hide Tracking Code in Link. Hiding the tracking code displays the final destination URL rather than the unreadable tracking URL, which can be confusing to readers. The tracking URL sends the reader to the right destination; it just does it by first linking through one of CJ's domain names. This doesn't work in all browsers, by the way, so if you test it when you're done and it doesn't seem to work, try a different browser to view your page.

e. The SID field is a place you can put your own additional tracking ID into the link. You may want to do this if you want to track more specifically where the final sale came from. I've done this when I wanted to see whether a certain blog post sent more sales than another one did that used the same link. I explain SIDs in more detail in the later section, "Tracking your affiliate links to improve your sales."

f. Set your Destination URL if you want to change the default page that you're linking to. Not all links have this option. It won't be visible if the option isn't available.

g. Enter an image URL in the Image URL field if you want to use a different image than the one that is offered. Again, not all links have this option, nor do I recommend changing it for a banner link. Banner links are fairly well maintained by most merchants — and will automatically change over time to reflect seasonal and store changes. Again, this option won't be visible if the option isn't available.

h. Click the Update Link Code button if you've made any changes.

6. **Place your cursor in the link code box, click the Highlight Code button, and copy it by pressing Ctrl+C or ⌘+C.**

7. **Place the banner ad in your template or blog post as follows:**

   • To place the banner ad in your template, paste the code into the prepared widget or template code. I show you how to do this in Chapter 11.

   • To place the banner in a blog post, make sure you're viewing the post in HTML mode and not the WYSIWYG mode. Place your cursor where you want the banner link to go, and paste the code into your post.

8. **Test your link by clicking on it and ensuring it directs your browser to the intended page.**

   It's worth repeating: I *always* test my links to make sure they send my readers to the intended destination. I take special care to do this if I made any changes in Step 5 or edited the HTML manually. I want to make sure I didn't somehow break the link in the process.

Tracking your affiliate links to improve your sales

As you start getting more established with using affiliate links, you'll find instances in which you want to know more specifics about how a sale took place. Especially if you use the same link on many different pages, you'll want to know which of those pages generated commissions for you. The easiest way to do this is by creating what's called a *Sub-ID* or *SID*. An SID is a bit of text that you can add to most affiliate links that will be tracked throughout the sales process. When the sale is complete, the affiliate network can tell you which link generated a sale by telling you which SID you used.

Because SIDs are optional, they aren't created automatically in your links. You have to add them yourself, putting them into the SID field as you create your affiliate links. The technical Step 5 in each of the previous sections will tell you how to add a SID in Commission Junction. In affiliate networks, you can add unlimited SIDs to your links.

I usually create a short abbreviation based on the blog name or page I am placing the affiliate link on to help me remember where I used a particular SID. But as you add more links, you will probably want to keep track of all your custom SIDs in a spreadsheet.

Amazon is a bit more limited, because it doesn't offer the use of SIDs to its affiliates. Instead, it offers the capability to create multiple tracking IDs. This accomplishes the same purpose, but Amazon limits its Associates to 100 tracking IDs per account.

Here's how to create a new tracking ID in the Amazon affiliate program:

1. **Log in to your Amazon Associates account at** `https://affiliate-program.amazon.com`.

2. **From your Associates Dashboard, click the Account Settings text link in the upper right corner of the page.**

3. **Under the Account Information section, click Manage Your Tracking IDs.**

4. **Click the Add Tracking ID button.**

5. **Type in a new tracking ID name in the text field and click the Search button.**

   Name the new ID in a manner that makes it easy to remember what it's for. If you want to use this tracking ID to track your links only in your Photography category, for example, name it something like JillPhoto. When a tracking ID is taken in the system, then no other associate can use the same ID. So basic names such as "photo" won't be available.

6. **If the tracking ID you selected is available, then click the Continue button to confirm the creation of the new ID.**

   If the name you want is already taken, Amazon will suggest alternative names for your ID that are similar to your original request. You can either select one of these or search for a new ID using the previous steps until you find one that's available.

When your new tracking IDs are available in Amazon, you can choose from any of your tracking IDs when you create your Amazon affiliate links. To do this, select the name you want to use in the Tracking ID drop-down list in the upper-left corner of the page. Any links you create while this selection appears will have the appropriate tracking ID in your affiliate link code. You can change this at any time. If you do not select an ID name in the Tracking ID drop-down list, then your links will be created with your default ID.

Using affiliate marketing tools to automate your work

Being a WordPress user has its advantages, especially when it comes to WordPress plugins. Quite a few plugins were created specifically to help affiliate marketers. One that I've found particularly useful is called Pretty Link Lite, which is free. Earlier in the chapter, I mention that product catalog affiliate links are usually your best bet for making an affiliate sale. The drawback to such links is that they tend to expire every few months.

With Pretty Link Lite, you can create custom affiliate links with your own blog URL. So, if my blog URL is www.bloggymom.com, a new Pretty Link Lite URL may look like www.bloggymom.com/favorite-products. After a new Pretty Link Lite URL is created, it never has to change. If the actual affiliate destination URL needs to be updated later, you can change it in the Pretty Link admin panel. Using this approach, you can update all your affiliate links in one place, rather than hunting down every one in your blog archives. You can see Pretty Link Lite in action in Figure 14-6.

Here's how to use Pretty Link Lite to create a custom affiliate URL for your blog:

1. **Download and install the Pretty Link Lite WordPress plugin at** http://wordpress.org/extend/plugins/pretty-link.

   For details on downloading and installing plugins, see Chapter 2.

2. **Go to the Pretty Link Lite admin panel by clicking the Pretty Link button at the bottom of the left column of your WordPress Dashboard.**

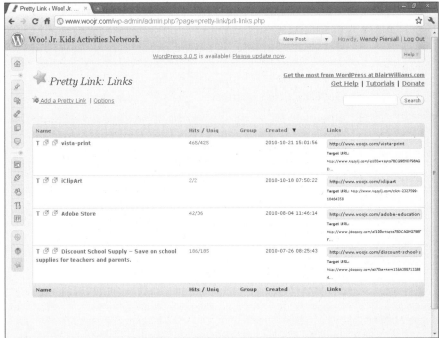

Figure 14-6:
Using Pretty
Link Lite to
maintain
your affiliate
links.

3. **Click the Add a Pretty Link hyperlink at the top of the page.**

4. **Create and copy an affiliate link from an affiliate network to your Clipboard, as described earlier in this chapter.**

   Make an affiliate link from any affiliate program, according to the steps in the previous sections of this chapter (they're headed "Adding a product catalog link to your blog post," "Adding a standard text-ad link to your blog post," and "Adding affiliate banner links to your blog").

5. **Go to Pretty Link and paste your affiliate link code into the Target URL text box.**

6. **Type in the Pretty Link name.**

   The plugin automatically generates a three-character suggestion, which I never use. Instead, I name the link with a few words that let readers know what the link is for. For example, you can use *doll-coupon-code* or *best-buy-laptop.* Make sure you don't use spaces, underscores, or slashes. Only letters, hyphens, and numbers will work.

7. **Type a title in the Title field so that you can remember what this link is used for.**

   You can do the same (optionally) in the Description text field. This is for your organizational purposes only; the title won't be viewable to your blog visitors.

8. **Click the Create button.**

9. **When you want to use one of your Pretty Link affiliate links in a blog post, simply go to your Pretty Link Dashboard and copy the Pretty Link URL and paste that code into your post.**

Discovering more about affiliate marketing

Affiliate marketing is a complex way to make money from blogging, but it can be tremendously successful financially when done well. I strongly advocate making money from your blog in a variety of ways — diversify. You'll also hear this bit of traditional wisdom often in this book: You never want to have all your financial eggs in one basket.

Many professional affiliate marketers — the ones who earn over six figures — will tell you that it took them two to three years to get their sites fully established and earning enough revenue to pay the bills. If you think your blog is a good candidate for affiliate marketing and it takes you a while to find some success with it, don't give up! Use some of these highly recommended resources to fine-tune your efforts and earn more over time:

✔ When I first started learning about affiliate marketing, I bought an e-book by the well-known affiliate marketer Rosalind Gardner. It was a wealth of excellent, honest information. Today the e-book is now a physical book on the subject of affiliate marketing: *Make a Fortune Promoting Other People's Stuff Online: How Affiliate Marketing Can Make You Rich.*

✔ Rosalind Gardner also runs Affiliate Blogger PRO, a very affordable paid training program that includes personal coaching, more tutorials, videos, webinars, community forums, and even technical support. Because she is one of the most respected names in the industry, I'm always happy to recommend her resources. See www.affiliatebloggerpro.com.

✔ Friends Missy Ward and Shawn Collins founded the Affiliate Summit Conference in 2003, and it is by far the biggest and most well-known affiliate marketing event in the United States. Over 7,000 people attended their two events in 2010. See www.affiliatesummit.com.

✔ ABestWeb is a very well-established affiliate marketing forum with over 80,000 members — and it's free to join. It also boasts members from all the major affiliate networks, as well as merchants' affiliate managers who provide resources and advice on just about any topic related to affiliate marketing. See www.abestweb.com.

Part IV
Expanding Your Blogging Empire

The 5th Wave   By Rich Tennant

"It all started when I was researching recipes for Baked Alaska and frozen custard for my baking blog."

In this part . . .

This is the part in which I show you all the ways you can take your blog and use it to open doors to new opportunities.

Whether you want to land a book deal, expand your blog into a network of blogs, hire writers, create multimedia content, get a "real" job, or even sell your blog someday, this part shows you what it takes to get there.

Chapter 15

Planning for the Future Growth of Your Blog

In This Chapter

▶ Thinking like a true entrepreneur and managing your blog as a business

▶ Building a blog that can grow into a larger business

▶ Forging partnerships with other bloggers

▶ Laying a foundation for future business opportunities

▶ Hiring writers

▶ Protecting your business interests

▶ Selling your blog

*O*ne of the things I hope I've hammered into your head in this book is that you can never really know how your blog will evolve as you become more successful. I've shared several success stories of people who never expected to become professional bloggers, some who have had to completely rebrand their blogs, and one who found her career in marketing and social media was best served if she closed down her blog altogether. In fact, as I've been writing this book, Google changed the way they rank websites — and effectively put several long-established Internet publishers out of business by cutting their traffic down by 90 percent. In other words: You have to expect the best but plan for the worst.

In my first few years of blogging, I wrote a lot about Internet business, building traffic, and how to monetize a blog. More than half of those posts are out of date by now. It really is challenging to stay on top of trends that affect blogging and social media-based businesses. That's why this chapter is indispensable to your blog business: It helps you structure your business in ways that will make it more resistant to outside influences and create a truly dependable, long-term blogging career. If you're only interested in creating a bit of side income from your blog, you can totally skip this chapter. But if you want that side income to last for the long term, then you'll probably want to read on.

My fear is that you may dismiss the information in this chapter, thinking that you don't need to worry about these things when you're just getting started. That fear is based on experience — because I was guilty of not planning ahead on several occasions. I can even admit that sometimes I still get short-sighted when overwhelmed with the day-to-day tasks of running a business *and* having a family life. But it's my hope that you *at least skim this chapter* so you're aware of the kinds of challenges that may be ahead for you. Then you can know when you need to seek help or additional resources before a situation blindsides you.

Creating Systems and Routines to Manage Your Time Effectively

The business problems I most often hear professional bloggers cite involve not getting enough traffic, not having enough advertisers, or having too much work. The biggest challenge they (and probably you) will face is time management. If you've been blogging for any length of time at all, you know it's a lot of work — probably a lot more work than you originally thought it would be. And if you want your blog to grow, the natural line of thinking would be to work more. The problem is that as humans, and especially as moms, working more isn't always an option. It sounds cliché to say you need to work smarter, not harder, but it's so, so true. And I say that with a little exasperation in my voice, because this is an ongoing challenge that never seems to quite be mastered the way I want it to be.

I've even done some consulting for some of the most successful mom bloggers out there, and this is where they need the most help. As you grow, I encourage you to start thinking in terms of being a manager, not an employee, of your blog.

The reason is that managers approach business differently from employees:

- ✔ **They see the big picture objectively.** Managers can make decisions based on what's best for the company, not on what is most fun or easiest to accomplish.

- ✔ **They delegate.** Managers evaluate people's strengths and weaknesses. They ensure that the right people are working on the right jobs, and will take them off any projects that aren't suited to their skill sets.

- ✔ **They keep an eye on the bottom line.** Managers know what parts of the business are most profitable and will dedicate more resources to that part of the business.

- ✔ **They streamline and consolidate.** Managers can analyze where time is spent in the company and make it a priority to invest in tools or projects that will reduce overhead and increase productivity.

I'll admit that these aren't easy shifts to make for *any* business owner who has spent years being a one-person show. It means letting go of control, giving up doing some of the things you love, and paying more attention to nitty-gritty details such as spreadsheets, tax write-offs, and legal protections. But here's what can happen if you *don't* manage your business instead of being your own employee:

- **Burnout:** Put this one in the "been there, done that, and don't want to be there again" category. When you're self-employed and you work too hard, your business can consume every aspect of your life. It's not like a job you can leave for the weekend or quit. You'll think about work while doing laundry, playing with your kids, and even while you're supposed to be on vacation. When I finally closed up shop on my freelance graphic-design business, I was so burnt out that I felt like I could now have my first day off in *four years*. I can assure you it's an awful way to run a company.

- **Mistakes:** When you get overwhelmed with the day-to-day work of running your business, it's so easy to make mistakes. These can be small, such as messing up your template and not noticing it for a week. Or they can be big — and you can find yourself redoing months of work or losing out on a lot of income.

- **Hinder your growth:** I know it's a common fear to think that running a bigger business means more work and more responsibility. So you may just keep your blog at a lower level of success than you're capable of. I've had this fear too. I've found, however, that when you step back and treat your blog as a manager would, it actually frees up more of your time and energy — not the other way around. It may take a bit of a time investment to get it to yield that reward, but it's so worth it.

- **Go out of business:** You may know the awful statistic that a little under half of new businesses go out of business in less than five years' time. Sometimes, this really isn't a bad thing — as was the case with Michelle Lamar (described in Chapter 18). Her blog was just a steppingstone to her dream job. But you can back yourself into a corner by the aforementioned mistakes, and ruin a great gig for yourself that could allow you to work from home and have more time for your family. If that's your goal, then preventing these pitfalls needs to be a priority for you.

So what are some of the ways you can be a manager of your business? Many of them are covered later in this chapter:

- **Outsourcing:** Do what you're good at. Hire others to do the rest.

- **Invest in technology:** I hound you to use WordPress in Chapter 2, or at least set up Blogger on your own domain. This is the biggest reason why: WordPress back-end technology and plugins can manage hundreds of tasks that you may be otherwise doing yourself. Many free or paid programs and tools can also make your life easier.

I mention premium themes in Chapter 2. These themes make it very easy to manage advertising, do software updates, make template changes, and search engine optimize your site.

✔ **Affiliate and advertising management tools:** I discuss these a little bit in Chapters 11 and 14. Juggling advertisers and hundreds of affiliate links can quickly eat up all your time. These tools help you to streamline these tasks and enable you to maintain these projects all in one place.

✔ **Custom administrative tools:** My biggest expense over the last five years has been my WordPress developer bill. It is the best money I've spent, paying for itself ten times over. My WordPress developer created several custom plugins that help me manage multiple blogs easily and efficiently. He also helps me to maintain the sites, because it takes him 15 minutes to do something that would take me 15 hours to accomplish.

Understanding What Scalability Means and Why You Should Care

Scalability is one of those absolutely annoying MBA-ish jargon words that you would probably never think would apply to a mom blogger — I used to think that, at least. Maybe you're more forward-thinking than I am. But what scalability really means is just that a business needs to have a structure in place that allows it to grow. Of course you want to grow your income — but you also want to increase the number of opportunities available to you, both personally and professionally. You also want to scale your business to avoid the problems I mention in the previous section.

In the mom-blogging world, scalability can refer to technology, content creation, traffic growth, advertising reach, publishing medium, diversified income sources, and marketing strategies. Wow, that's a lot in one sentence. Let me break those down further for you:

✔ **Technology:** I talk about technology a lot earlier in this chapter and in Chapter 2. For most blogging businesses, you need a website capable of many different potential features. These could be adding a shopping cart, a forum, or community; integrating Facebook or Twitter applications; adding custom advertising placements; or streamlining administrative functions.

✔ **Content creation:** For some blogs, you are and will always be the only writer. Other times, you may want to bring in more writers to increase the volume of content you publish. But even if you wish to remain a one-woman show, you still need to devise ways of creating more content beyond your regular blog posts. Ways of doing this are various: Add a photo blog, add videoblogging or podcasting, or create resources for your readers such as free downloads.

✔ **Traffic growth:** One of the harder lessons I learned when I first converted my blog into a blog network was that the online marketing skills I had developed to grow my blog up to that point were not the same skills I needed to grow *beyond* that point. To reach increasing levels of traffic, you need to get more sophisticated with (well, yeah) your traffic-building skills. These include search engine optimization, link building, syndication partnerships, and purchasing online advertising.

✔ **Advertising reach:** As you find advertisers and sponsors to work with, increasing traffic will (for the most part) increase your revenue. But as social media get more integrated into our daily lives, you also need to ensure that you have a growing presence on sites such as Facebook and Twitter. You can also expand your advertising reach by publishing multimedia or mobile-enabled content.

✔ **Publishing medium:** Many writers find their blogging careers take them beyond writing just for themselves. You may start writing for other blogs and online publications, and move on to writing for magazines or get a book deal. These all require skill sets other than those you need for writing on a blog.

✔ **Diversified income sources:** I warned about the dangers of having too many eggs in one basket in Chapter 4. Things change too quickly in the online world to rely on only one or two sources of income from your blog. It is critical that you work hard to diversify how you make money, including working with multiple advertisers or multiple sponsorship packages, selling different categories of products, adding affiliate marketing links, or running multiple websites. You can see in Chapter 18 that nearly all the financially successful moms I profiled earn income in multiple ways.

✔ **Marketing strategies:** Having all your traffic or publicity come from one place is a similar problem to having all your revenue come from one place. That source can go away at any time. You never want to build your blog on a foundation that relies solely on another business to succeed. Strive to grow your blog and brand in multiple ways, such as search engine optimization, PR, networking, speaking at events, and via social media.

Planning for success

I feel like a broken record saying this again, but most successful bloggers didn't start out planning on being successful bloggers. They started a blog for fun and then found that they could continue blogging for profit. That means many of the most successful bloggers you know didn't start out with a plan to get to where they are today. They had to figure it out along the way, much of the time taking many detours and making many course corrections. The one thing we bloggers have in common is that we all wish we knew what we were getting into when we first started blogging, because we all would have been a little more conscientious about the decisions we made that ended up having a long-term impact on our blogs.

A great way to illustrate this is to show you the steps I took when launching my last blog. With the benefit of five years of hindsight, these are the things I made a top priority before I ever invested a second in starting the blog:

✔ **Chose a catchy name that meets the following criteria:**

- *It's brandable.* I came up with a name that was unique, memorable, and easily conveyed the nature of the content of my site. This doesn't have to be too literal, because remember that your tag line and logo can convey the nature of your site as well.

- *A good domain name is available.* My criteria for a good domain name: ends in a `.com`, is as short as possible, is not easily misspelled, has no hyphens, and is not too similar to the names of directly competing sites with similar domain names (which could confuse people). It's a bonus if the domain name has at least one good keyword in the URL; you can also buy commonly misspelled variations (such as WooJr.com and WooJunior.com, or CopycatCraft.com and CopycatCrafts.com).

- *It's not already used.* Make sure the name isn't being used by another blogger who writes on the same topic as you plan to write about. Even if the domain name is available, you should check to make sure that someone isn't using that name on a `blogspot.com` URL or as a Twitter handle. Also, make sure that an appropriate Twitter name is available for the blog and register it immediately, even if you don't plan on marketing via Twitter for several months. Twitter names disappear fast.

- *It isn't going to be your own nickname.* This is a personal choice, and you may feel differently about this. It works for Heather Armstrong, also called Dooce. This choice has everything to do with an *exit strategy* (what you do with your blog when you don't want to blog anymore), as I discuss later on in this chapter. Heather can never sell the domain `dooce.com` to anyone else, because its worth is directly tied to her personal brand. And unless she wants to radically change her business model or get a nine-to-five job somewhere, she can't retire without losing everything she has built. I asked about this matter in my interview with her, and she absolutely knows that this is the right business decision for her, and for her family. She knows deep down inside that she's found her calling, so to speak, and she wouldn't change it even if she could.

  I, on the other hand, know myself well enough to know that I could never blog about one topic for the rest of my life. So I'll never again brand a blog in a way that ties it too closely to my personal brand.

- *It isn't in use by another company.* Even if the other company has a very minimal online presence and is in another industry, if the name you're considering is being used, choose a different name. There's just too much potential for problems in the future with confusion — or even copyright and trademark issues.

  I also would never choose a name that is a spinoff of a popular brand name. For example, my husband once had a band he named Salvation Amy. The "actual" Salvation Army didn't take too kindly to this, and sent a cease-and-desist before the band had more than a few gigs under its belt. They had to start from scratch, building name recognition all over again, throwing away three months of work.

✔ **Have a monetization plan of action before you launch:** From a business perspective, I absolutely will not start any new project without knowing how it will sustain itself. Even if the idea is the best thing since sliced bread, if I can't make money from it, I can't justify spending time on it.

  Here's another thing I learned the hard way: Being in a great ad network doesn't mean that it will automatically allow you to use its ads on any site you launch. There are a lot of factors that influence when an ad network will allow you to run its ads on your site, including whether the site draws the right kind of audience, whether the network is already working with established competing sites, and whether the network has enough ads for you to run. I invested a whole week in setting up a sixth site addition to my Woo! Jr. network, only to find out that my ad network didn't have the inventory to add that site at that time. That was a week's work — and a decent-size developer bill — down the drain.

✔ **Focus on an underserved market or topic:** I've found it's far easier to build a name for yourself and become a valuable resource in a niche or topic that isn't already oversaturated with other bloggers. For example, unless you're an amazing chef and food photographer, I would not start a *general* food blog today. Instead, focus on a much smaller topic that you can truly dominate, as Bakerella does with her cake-pops blog (www.bakerella.com).

  If I was starting this blog to support a business such as being a consultant or coach, I would be sure to focus my client practice on an underserved niche. For example, there are plenty of small-business coaches, but not many are just for women entrepreneurs who want to build a seven-figure business, as my friend Marla Tabaka did. Marla has built a profitable and stable coaching business in the midst of the Great Recession by focusing on a very small group of potential clients. It is always easier to make your mark when you're a big fish in a small pond.

✔ **Look for a market that has potential for large growth:** Even though I chose something that is underserved (as in the previous bullet point), I also need to ensure that eventually this blog can attract the kind of traffic and revenue to become a viable business. I may be able to make the most incredible blog in the universe on underwater basket weaving, but I'll never find enough readers to make it worth my time — or worthy of the attention of advertisers — as a business.

✔ **Get set up on WordPress:** I know, I know. I sound like a broken record on this point. (See Chapter 2.) The truth is, you don't know what will be the true ticket to long-term success with any blog. You may want to expand it into another blog network. You may find that you want to build an affiliate store on the blog. You may find that you want to create a community and add Facebook Connect to allow people to sign in with their Facebook accounts. You can't do any of these things on Blogger. I'd rather have the option to do whatever the business dictates in the future, instead of having my blogging platform dictate how I can (or can't) expand.

✔ **Get a premium WordPress theme:** I don't have time to mess around with code. Premium themes make setting up a great-looking blog brain-dead easy — and you usually don't have to hire a developer to customize it. If you do, then it's usually only for very minor changes that are affordable. Premium themes also look professionally designed straight out of the box. I would absolutely not launch a blog that doesn't look professionally designed.

✔ **Get a logo:** I'll admit I have an advantage here because I used to be a logo designer. But there are resources I mention in Chapter 6 that anyone can use to get a good-looking custom logo for cheap — or even free in some cases.

Forging partnerships with other bloggers

Another way to grow your capabilities as a blogger is to form partnerships with other bloggers. Combining resources is a powerful way of building traffic and revenue — or of getting an entirely new project off the ground. I've seen several bloggers partner up to build and promote new events and conferences, such as Allison Worthington and Barbara Jones. Allison had the blogging experience and had built a strong community; Barbara had a lot of experience working with brands that wanted to get more involved in the mom-blogging community. The Blissdom Conference — their joint effort — is now going on its fourth year, and has expanded to Canada as well.

Another way of working with other bloggers is to pool your advertising sales together. Chic Chick Media (www.chicchickmedia.com) is the partnership among three bloggers: Laurie Turk of Tip Junkie (http://tipjunkie.com), Cindy Lou Hopper of Skip To My Lou (http://skiptomylou.org), and Kim Demmonof Today's Creative Blog (http://todayscreativeblog.net).

They write on similar topics, have the same target audience, and are quite successful individually. Yet it was difficult for any of them to find long-term advertisers, because most large advertisers seek to buy ads on sites that can deliver a significantly higher volume than most individual blogs can generate. Yet together, as Chic Chick Media, they could promote their blogs as one advertising package, reaching nearly half a million readers a month. This is extremely attractive to advertisers who don't want to (or can't) manage advertising buys on multiple smaller sites.

It is important to note here that business partnerships require a very clear understanding of how you and your business partners will work together. At the very least, you should have a written agreement stating who is responsible for what, how recordkeeping will be established, how costs will be shared, and how revenue will be split. This doesn't need to be a complicated legal document, but it *absolutely* should be in writing. For the best protection, I strongly recommend having a lawyer get involved to ensure that all parties' interests are protected. Much of the time, you don't know what you don't know — and you don't want to find that out after a disagreement occurs.

Understanding What an Exit Strategy Is and Why You Need One

I mention earlier in this chapter that an exit strategy is definitely one of those super-businessy terms that can make your eyes roll back in your head. "Exit strategy," honestly, wasn't even a part of my vocabulary until a few years ago — when I heard big, important entrepreneurs tossing this term around, and I was left scrambling to figure out what the heck they were talking about. An *exit strategy* is simply what you plan on doing with your business when you don't want to do it anymore. Will you just close up shop? Will it be the foundation for a different business in the future? Will you want to sell it someday? Or will it merge with another company?

These concerns probably seem far-off, as if they didn't have anything to do with your business today. But as an entrepreneur, I would encourage you to think differently about this topic. If you want to transition your blog to have others write on it, you will need to ensure that you have the revenue now to pay for content — *and* make sure that you can earn that money back. If you decide you want to sell your blog someday, you may need a year or more to make changes to your site so that someone else can run it.

Both of my first two businesses ended when I shut them down. While this is an absolutely appropriate (and common) way of ending a business, it isn't your only option. If you want your blog to be the foundation for a different business in the future, or if you even want to sell it someday, there are things you need to take into consideration *now* to prepare for that end goal. In the following sections, I show you some of the ways to create a blogging business that can continue to thrive even if you get to the point that you don't want to create content anymore.

Determining how to build your business to match your future goals and plans

This is the section where I take off my mom-blogging hat and put on my "career counselor" hat. I was, in fact, a recruiter for a few years, and I learned quite a bit during that time about taking a long-term approach to putting together a great lifelong career. I don't underestimate the power that one great blogger has to create the career of her dreams. I've seen so many women do it, and my biggest goal in writing this book is to help more women do the same.

When I used to screen candidates for jobs I was trying to fill, I always asked them where they wanted their careers to be in five to ten years. I asked because I really needed to know if the position they were applying for would help them get from where they were to where they wanted to go. Sometimes that meant passing up highly qualified candidates because I knew that they wouldn't really last in that position.

Blogging is an extremely powerful medium, and can be like that perfect job that can take you to where you want to go. In order to do this, you'll need to take a long-term approach to the decisions you make about how you build your blog today.

Here are just a few examples of how your short-term goals may need to change to accommodate your long-term goals:

- ✔ **Write a book.** If your long-term goal is to write a book someday, it will be important now to build a following and establish yourself as an expert in your craft. These aspects of blogging are very important to publishers who scout for new writers. Getting there may mean (in the short term, at least) that you don't have the time to build advertiser relationships.

- ✔ **Own a blog that earns passive income from advertising.** If your long-term goal is to build a business that generates passive income from advertising and affiliate marketing, then it will be crucial now to build a blog that has a lot of traffic — and that means writing with search engine optimization in mind. Focusing on advertising income may mean (in the short term) that you won't have time to build an active community around your site.

✔ **Be a marketing consultant.** If your long-term goal is to be a social media marketing consultant, it will be important now to be extremely active on Facebook and Twitter, and to get involved with brands that are developing high-profile blogger-outreach campaigns. This focus may mean, in the short term, that you won't have time to build a lot of traffic to your own site or do your own projects.

Laying a foundation for a range of opportunities

In Chapter 4, I show you how different kinds of blogs need to be promoted in different ways. But if you take a step back from just promoting one blog, you may want to build up a way to open the doors to many career opportunities, not just success with one blog. If I had to zero in on the most important elements to include if you're using your blog as a launch pad for other opportunities, I'd suggest you focus on these:

✔ **Build a strong personal brand.** Building a great reputation can take years of hard work and dedication. But having a strong personal brand is an asset no matter where you go or what you do. It will help you build goodwill when you launch new projects, and it will help you get your foot in the door for future opportunities. Plus, it's one of the most important things that book editors, TV producers, or brand representatives look for when they're deciding who to work with.

✔ **Become a recognized expert in your field.** This is related to building a strong personal brand, but is specifically important as you develop what you're known for. When you're a leading voice in your chosen field, it means that when you talk, people listen.

✔ **Be professional, all the time, even when you think no one is watching you.** The Internet offers a level of anonymity that sometimes makes people feel that they're safe when they act in (ahem) unflattering ways without other people knowing. Yet everything you put online is practically permanent — and you may never know when your words can come back to haunt you and undermine your credibility. A friend just mentioned the other day that she used to moderate a forum in which a member was always helpful and courteous when participating in conversations. Yet that same person would go around to forum members' blogs and leave scathing, nasty comments anonymously. For someone who is tech-savvy, it isn't hard to trace online activity to one person. In other words, make sure that every interaction you have online is one you would be willing to have others watch, because there is no such thing as complete privacy on the Web.

✔ **Be very active in social media.** For any personal or business endeavor, it's always advantageous to have a large circle of friends to help you spread the word. Word of mouth is the most effective marketing strategy that exists, and it only gets more effective as social media becomes more widely adopted by people in general.

✔ **Always be networking.** You'll never know where that next opportunity will come from. There have been several examples in this book in which I was fortunate to meet the right people or be in the right place at the right time. If I can get onto the *Today Show* from an initial conversation on Twitter, think of all the other ways new connections can make a huge impact on your career.

Hiring (and Firing) Writers

The longer I work in the blogging industry, the more value I find in bringing other people's voices onto my blogs. Writers bring a completely different perspective on your blog topics, based on their various backgrounds. Sometimes I'll also hand-pick people to help with specialized content that I am not qualified to write myself. Ultimately, I think this adds a lot more richness to the content I'm providing to my readers.

Hiring writers, however, doesn't mean that *all that work* is off your plate and onto theirs. Most writers need input and guidance, especially if they're writing for you on a regular basis. Managing people is a skill that definitely takes practice and patience — especially because the people you're likely to work with will be people you consider friends. Being their employer (whether those folks are true employees or contractors) changes the dynamic of their relationship with you, and that can be tricky to navigate. Many friendships can handle such a temporary shift in power, and be better for it. Unfortunately, sometimes the opposite is true as well. So if you want to hire someone you consider a dear friend, be sure your relationship is strong enough to withstand some tension and disagreements along the way. If you have any doubt in that department (even if you're really close to the person), hire someone else.

Knowing when to hire help

One of the harder lessons I learned about working with hired writers is that it can be difficult to make enough money from the paid content to cover your costs. Sometimes you have people writing for you for free, which I talk about that later in this chapter; this section talks about paid writers. The point at which you think about hiring writers should not be *when you need more content,* but instead *when you know you can turn that content into dollars.* The hard part of this lesson, for me, was that I thought I could make money from my writers' content, so I invested time and money in them with that goal in mind, in hopes of earning that money back someday. That was a $10,000 mistake. But don't worry; my story has a happy ending. It took a little time, but my business is definitely in the black now.

Note: I should state here that I am making an assumption about the kind of blog you may have that requires you to hire writers. If you're focused on creating more content, you should *already* have a way to make money from that content — namely with advertisers. If you don't already have advertisers in place, don't hire anybody else until you get them. I'm also assuming that if you hire writers, you have been blogging for more than just a few months. Hopefully, that means you have a track record and have established analytics in place to help you with the rest of this section.

So, how do you know if you can make enough money to justify hiring help? I don't have a foolproof equation, but I have a way to estimate future revenue — which in turn helps me to know what my budget is for any writing project I have. It involves looking at past performance and projecting future profits based on estimated traffic.

For this example, say you want to know whether paying $50 for a tutorial on a sewing project is worth the cost. You'll need to have an ad network or current advertisers that pay you according to the number of impressions you can deliver, not on a per-month or per-week basis. To crunch the numbers, use the following steps:

1. **Pull your Top Content report up in Google Analytics: Go to your Google Analytics Dashboard, click Content, and then click View Full Report at the bottom of the page.**

2. **Change the date range to a full year's worth of data: Click the drop-down list next to the current date range and type in today's date last year as your start date. Click Apply.**

3. **Find a page that already exists on your blog that is a close approximation of the content you want to pay for and click on the page URL to view the Content Detail page.**

   In this case (as shown in Figure 15-1), I have a simple sewing project that I wrote myself, which is generally a good indicator of the kind of traffic a new sewing-tutorial post could expect over the same period of time.

Figure 15-1:
Singling out
the history
of a page
to predict
future
earnings
on similar
pages.

As you can see, this one page has been viewed just over 24,000 times over the last 12 months.

4. **Estimate past advertising earnings by adding the number of ads on the page and the average rate you're paid for each ad.**

This doesn't need to be a complicated analysis of the average from every cent your blog has earned (though it could be if you're as into spreadsheets as I am). On my page, here's the hypothetical breakdown:

a. Three ad units from two different ad networks. The average rate they've earned per 1,000 impressions is $1.

b. AdSense ad units that earned an average of $0.65 per 1,000 impressions.

c. $(3 \times \$1.00) + \$0.65 = \$3.65$ per 1,000 impressions.

d. 24,000 views with an estimate of $3.65 per 1,000 impressions means that this post roughly earned $85 over the course of the last 12 months $(24 \times \$3.65 = \$87.60)$.

5. **Weigh your final calculation against your costs.**

If you estimate that you can earn $85 over a reasonable period of time, paying $50 for a sewing tutorial probably works for your budget. If you think that page will get about 24,000 views, you can definitely expect to earn your money back in less than a year.

So: Say you've established that you have a budget to pay for content. What other indicators signal that it's time to hire help?

- ✔ You can't dedicate any more time to writing than you already are.

- ✔ You have the time to commit to hiring, training, and managing writers.

- ✔ Your readers have expressed an interest in content you can't or don't want to write.

- ✔ You have money you can front and not earn back for 6–12 months.

- ✔ You're ready to take your business to the next level, and are willing to do *all* the work that goes along with it.

Finding good writers

There really is no shortage of writers to hire on the Web. The challenge is finding *good* ones. The way I find my writers is typically through word of mouth. When I went through my first round of finding writers for six new blogs, I asked a few friends to write about it on their blogs and have anyone interested in writing for me to contact me. I was overwhelmed with more than 100 applications in less than 48 hours.

While this is a good problem to have, it's still a problem. I really didn't have the resources to be able to interview and review every single applicant. So I set up a system in which I let the ones who were the most serious about the job stand out from the crowd. I did this by asking the applicants to participate in a conference call and send me a proposal to let me know what they were most interested in writing about. Interestingly, only 20 people out of the 100+ applicants did these two things, which made it much easier to filter down to the people I knew I could rely on.

Today I only have one or two regular contributors, but still hire out writing for my blogs on a per-project basis. This way, I can obtain multiple blog posts at one time and post them whenever I need them. This is a great arrangement; on days that I don't feel like writing, I still have fresh content to post.

The best way I have found to hire project writers is to use a website such as Elance (www.elance.com) or Guru.com (www.guru.com). You can also post a help-wanted ad on the ProBlogger job board at http://jobs.problogger. net for a nominal fee. It's important to clearly state exactly what you need a blogger to do in your job descriptions. Plus, give some indication of the kind of writer you're looking for — do you need someone who is very affordable (inexperienced) who will need guidance from you? Or do you want to pay a higher rate for someone who is more experienced and can work with very little oversight? Offer a way for applicants to get in touch with you in case they have questions about things you may not have addressed in your help-wanted ad.

Determining how your writers will be compensated

The amount of diversity in the ways bloggers are compensated is enormous. Some bloggers write for free, some are paid per post, some are paid a monthly fee, some are paid for a specific number of words or pages, and some are paid based on a percentage of advertising revenue. Then there are those who occupy the in-between pay scales in all these approaches, or use a combination of different approaches.

I've worked with every kind of writer paid as mentioned here, and can confirm that are pros and cons to all situations, as described in the following sections.

Writers work for free

Pros: Having writers work for free only works when you have something else to offer besides money. It may be exposure, prestige, experience, or mentoring — but no writer's work is truly *free*. The other good thing is that if you have so much going for you that people are willing to write for you for free, you can probably find more than one person to do it.

Cons: Without the incentive of money, you can't rely on your writers to produce consistent content. Plus, you'll usually be last on their priority lists after they've written for their own blogs and for paying clients. Plus, the turnover rate is extremely high. When they don't need your exposure, prestige, experience, or mentoring, they'll be gone.

Writers are paid per post

Pros: Paying writers per post is a great way to budget your expenses and predict revenue. Plus, you can dictate what topics the blog posts are written about, filling in your editorial calendar around the things you don't have time to do yourself.

Cons: Once your writers have published their posts, they aren't likely to be invested in helping you to promote them. They've already done what they've been paid to do. Plus, if a writer gets sick or busy with other clients, you may only get three posts that month instead of ten.

Writers are paid a monthly fee

Pros: Paying writers a monthly fee is another great way to budget expenses and predict revenue. It should be clear that you expect a minimum amount of writing or hours worked within that month. You might also be able to have these writers help with other aspects of the business, such as promotion or site maintenance, if they can still do it all in the agreed-upon time frame.

Cons: Again, if your writer gets sick or busy, you've lost out on content — and in this scenario, you're paying for content you aren't getting. Rarely, you'll find writers who will milk the agreement by writing extremely short posts, or dragging out the time it takes to complete tasks.

Writers are paid per word or per page

Pros: Paying writers per work or per page gives you the most control over the quality and quantity of the content you expect to receive, and (again) is very predictable in terms of payments and income. Freelance writers who work in this manner tend to be more experienced, and will make your work a priority.

Cons: As with writers paid per post, these writers are not typically invested in your business beyond delivering the content you hired them to write.

Writers are paid a percentage of advertising revenue

Pros: Paying writers a percentage of ad revenue means that the writers have a vested interest — not only in creating great content, but also in helping your blog succeed overall. When you can find the right writers, they're the most motivated — and usually go above and beyond the scope of what any other writer will do for you.

Cons: It is very difficult to find good writers who are willing to work based on pure incentives, because there is no guaranteed income. Additionally, these writers can get so invested that they feel like they're entitled to more than just the advertising income, and can become increasingly demanding to the point of being inappropriate.

Writers are paid a combination of flat rate and incentive percentage

Pros: Paying writers with a combination of a flat rate plus a percentage of ad revenue can only be truly effective *if* you ensure that the base amount you pay will be completely covered by the revenue generated by the writer.

Cons: In theory, this should be the best of both worlds, right? Maybe it can be, but I found it to be the worst. This combination accounts for over half of that $10,000 mistake I mention earlier in the chapter. I paid a base that I never recovered, and then still had to pay out advertising percentages on top of a loss. I'm a much smarter businesswoman today because of this lesson.

Putting contracts in place to protect yourself and your writers

There was a time in my career in which I would have skipped reading this chapter. I thought the people I worked with were all rational, smart, talented people whom I treated well, so I was sure they'd want to treat me well, too.

My perception was that putting together written agreements was a headache that would probably command large legal fees.

But when I launched my blog network, I was sufficiently paranoid about leaving these kinds of things undone that I did take the time and money to create legal agreements with all my writers. I took a copy of an agreement a former client had given me, made some adjustments to it to reflect the nature of my business, ran it past a lawyer (who was family and not familiar with contract or copyright law), and had all my writers sign and agree to it. I was really quite proud of myself, actually, for not blowing off this very important thing (the way I used to do). I was treating my business like a *real* business.

Unfortunately, one of the people I had hired didn't work out, and I had to fire her. I learned a lesson that many other entrepreneurs have learned: You never know what you should have done until it's too late to do it. My legal agreements were strong enough to defend in court, but weren't as solid as I thought — and I paid the price. I was forced to find a really good lawyer who specialized in copyright and contract law to help me navigate through this unfortunate situation in the hopes of coming to a resolution.

This lawyer is now my friend Evan Brown from Internet Cases (`http://blog.internetcases.com`). He spent several hours helping me to ensure that this section of my book will give you the best possible advice on this subject. Because — even after everything I've gone through — I'm no lawyer. Copyright law is weird and tricky, and often defies common sense.

Here are the most important things you need to know when you are crafting a legal agreement with your writers:

- ✔ **Who owns the copyright of written works?** Even if you pay for content, you do not own the copyright to that content unless you have an agreement in writing that states that the author *specifically* assigns copyright to you. This can be done via e-mail or actual documents, but must be agreed to in writing by both parties in order to be binding. This does not apply when a person is a legal employee of your company, when the employing company is the automatic copyright holder. I cover the difference between employees and independent contractors in a bit.

- ✔ **What is the difference between copyright and publishing rights?** Copyright is automatically held by the author unless specifically assigned otherwise in writing. Publishing rights can be communicated orally or even assumed by the author's conduct — if the author is posting directly on your blog on a regular basis and taking your money, this is enough to presume that you have legal publishing rights. But in cases where there are disagreements, it's best to have publishing rights established in writing or granted in an e-mail.

✔ **What is the difference between an independent contractor and an employee?** According to the IRS, "You must withhold income taxes, withhold and pay Social Security and Medicare taxes, and pay unemployment tax on wages paid to an employee. You do not generally have to withhold or pay any taxes on payments to independent contractors." Nearly all blogging working relationships are set up with independent contractors. Here are some of the primary things you would have to do in order to be considered an employer: You must dictate the schedule that specifies when your writer works, control what that person does for you, how he or she does it for you, and specify that the writer work on materials or goods that you supply, which must be returned to you.

✔ **How can I enforce a copyright?** If you believe that another website is illegally publishing the content you own, you can file a Digital Millennium Copyright Act (DMCA) takedown notice with both the website's hosting company and/or with Google. The way that a DMCA notice works is that after you file it and specify the content that you wish to have removed, the hosting company where the site resides must take down the material in question, or Google must remove it from its index. You must be the actual copyright holder or authorized representative (a lawyer) to file a DMCA notice. If you believe that someone has filed an unjustified DMCA notice against you, you can also file a DMCA counter-notice. *Only do this if you're prepared to defend your counter-notice in court,* because the counter-notice effectively swears that you legally do have the publishing rights of the material in question.

Parting ways with writers without burning bridges

Nothing can really soften the blow of getting fired; it's a humiliating experience that nobody wants to have happen. Here are some of the things you can do to part ways with a writer without having to get to the point of firing — or to manage a working relationship that starts deteriorating:

✔ **Scale back the writer's work.** If you feel that a writer isn't working out, cut down his or her assignments significantly. This may just encourage the writer to move on.

✔ **Suggest more appropriate work.** Often a writer just has strengths and weaknesses that aren't a good match for you. In this case, suggest that the person try writing for a different blog or pursuing different work where you think they'll excel.

✔ **Don't sweat the little things, but don't let them go unaddressed.** There's no reason to get worked up about small stuff — the stress isn't worth it. But be sure to communicate problems when they happen, so they don't become an accepted way of working with you.

✔ **Read between the lines and trust your gut.** If there are frequent miscommunications or misunderstandings, these are clues to where this writer is coming from. Take the time to ensure that your writers understand your position and their roles clearly, especially when repeated misunderstandings occur.

✔ **Err on the side of generosity.** It's worth more to pay a disputed amount or accept less-than-perfect work if that means it keeps the peace. But if this happens, it's a signal that it's time for this person to move on. I'm not advocating that you allow yourself to be taken advantage of — in that situation, it's important to stand your ground.

✔ **Be empowering, but not misleading.** It's always best to do what you can to help your writers grow and be more successful, and to encourage them along the way. But don't allow them to take credit for things they did not do, or let them believe they've accomplished more than they really have. You may think it's a confidence-booster to fib about whether a piece of writing fills the bill — but instead, it can set you up for unrealistic demands or expectations from your contractor.

✔ **Always maintain your professionalism.** Even if things turn very ugly, don't lose your cool in public. Your reputation is worth more than getting in the last word, even if that means not everyone hears your side of the story. Your professionalism will speak for itself. As long as you maintain your integrity, nobody has any real power over you.

Ultimately, the only things you can control are your own thoughts and actions when a dispute arises. In one situation in which I had to fire a writer, I endured short-term pains for long-term gains. I was out over $4,000 for content by this writer, but ultimately, it was a small price to pay. I walked away from the situation with my professionalism and self respect intact, no legal gray area hanging over my head, and *lots* of good karma on my side. It also provided a lot of the emotional fuel I needed to make my second blog network successful, and that alone was worth it. You can always turn a bad situation into a good one, as long as you're willing to look at it from another point of view.

Selling Your Blog

I love talking about selling a blog — I learned so much about myself, entrepreneurship, and business when I sold Sparkplugging in 2009. It is one of my proudest achievements, but it was a grueling process that took quite an emotional toll. Selling a blog is not for everyone, and it can be quite a challenge. Most things that make a blog great also make it harder to sell. Most bloggers wisely do things like writing with passion, creating a strong personal brand, and using a blog to build a platform for other career opportunities. This kind of blog promotion creates a blog that is less valuable to everyone *else* in the world other than yourself. If you think you may want to sell your blog someday, you'll probably have to do quite a bit of work to get it to the point that it holds its value without you at the helm. I explain those things in the following sections. I also answer some of the most common questions asked about selling a blog — such as how you find a buyer, determine a selling price, and negotiate the best deal for yourself.

Building a blog that can maintain its value under a new owner

I explain in Chapter 6 that part of the goal of changing the name of my first blog from eMoms at Home to Sparkplugging was to create a blog network that wasn't directly associated with my personal brand. Because my nickname is eMom, eMoms at Home could never be a brand that would be separate from me. That was my first step toward building a blog that could be owned by someone else someday, even though that wasn't my primary goal at the time.

A blog that can be valuable with any writer at the helm needs to meet most, if not all, of the following criteria:

✔ The blog is focused on a mainstream topic, or group of topics.

✔ The blog already has a team of contributing writers.

✔ The blog has an established track record of predictable income.

✔ The blog has an existing readership and consistent high volume of traffic.

Additionally, if your current blog is successful in any of the following ways, it could limit your ability to sell your blog:

✔ **Your blog has a vibrant reader community that is invested in a relationship with the writer.** That means if your blog's readers come to interact with you, or because of you, they probably won't come back to your blog if you sell it to someone else. Additionally, if your readers are more interested in you and your community than in your specific content, they'll probably follow you to wherever you go next.

✔ **Your blog's primary source of income comes from anything except straight advertising, affiliate marketing, or product sales.** Endorsements, blogger-outreach campaigns, spokesperson positions, and integrated social media campaigns can pay very well. But when the campaign relies specifically on your participation, brands are paying to be associated with your personal brand, not with your blog's brand. Personal brands are definitely not transferable. The only income that another person can replicate comes via methods that do not rely on you.

✓ **Your personal brand is very well known and you don't plan on remaining a part of the future of the blog.** When I think of extremely well-known blogs such as Mashable (`http://mashable.com`) and the Huffington Post (`www.huffingtonpost.com`), it's clear that those blogs rely heavily on the star power of Pete Cashmore and Arianna Huffington. The Huffington Post was recently sold, but Arianna is still a part of the company. If she were to leave, the value of her blog would be greatly diminished. If Arianna were to not be a part of the blog under the new ownership, I'm sure she would have had to sell it for far less than the $315 million she actually received.

Knowing when it's time to sell

When I was first approached to sell Sparkplugging, I really wasn't sure I wanted to sell my blog network. I had built the site from the ground up, and it had become very well known in the business-blog community. I had a solid platform with which to get clients, do more professional speaking, get a book deal, or develop and sell my own products. I had a powerful brand in my possession, and I wasn't sure it was such a good idea to let that go. I was quite scared that without it, I could totally and completely fail in my next endeavor. I also really had no idea what I would do with myself if I didn't own Sparkplugging anymore. I didn't have a "next endeavor," and I thought it would be pretty darn foolish to give up what I had without a safety net.

As I considered the idea, I realized that the platform I had built wasn't one that was getting me where I wanted to go. I had set out to build a business that earned revenue from advertising and affiliate income. Sparkplugging wasn't that business. I made some money through these means, but the blog's biggest potential was in getting clients, landing professional speaking gigs, writing a book, or developing my own products. I had to be brutally honest with myself: That was then, and this was later on; I had tried almost all those things, and I *hated* doing them. I didn't want clients. I was tired of the travel required for speaking. And though I enjoyed creating my own products, I hated selling them and dealing with customer-service issues. And back then, I really had no desire to write a book, knowing what a huge amount of work it would be.

The choice became clear — I could continue to work on Sparkplugging, which I finally realized had become a business I didn't want to be in. Or I could risk giving it up for creating the business I really wanted. I chose the latter.

I admit it was a big risk, and that kind of risk isn't for everyone. The payoff, though, was potentially creating what I'd consider *the* perfect business. I look back now on Sparkplugging as the precursor to the biggest success story of my life. Because everything I learned when I ran that business enabled me to start the Woo! Jr. Kids Activities Network that was profitable after less than 30 days.

That's my story of how I knew when it was time to sell. There are many other reasons why a mom blogger would want to sell her blog:

✔ Family circumstances can change; you may not have the time to dedicate to your blog anymore.

✔ You may get burnt out and need a change.

✔ You may get a purchase offer that is too good to pass up.

✔ A better business idea may come along and take priority over your old blog.

No matter why you sell, be prepared for an emotional roller coaster as part of the sales process. Building a blog is a little bit like raising a child. Selling it is like what happens when your child is 18, all grown up, and heading off to college, never to live with you again. Your blog has been a part of you and your life for several years; selling it is a true letting-go process, fully accompanied by tears and a little heartache.

Evaluating your blog's assets

There are some obvious aspects of a blog that would make it valuable to a buyer. Lots of traffic, regular advertisers, and quality content are pretty much the three biggies. But because lots of traffic can be a very relative term, you can do a lot of other things to build value for a future buyer:

✔ **Good search engine rankings:** If your site is on the first page for a very competitive term, you may get offers to purchase your blog based on that alone. It definitely pays to have solid search engine traffic. But you don't want traffic from search engines to be a very high percentage of your overall traffic. That is a risk that most buyers would avoid.

✔ **Solid social media presence:** This doesn't refer to your personal profiles on social networking sites, but to your business profiles, such as a Facebook fan page or a Twitter account just for your business. These are things that prove your readers are engaged with your brand, and will be an asset to any owner.

✔ **Established mailing list or RSS readers:** A large RSS subscriber base is a guaranteed source of traffic and repeat visitors. Mailing lists are even more valuable, and can generally be transferred to new owners. Subscribers are a group of individuals who are invested in your content and have already stated they're open to your marketing initiatives.

✔ **Great domain name:** If your domain name has value by being short, memorable, or having good keywords, this adds value to your Web business.

> If you also bought common misspellings of your domain, this is a bonus, but not likely to affect your sale price.

✔ **Special applications or technical functionality:** If you've invested in having a custom function developed for your site, this is also valuable to a new owner. Examples would be custom plugins, integrated Facebook applications, a job board, or a shopping cart.

✔ **An established membership community or forum:** Active online communities are hard to start and hard to grow. Forums are also very sticky features on a site; they draw visitors back regularly, especially those who view many pages.

When you reach the decision you want to sell your blog someday, you should do everything you can to build up these assets along with your traffic and revenue. That way, when the day comes that you do have an offer, you'll have plenty of advantages working in your favor.

Determining the value of your blog

The most common question I get when people ask about how to sell a blog is "How do I determine the value of my blog?" This can be a very subjective number, especially when you can consider many of the factors described in the previous sections.

The accepted standard you can use to determine a baseline value to work with is as follows:

1. Total the monthly revenue of your blog from ongoing advertising revenue, affiliate revenue, and ongoing product or service sales (such as membership fees, classified ad listings, downloadable purchases, and so on).

    • You can only count revenue that can be earned by anyone. Any consulting fees, personal sponsorships, or opportunities you received because of your blog are not likely going to transfer over with a new owner.

    For example, $500 advertiser revenue + $250 AdSense revenue + $250 in product download sales = $1,000 per month.

    • If your revenue has steadily grown over time, use an average amount from the last three months.

    • If your income fluctuates or is seasonal, you'll have to determine your annual income instead of your monthly income.

2. Multiply the monthly income by 24 to determine two years' revenue.

- For example, $1,000 per month × 24 = $24,000.

  Two years' revenue is a commonly accepted starting point to determine the estimated earnings a buyer can expect after they take over your site, so this calculation assumes it will take them two years for them to break even.

- Of course, a new owner can be expected to work on growing that revenue, so they may break even sooner.

For small sites that change hands between individuals, two years may be too long a time to use in this calculation. In that case, you may only get 12–18 months' worth of income. When the economy is great and you have multiple parties interested in buying your blog, you may get three or four years' worth of income.

And again, this is a starting point. If you have a mailing list with 100,000 subscribers, have a sophisticated application up and running, or you've lucked into a highly coveted domain name, you have a lot more negotiating room beyond just your blog's monthly income.

Finding a buyer for your blog

Ironically, I've never had to go out and find a buyer for a blog. All my potential buyers — and my actual buyer — came to me. But I already knew most of these people, so consider this just one more time in the book that I point out how important it is to be constantly networking. One prospective buyer approached me blindly through my website contact form, and I didn't pursue it because I didn't want to sell the site to someone I didn't know. One of the things I realized was that I really cared deeply about who would take over Sparkplugging, and would even take a lower offer if it meant that I knew the site would be well cared for, or could ensure the new owners wouldn't use my site for spamming or scamming purposes. Today there is also a website called Flippa (`https://flippa.com`), which is a marketplace just for people who want to buy and sell websites.

When you find a potential buyer, the time from initial conversation to actual purchase can take weeks or months. A buyer will have to do due diligence and ensure that all your stated traffic and income figures are indeed accurate. Plus, the negotiating process is not easy — and for many people it can be quite humbling. Most people think their business is worth more than it really is — and I was guilty of that as well. If I could have sold my site to myself . . . well, I could have commanded quite a sum, and I might not have been able to afford me, so to speak. But again, that's because Sparkplugging was worth more to me than it was to anyone else on the planet.

Because every transaction is different, there's no way to predict the pitfalls you may face in the sale of your own blog. But here are the things I learned during the sale of mine:

- ✔ **Steer clear of revenue-sharing deals.** The first buyer I talked to wanted to give me very little money up front, but give me a healthy percentage of the profits earned. There are two glaring problems with this approach:

  - Once the site was sold, it was out of my control. I would not be able to have any influence over the profitability of the site.

  - If there was very little upfront investment, potential buyers could feel they'd have little to lose by walking away from the project if they got too busy or their business plan didn't work out on the first try.

- ✔ **Be wary of extending a payment plan.** Unless you know your buyer has great credit, I suggest not allowing the buyer to pay you over time. At the very least, minimize the payment period to a short time frame, such as six months. Circumstances can change too easily — and you could either be out the remainder of your payments, or have to go to court to collect them. Neither of those is a very fun option.

- ✔ **Make sure your advertisers will allow you to transfer the sale of your blog.** Some ad networks will not let new owners of a site be a part of their network. I've heard of one ad network that will not even allow you to sell your site without giving the network the first right of refusal. If you work with your advertisers directly, be sure to discuss the sale with them before the sale is finalized. If you're worried about information leaking before the deal is done, you can ask the ad network to sign a Non-Disclosure Agreement (NDA) to keep the potential sale of your site confidential.

- ✔ **You might be asked to sign a *non-compete agreement*.** A non-compete agreement generally prevents you from starting up another website that would compete directly with the site you just sold for a certain length of time. Personally, I think this is a totally fair request, especially because if you want to sell a site, why would you want to turn right around and do the same thing again?

You *must* have a lawyer review your sales contract. There are plenty of legal loopholes you would never know to look for. A friend of mine sold her coffee shop to a new owner who decided to stop paying rent on the shop. There was an overlooked technicality in the wording of the contract, and my friend was stuck with a $50,000 bill for past-due rent on a shop she didn't own anymore. I would never trust anyone but a lawyer with the technicalities of legal liabilities in the transfer of a business ownership. Even the word *liability* scares me!

Chapter 16

Exploring the Ways You Can Expand Your Reach

In This Chapter

▶ Growing your blog into an online magazine by starting a blog network

▶ Building a forum or community as an extension of your blog

▶ Developing multimedia content to reach a new audience

▶ Getting a book deal

*A*t some point in your blogging career, you probably will want to find ways to grow your business in new ways. You can do a lot of things to take your blog to the next level, such as build a blog network, create a community, add multimedia content, or publish a book (or maybe move on from your blog to a new job). I describe all these ways to take your blog to the next level in this chapter. All these things are closely related to blogging, but do require a pretty different skill set. You may experience a learning curve, but I share some tips on how to handle that, too.

Most of these ideas involve a rather big undertaking, requiring many hours of work *on top of* the hours you spend blogging already. So I do recommend waiting until you have a blogging work schedule firmly in place and have been established for a while, so you aren't struggling with an existing blog while trying to start a new project as well. I also recommend waiting until you're in a position to coast for a while financially before you take on these projects. When you do dive in, you probably won't have time for several weeks or months to increase your income in other ways.

I can say with certainty that while these projects are challenging, there are great rewards to be had as well. Over time, they can have significant positive impact on your career. Expanding your blog may mean increasing your traffic, getting in front of a whole new group of readers, or opening doors to opportunities you might not otherwise ever have had the chance to pursue.

Building a Blog Network

After building two blog networks, this is a topic I know quite a bit about. If you want to expand your blog into a blog network, it will take a significant investment of time and some money to find success with it. Several aspects of running a blog network are quite different from running just one blog, the most important of which are

- ✔ **Technological challenges:** Building and maintaining a set of blogs is a *big* undertaking; even if you could do the job yourself, you might not want to. You'll need to decide whether you want to create separate websites, or to build multiple blogs on one website. You'll need to create a consistent design across all your blogs that also allows them to be distinguished from each other. Ensuring readers can easily find what they are looking for over multiple blogs presents site navigation challenges such as how to create a search function that includes all the blogs in your network.

    Maintaining multiple blogs can get out of hand fast when all of them need updating at the same time. If you're on WordPress, that may mean you have to update hundreds of plugins all at once instead of just one set for one blog. You'll also need a way to track revenue across each blog individually, so you know which blogs are making money and whether any are losing money. You might also need to set up your blogs on a dedicated hosting server, because multiple blogs pull far more resources from a Web host than just one.

    This is when I strongly suggest consulting with a very experienced developer who can understand all your blog network requirements and offer the best possible solution for you. You'll want to ensure that you minimize any possible duplication of maintenance tasks, while maximizing usability and functionality.

- ✔ **Marketing challenges:** After I launched my first blog network, I pretty much went through a six-week panic attack as I realized what I'd gotten myself into. I knew a lot about marketing my own blog, and I assumed that I could use those same techniques to market all my blogs. I was wrong. Even though all the blogs were on closely related topics, they all had to be promoted in very different ways.

    Additionally, even if what you've learned about promoting yourself and your blog has taken you very far, it's likely that you'll need a higher level of marketing strategy to promote a blog *network*. Bigger businesses need bigger marketing campaigns in order to make a difference. You can't rely on simple word of mouth and good traffic from social media sites in order to grow. You'll probably need to advertise, do much more social media marketing, increase your PR workload, and learn much more advanced search engine optimization strategies.

✔ **Personnel challenges:** A client of mine asked how I hired writers and ensured that they stuck with me. I told her I didn't. I never planned on having any of my writers work with me forever, because I knew they would all outgrow working for me someday. If I found someone who wanted to continue to write for me for a very long time, I considered myself lucky and blessed. As a Web publisher, you need to plan on *heavy turnover* with your writers: They'll come and they'll go. So you'll need to have a backup plan when one of your blogs doesn't have a writer, taking into account that it may take you several weeks to find a new one.

On top of this, you'll have to deal with regular managerial issues — say, when a writer gets sick, when the content you're getting isn't up to par, when someone doesn't feel like writing, and when writers do things they aren't supposed to do. Once a person writes for you, their actions can reflect on you, so you need to ensure you have clear writer guidelines that state what writers can and can't do when they're blogging for you.

In Chapter 15, I also talk about some of the challenges you may face while hiring (or firing) writers, and some of the copyright issues you'll need to address when you're publishing someone else's work. (Yep. Barrels of fun.) It's no wonder I try to do a lot of the writing for my blog network all by myself.

✔ **Time management challenges:** In case you haven't figured it out by all the things I just talked about, running a blog network is a lot of work, sometimes in ways you can't expect or prepare for. And realistically, it's pretty difficult to undo things if you find that running a blog network is not for you.

In other words, if you're going to launch a blog network, you need to be in it for the long haul and go all out, as they say.

Exploring the benefits of different kinds of blog networks

I mention in the previous section that you face a lot of technical challenges in setting up your blog network. There are also many ways to set one up. Technically, a *blog network* is a group of blogs working together to build traffic and revenue. So in some cases, a blog network could be as simple as a loosely associated group of bloggers who promote each other or sell advertising together. This is how the Double Duty Divas blog network (www.doubledutydivas.com) got started in 2010 by Cecelia Mecca and Bridgette Duplantis. They now boast a membership of over 300 individually owned and operated blogs that pool their resources to attract advertisers and grow traffic.

B5Media (www.b5media.com) is one of the older blog networks around, and has gone through several different structures over the years. Early on, the network established multiple blogs on different websites and hired writers to write on the blogs. Some of the blogs were also started by others, joining the network with the condition that they could leave again someday should the need arise. After a while, B5Media began to group the blogs into related topics, selling advertising on the blogs as a group. Through some management changes, B5Media decided to change its format altogether. Today, it has merged each group of blogs into just a few multi-blog sites. The changes were due to many factors, mostly making them easier to maintain and to consolidate their content into fewer domains. From the viewpoint of search engine optimization, this is positive — there are more links pointing to just one domain, instead of to 5–20 domains.

For Sparkplugging, I decided to build several blogs all on one domain, mostly for the same reasons that B5Media evolved into more consolidated websites. Doing so made it easy to make updates across all the blogs at once — and it built up Sparkplugging as a brand, rather than as a group of brands. The benefits to this setup are great, but there are some drawbacks, too. A great example is how my Woo! Jr. Kids Activities blog network is set up: It's on five domains, each with a separate name, all of them tied together with a hub site. Having sites focused on narrower topics make them easier to market to the most appropriate audience for each one. The readers of my Classroom Jr. blog are pretty different from my Craft Jr. readers, though there is a little overlap between the two. Additionally, if you have a technical problem with one of your blogs, it doesn't affect all of them. In a recent Google update, two of my websites lost a little bit of search engine traffic and two others gained traffic. Had they all been on one domain, all my sites could have lost traffic.

There really is no one answer that's right or wrong. You'll need to decide on a structure that's right for you, based on all these factors. I encourage you to look carefully at existing blog networks and note what you like and dislike about each of them. Ultimately, you'll be able to put together a plan that combines all the elements you think will bring you the best chance for success.

Finding new topics in your niche

If you're expanding by adding blogs to your existing blog, or by putting together a new group of blogs, be sure you continue to focus on a niche, just as I encourage you to do with a single blog. This way, even though you may be marketing each of your blogs differently, you'll attract readers who are interested in all of your content, not just some of it. Almost half the traffic on my blogs comes from other blogs in my network, so you can readily understand why it's beneficial to know who your audience is — and give them the content they want.

Every blog I've ever started began as an idea hatched in a previous blog post. When I chose the first group of blogs to add on Sparkplugging, I analyzed my existing content to see what got the most traffic or response from readers. Some of my slightly off-topic blog posts were surprise hits, and it didn't make sense for me to expand my own blog to cover these other topics. I also looked at the keywords people were using to find my site to identify content that I hadn't written very much about. Lastly, I made some educated guesses. Because I was writing about being self-employed and running an Internet business, it made sense that my readers would also be interested in a blog focused on freelancing, eBay selling, and selling crafts online. Those guesses weren't always accurate, but I was right about my hunches about 75 percent of the time.

Mostly, when expanding into multiple blogs, you really need to build on things that are already working for you. I wrote a blog post in desperation one summer day, with 101 kids' activities for work-at-home parents, mostly because I needed a go-to list to find things for my kids to do while I worked. I wasn't sure people would really appreciate it very much, but it became one of my all-time most popular posts. That led me to add a kids' activities blog to Sparkplugging — and that, in turn, led to my starting a whole new blog network on the subject. When you find a recipe for success, it makes sense to continue to use that recipe as much as possible.

Adding a Forum or Community

If you have a blog with a very connected community of readers, you may want to consider adding a forum or member community. For this section, I just call any section of a blog that has conversation threads and requires membership a *forum* for simplicity.

Done right, forums are an extremely valuable addition to a blog, because they attract large volumes of repeat visitors who spend a significant amount of time on your site. This can greatly increase your traffic and page views, which translates to more advertising revenue. Forums also create a significant amount of *user-generated content,* which means your site visitors are creating content for you. Ree Drummond has a large member community called Tasty Kitchen (`http://thepioneerwoman.com/tasty-kitchen`); Heather Armstrong also has a member community on her blog Dooce (`http://community.dooce.com`). You can see them in Figures 16-1 and 16-2.

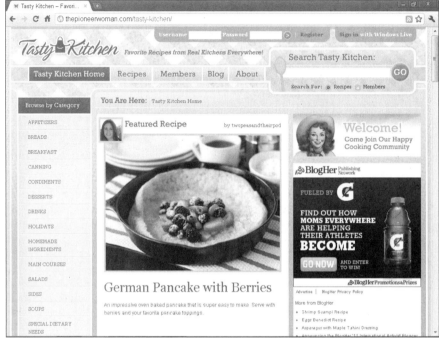

Figure 16-1:
The Tasty
Kitchen
community
on The
Pioneer
Woman
blog.

Figure 16-2:
The Dooce
community.

Keep in mind, however, that forums require a lot of work to maintain — and they are not the best feature for everyone. You'll need to set up software such as phpBB or vBulletin forums or a more recent option such as the BuddyPress add-on for WordPress. Getting a forum set up is fairly easy — it's similar to setting up a self-hosted WordPress blog. But customizing a forum is a little trickier; either you'll need to hire a developer or learn how to do it yourself — fast — to get your community to look and function the way you want it to.

Just because you have an active community doesn't mean that a forum will be successful automatically. You'll still have to promote it, participate, actively work on adding members, and foster conversations to get it established. Additionally, forums need to be constantly and actively monitored with moderators. This is to ensure that conversations remain on topic, spammers don't post unwelcome messages, that inappropriate content doesn't appear, and that disagreements between members don't erupt into senseless arguments (known as *flame wars* on the Internet).

For more about how to set up and grow an online community, I highly recommend *Managing Online Forums* by Patrick O'Keefe (AMACOM) or the soon-to-be-published *Online Community Management For Dummies* by Deborah Ng. (Both authors are friends, and they really know their stuff.)

Developing Multimedia Content

There are a lot of benefits to creating content beyond the written word. People have different preferences as to how they get their information. My husband (for example) wouldn't pick up a book or read a blog to save his life, but listens to talk radio and music constantly. I, on the other hand, can probably count the number of podcasts I've listened to on one hand. But I am an avid reader and watch plenty of video content.

A big benefit to developing multimedia content is that you have the opportunity to get your message in front of a completely different audience from the one your blog attracts. iTunes and YouTube have their own massive audiences who might never find your blog any other way.

Because this is not an area of expertise for me, I interviewed two amazing mom bloggers who are also podcasting and videoblogging pioneers, Kelly McCausey and Danielle Smith.

Amplifying your blog with a podcast

Kelly McCausey started the very first work-at-home-mom podcast in November 2003, and I've heard her frequently say, "Podcasting *made* me."

Although Kelly was an early adopter, it has been her consistency and perseverance that has really brought her success. As of early 2011, she has created over 325 episodes, and both her readership and number of listeners continues to grow.

At the beginning, Kelly used her podcast to establish herself as an expert and worked with a few advertisers who stuck with her for many years. Today Kelly doesn't accept advertising, but instead can promote her own products and services as a part of her show. Because Kelly is a WAHM (work-at-home-mom) coach and her products are *for* work-at-home moms as well, the podcast has given her substantial credibility and has set her apart from others selling similar products. (See Figure 16-3.)

Kelly's podcasting tips for success follow:

- **Market your podcast the same way you promote your blog.** Twitter and Facebook are just as important for this medium as they are for any other.

- **Experiment with show length.** When she first started, she was creating shows much longer than they needed to be, and has now settled into a shorter and more successful show length ranging between 40 and 60 minutes. I know several other podcasters who feel their optimum show length is about 20 minutes.

- **Optimize your podcasts for search engines.** Kelly posts every show with a write-up of the names of guests, a show guide, show highlights, and links to resources mentioned in the episode. Because search engines can't listen and index a podcast, it's important to put this information into writing so listeners can find your content.

- **Best podcasting tools.** BlogTalkRadio (www.blogtalkradio.com) is best for live podcasting. If you're going to record and edit your podcasts, Kelly recommends using Skype (www.skype.com) for clear-sounding interviews, Pamela (www.pamela.biz/en) for recording, and Audacity (http://audacity.sourceforge.net) for sound editing.

- **Establish a presence on iTunes.** iTunes can bring in 20 percent to 50 percent of your new listeners, because iTunes users actively seek out new audio content to download.

- **Tap opportunities that are unique to podcasting.** Kelly says there's still plenty of room to be a big fish in a small pond in the podcasting world, because fewer people develop good podcast content. It takes a lot of work and time to develop a regular audio show, and it can open doors that blogging alone can't do because you have a whole other content channel to distribute content through.

Figure 16-3:
Podcasting
expert Kelly
McCausey's
blog.

✔ **How to find advertisers.** Finding sponsors for your podcasts is the same as finding sponsors for your blog. The fact that an advertiser can reach both your readers and your listeners is definitely an extra value for them, so it would benefit you to create various advertising packages to promote both your podcast and your blog.

Additionally, some people are great talkers, but not such great writers. Podcasting offers a medium that's better suited to these individuals (who might not even be blogging otherwise).

Kelly can be found at www.kellymccausey.com, where she has even more resources for aspiring podcasters and work-at-home moms. You can see her website in Figure 16-3.

Enhancing your blog with video

Danielle Smith started her career as a television anchorwoman and has always been at ease in front of a camera. She also has been creating video content for three of the three-and-a-half years she's been blogging. She has worked hard to establish herself as an expert on video content, and that work has paid off. In 2010, Procter & Gamble hired her to be a videoblogging correspondent for the Vancouver Olympics. She has also created video content for clients such as ConAgra, Fisher-Price, Huggies, and Kraft Foods.

Danielle refers to videoblogging as "storytelling" or "show and tell." She notes that brands pay very close attention to how moms create content and communicate online — and (as Kelly says about podcasting) they're aware that video can absolutely help you stand out from the crowd. She also says that viewers get to know you better than when they just read your content. Your mannerisms, tone, style, and appearance allow people to understand you and your message more completely than via the written word. (See Figure 16-4.)

Danielle's tips for videoblogging success follow:

- ✔ **Pay attention to video quality.** She says you don't have to have an expensive camera, but it helps. Lighting and sound quality are really critical components that can make or break a video.

- ✔ **Pretend you're talking to a friend.** When you look into the camera, don't talk into it as if you're talking to an audience; talk like you would talk to a friend. It's okay to look away from the camera momentarily, like you would in a normal conversation, but keep eye contact as much as possible.

- ✔ **Watch yourself and get critiqued.** You may not realize that your speaking or presenting habits could use some freshening up until you actually see yourself in action. For example: *um, ah, so,* and *okay* are fine now and then, but can quickly become irritating if you say them too frequently. Have friends watch your videos before you put them online and give you feedback on the points you may miss on your own.

- ✔ **You don't have to be on camera all the time.** For those of you who are nervous in front of a camera, Danielle suggests starting out by filming the things around you and doing a voiceover instead. This gets you comfortable with the editing-and-production process and builds your confidence to get in front of the camera.

- ✔ **Tap the power of YouTube.** Use YouTube to market your videos the way you'd market your blog to other bloggers. Comment on others' videos, title and tag your videos with appropriate keywords and descriptive text, and use YouTube's video-response feature to interact with other videobloggers.

- ✔ **Use the best free or low-cost videoblogging tools.** Danielle recommends the easiest, free tools that already are on your computer: Windows Movie Maker for Windows machines and iMovie for Mac machines.

- ✔ **How to find advertisers.** Because of her expertise, Danielle mostly does custom video for clients and doesn't work with many advertisers in her video work. But on YouTube, she says that if you can build up enough video views, you can apply to join the AdSense for Video program at `www.google.com/ads/videoadsolutions/publisher.html`.

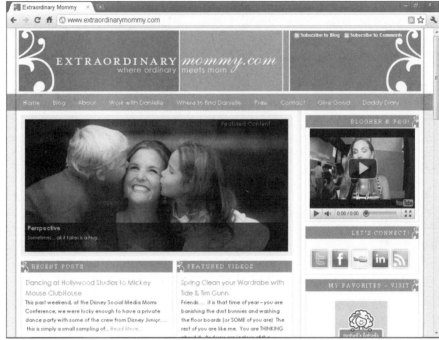

Figure 16-4:
Video-
blogging
expert
Danielle
Smith's
blog, Extra-
ordinary
Mommy.

Danielle Smith can be found at `www.extraordinarymommy.com`, and at
`http://youtube.com/extraordinarymommy`. You can see her website in
Figure 16-4.

Landing a Book Deal

Blogging is one of the best ways to get a book deal and is also the very best
way to prepare for writing a book as well. I can say from experience that
both blog-writing and book-writing take an incredible amount of work and
discipline, probably more than you might imagine. At the BlogHer conference
in 2007, I saw Gina Trapani speak on writing her LifeHacker book that had
just been published. I had imagined that writing a book was a pretty glamor-
ous deal that earned writers quite a bit of money. Gina gave her session
participants a dose of reality:

> ✔ **You don't write a book for the money; you write it to build your plat-
> form.** I think I almost fell off my chair when she said this. I had always
> thought of writing books as an end goal. Gina made it clear that books
> are much more frequently used as a means to an end — to get clients,
> jobs, or publicity.

✔ **You may or may not get a book advance.** If you get an advance, it's only against book sales. That means you have to sell a lot of copies to earn anything on top of your advance.

✔ **A publisher won't really market your book for you.** I was so surprised to learn this — it's pretty much up to the book author to do all the marketing and promotion for the book. You may get a little bit of help and guidance from your publisher, but sales fall on your shoulders.

✔ **Writing a book is way different from writing a blog.** Writing a long-form book is far different from writing short-form blog posts. It also takes discipline above and beyond what it takes to write for a blog.

✔ **Writing a book is a full-time job.** She was so right. I knew that writing a book would be a lot of hard work, especially because I would have to continue working on my business full time. But I didn't think it would be like working *two* full-time jobs for several months in a row!

So, if you're still interested in writing a book, keep reading — and make sure you're ready before you jump into it. Ironically, after I heard Gina Trapani's advice, I decided (at that time, anyway) that writing a book wasn't for me. At all. I met someone from Wiley publishing in 2008, but I waited almost three years until I was ready to take on the challenge of writing a book. Now that I know what's involved, I'm so glad I waited. Having a steady income from my blog made it much easier to cut back on my working hours so I could fill up my schedule with book-writing and promotion.

Understanding what publishers are looking for

When I signed my own book deal to write *Mom Blogging For Dummies,* I had an idea of what a publisher was looking for when they chose which authors to work with, but I didn't know the specifics. Was there some magic formula that editors used to know when to hire one writer and reject the next? So I asked Connie Santisteban, Associate Editor of General Interest Books with John Wiley & Sons for her input.

Connie confirmed my number-one expectation of what a publisher is really looking for — an author who has a sizable and dedicated readership and who also has a great book idea. I asked what she does when she comes across authors who have a killer book idea but don't really have a following. She explained that not having a built-in audience makes it very difficult for your book to compete against other books in the marketplace. She has done it successfully in the past, but only when the book caters to a very specific, well-defined niche that's generally underserved in the book marketplace. I loved that she said this, because it reinforces (again!) just how important it is to carve out your niche and *own* it.

I had assumed that Connie's job mostly consisted of sifting through book proposals that are submitted to her for review. Interestingly, she spends far more time hunting down bloggers and writers with an established readership in the hopes she can successfully pitch the idea of writing a book *to them*. As she evaluates potential authors, she looks at a lot of metrics to gauge a writer's influence among peers, such as RSS subscribers, Twitter followers, site traffic, number of Likes for an article you've written that's posted to Facebook, or number of votes it receives on sites such as Digg or Reddit, and whether or not your site has a robust community of commenters.

Ultimately, an editor has to prove to the publishing company that a book he or she wants to publish with an author is one that can turn a profit. A book can only be successful if readers know how to find it, so authors have to be extremely proactive about promoting the book when it hits the shelves.

Developing a book idea as an extension of your blog

Because Connie made it clear that a book is likely to be most successful when an author has an engaged audience, it stands to reason that your audience is going to expect that any book you write is similar to your blog — a familiar approach to a familiar topic. It would be much harder for (say) a business blogger to write and promote a craft book than it would be for a craft blogger to do so. Your readers have come to enjoy your voice, your ideas, and the topics you already write about. So if they want to buy your book, they'll want more of that.

At the same time, keep in mind that they'll want new stuff. You can't really take all your past blog posts and just repackage them as a book. Your readers would likely feel a little betrayed that they paid for a book when they could have read the same content for free on your blog. So any book you write can be based on your blog content — but really *must* add value above and beyond what you've already published online.

Some authors have mixed previously published blog content with new content in their blogging books. The idea is to provide the people who haven't yet read their blogs with some benefit from the older material, and it seems a little easier to pull a book together if you don't have to write the entire thing from scratch. It may sound okay, but let me point out a cause for concern: I've seen several poor book reviews written on Amazon by blog readers who felt that the new material in a book wasn't enough to justify purchasing the book. (Ouch.) Finding a balance between building on your existing content and creating a new body of work can be tough. But no matter how you pull a book together, it should still be based on the same topic as your blog. Otherwise the benefits you get from having a following are negated by writing a book that your readers might not be interested in buying and reading.

Pitching a book idea to a publisher

In the fall of 2010, Wiley was at the BlogWorld Expo conference in Las Vegas and ended up signing book deals with over ten bloggers they talked to at the show. In my experience, and that of a few other people I know who were a part of this group, the bloggers didn't specifically come to Wiley with a book idea ready to roll. Instead, Wiley saw the potential in this group of authors, and then worked with each one of them to help develop a book idea based on each writer's strengths — and on what they knew could be a good, marketable book for their customers.

If you have a book you want to write, but you don't have an established audience, you can greatly increase your chances of getting a publisher to say yes to you by taking a year to get an established presence online. You can also find a book agent who will work with you to present your idea to several publishers. Agents are far more experienced in selling book ideas than the rest of us, and this may be a great route to take. Some publishers will only work with agents and not with authors directly — so if you're dead set on getting that book deal, getting an agent will certainly increase your chances. The trade-off is that a portion of the earnings you receive from your book goes to the agent for setting up the book deal.

Putting together a formal book proposal for a publisher is a pretty big undertaking, and many editors will even help you with it. This is because the editors need to take your book proposal and their market research and pitch the entire idea — on your behalf — to their companies. If you can get to this point of working with an editor to draw up a formal proposal, that means your editor believes you have a strong chance of moving forward with writing the book. But only when the editor gets the final approval from the top decision-makers can he or she officially offer you a book deal.

Knowing everything that I know now about getting published, if I were to start from scratch all over again, these are the things I would do to pitch a book idea to a publisher:

1. Establish a blog and focus on writing really high-quality content that showcases your expertise, and target your content to a very specific audience.

2. Promote your blog and get very involved in the community of bloggers who also write about your topic.

3. Build a strong presence on Facebook and Twitter.

4. Network like crazy — both online and offline at industry events.

5. Develop a book idea based on

- What you want most to write about

- What your readers know you for

- What you know your readers would be interested in learning more about

- How you would differentiate your book from the existing books on the same subject

6. Look at books already written on this subject and determine which publishers have experience with putting out books on the subject.

7. Reach out to the editors who work for these publishers via e-mail, phone, or their social media profiles.

8. Write a short, one-page introduction explaining who you are, what book you want to write, and why you're the one to write it.

Highlight your accomplishments, press coverage, your blog's traffic stats, and your friends and followers on Facebook and Twitter. If you really want to go for the jugular, let the editor know about how you plan on marketing the book once it's published.

If you really do have a following and a great book idea, it will only be a matter of time before that book gets published. If you get any initial rejection letters, your best bet is to spend your time working on getting more established as a blogger and building a stronger community around your content. As Connie said, she spends most of her time looking for people who go through a process just like this to prepare for writing a book.

Getting a Job

Okay, I know that getting a job isn't truly an expansion of your blog, but think of it as more of an expansion of your *career*. I've watched several bloggers, moms included, build up so much trust and credibility in social media that companies have hired them to fill some great social media marketing and other management positions. When you have a track record to prove results for yourself or for freelance clients, a company knows that hiring you is a low risk with high rewards.

There's another reason this section of the chapter is near and dear to my heart: I know firsthand what it's like to choose to put your career on hold (or in slow motion) to raise a family. When your children are older, it can be *extremely* challenging to re-enter the workforce if your skills have become out of date. In a poor economy, it can be next to impossible to prove you're qualified for a position at the same level as the one you occupied when you left. Usually, that means moms need to step down their job expectations and prove their qualifications all over again. This is a hard, intimidating task, and it can be downright demeaning.

Blogging is an *ideal* way to ramp up your professional experience and networking efforts to prepare yourself to get hired again — for the following reasons:

- ✔ Your blog will show off your talent and smarts.
- ✔ Starting a blog and marketing it will add skills to your repertoire or refresh marketing skills you already had.
- ✔ Blogging gets your name out there in front of potential employers.
- ✔ Your blog posts on your areas of expertise will get found in search engines by companies and peers.
- ✔ The networking that you do as a part of blogging will constantly put you in touch with people who may be hiring.
- ✔ The longer you blog, the longer you have a new professional track record building up.
- ✔ The successes and results you can achieve for your own blog can be turned into case studies that you can use to showcase your experience.

Even if you aren't returning to the workforce after a break, a blog is still a powerful tool for getting hired. This is especially true as social media marketing becomes more widely used by both large and small companies. Your experience with promoting a blog and using Facebook and Twitter as marketing tools gives you some highly sought-after skills that companies and ad agencies know they need. Companies that market to moms consider it a serious advantage to hire people with direct experience working *with* moms in the social media space.

Often small projects can lead to bigger opportunities. So I encourage you to read Chapter 8 and use your blog to find short-term or freelance projects with the kinds of companies you hope to work for. If you can prove that you can deliver results and are easy and fun to work with, those companies will come back to you when it comes time to add a member to their teams.

Part V
The Part of Tens

The 5th Wave   By Rich Tennant

"I'm sorry Mr. Garret, a 35 year old tattoo doesn't qualify as a legal trademark for 'Mother.com.'"

In this part . . .

This is where I get to share two very important Top Ten lists.

The first one is a parade of mistakes you don't want to make. How do I know you don't want to make them? Let's just say I've been there, done that.

The second list profiles ten mom bloggers who are making a **substantial** living with their blogs — many of them make over six figures. I also show you exactly how their blogs earn money so you can see how all the information in this book works in the real world!

Chapter 17

Ten Blogging Mistakes to Avoid

*T*alking about blogging mistakes is kind of fun, because I get to share with you some of my more embarrassing moments on my road to success. Even though blogging has been part of mainstream media for over seven years, in many ways I consider blogging still in the Wild Wild West stage of the evolution of the industry. There are still clashes between traditional journalism and the new media information world. There are still big disagreements about what truly constitute best practices. That means not only have a lot of mistakes been made, but many more will be made for many years to come.

In this chapter, I show you some of the big mistakes I've made or seen others make that had an actual impact on how successful a blog (and the blogger) could be. Sure, you can make a template change that causes you to start your blog design from scratch again, but that kind of thing isn't going to keep you from your goals. Additionally, all these mistakes, if caught and corrected, won't hold you back in the long term. But if allowed to persist, these mistakes will not only hold you back, but could also put your blog out of business.

Not Asking for What You Want

Most blogs are a business of one, which means you're the only one who can stand up for yourself and go after the things you need in order to make your blog successful. That doesn't mean you don't have any support — the folks in the mom-blogging community are extremely supportive of each other.

Part of the problem of not asking for what you want is that you might not know what you want nor know what's appropriate to ask for. Other times, bloggers undervalue what they offer and sell themselves short. This was one of the bigger reasons I wanted to write this book: to give mom bloggers the tools they needed to make smart and empowering decisions that will end up helping the entire mom-blogging community.

At the BlogWorld Expo in 2008, I heard something in a panel presentation that forever changed how I perceived my own value and that of other mom bloggers. The panelist stated that in the corporate and agency world, it's easier to get approval to spend $20,000 than it is to spend $200 on a campaign. In the world of big players and big budgets, a $200 blogger campaign isn't perceived as a serious and viable marketing initiative. The ad execs don't yet value that blogger's work as something that could possibly deliver the high-value results they need to deliver for management. It would cost them far more than $200 in hourly wages to manage the project in the first place.

That doesn't mean you should increase all your rates by 10,000 percent. It means that if you know you can deliver real value to a company or brand — value that will affect its bottom line — then you should charge what you're worth. This usually means going way outside your comfort zone. Unfortunately, the very nature of going outside your comfort zone means you'll be . . . well . . . extremely uncomfortable. But here are some ways I cope with feeling completely out of my element:

- ✔ **Talk it out:** The doubting voices in your head sound a lot less valid when voiced.

- ✔ **Accept where you are:** It's natural that being outside your comfort zone doesn't feel good — so feeling scared, insecure, or full of self-doubt doesn't necessarily mean that something is wrong.

- ✔ **Trust yourself:** If you *really* get off track, you'll know. Really.

- ✔ **Remind yourself of the positives:** No matter how hard it is to think positively, you really have to just commit to doing that. "Fake it Till You Make It" really does work. Also, now would be a really good time to recap your accomplishments to yourself.

- ✔ **Don't give in to your fears:** If you've gotten this far, you already know that following your fears is a bad move, so don't start now.

- ✔ **Failure is always an option:** Nobody ever did anything great without taking a risk. The greatest successes never come on the first try.

Pursuing Fame for Fame's Sake

I cover the topic of striving for fame in Chapter 4, but it's such a potential red herring that it needs to be included here too. When really successful mom bloggers appear on TV, in magazines, or are mentioned in the *New York Times,* that level of media coverage seems to be all a blogger needs to ensure success. When that many people see you in the national spotlight, you naturally assume that it means traffic will roll in, advertisers will line up, and publishers will fight over who gets the book deal with you. Well . . . The reality is that the traffic comes when you're on TV, and the next day it's gone. Advertisers rarely — if ever — come knocking on anyone's door (even the largest Internet media property, Yahoo!, still needs a sales team). And if you really have what it takes to get a great book deal, you'll get it whether or not you've appeared on the *Today Show.*

It takes a lot of time and energy to become Internet-famous. It takes even more time and energy to *stay* Internet-famous. Pursuing publicity for yourself and your blog can be a full-time job, and publicity doesn't pay the bills. Only a strong and active business model can do that.

Publicity is something to pursue only *after* you have something to sell. That "something" may be your own products, your own services, or advertising and sponsorships. You must have a goal — and be able to get something tangible out of getting your message in front of thousands (or millions) of people. Publicity will certainly help to build awareness of your blog, but if you don't have existing advertisers or a product to offer, all those people may come to your blog, but then they'll go, leaving nothing behind. Make sure your blogging business model is in place before you take the time and effort to publicize yourself. Otherwise you have a horse with no cart to pull.

Using Your Blog as a Weapon

There's a fine line between voicing valid complaints or criticisms and using your blog as a weapon. I talk about some real examples of blogging influence gone wrong in Chapter 10, and I think we can all agree that extorting or black-mailing anyone — or even the threat of it — is absolutely wrong and has no place in the world of professional blogging.

Nor do I think it appropriate to use your blog as a tool for revenge. Just because a big appliance brand delivered the wrong refrigerator to you doesn't mean you should write vicious blog posts about the company in hopes that your readers will stop buying that brand. Every company makes simple mistakes and doesn't deserve a dose of horrible PR and an angry mob without being given the chance to make it right.

This is where the gray area appears — what if the company had the chance to make things right, and yet it continued to blow it? What if its customer service continually overpromised and underdelivered? What if you've found evidence that this isn't an isolated episode, but a systemic problem within a company that's truly affecting its customers in a negative way?

I know people who have voiced these kinds of complaints on their blogs or on social networks. And I know people who have threatened to voice their complaints in the hopes that the company does the right thing rather than deal with the bad PR. When is it acceptable to call a brand or a person out for negative behavior? That's a hard one. Because this is a very personal decision, here are some questions to seriously consider before taking such drastic action:

✔ **How will this affect my personal brand?** Consider whether writing a critical post is congruent with your personal brand. You have to decide whether you want to be known for calling people out on their incongruent behavior. Also consider that if your brand usually focuses on the positive side of things, your readers might view you differently if you write this kind of negative blog post.

✔ **Is the company/person active online and in social media?** If not, you need to decide whether it's fair to voice your complaints in a medium where you clearly have the upper hand.

✔ **Will my blog post *really* help protect other consumers?** If your intentions are to honestly warn your readers, consider whether there are other ways you can achieve this goal without writing negative things.

✔ **Am I willing to have this blog post published forever?** After you publish your post, there's no turning back. Even if you delete the post, it will live on in Internet archives permanently.

✔ **Am I sure there will be no legal consequences to my actions?** Big companies have big legal departments. If any part of what you write isn't strictly the truth, you could be sued for libel.

✔ **Could this complaint backfire on me?** There are hundreds of ways this kind of situation could backfire on you. You could experience backlash from other bloggers, reduce the level of trust people have in you, or become the target of attacks yourself. This is especially true when your problem is with another person instead of with a company — when there's inevitably another side to the story that may ultimately get more attention than yours.

Becoming a 24/7 Infomercial

When I was struggling to figure out how to make money from my blog, I was willing to try just about anything as long as it was ethical. The longer my blog went without earning much money, the more desperate I got to find a solid source of revenue. I felt as though I couldn't turn down any legitimate opportunity that came my way.

As my readership grew, more opportunities did come my way — so, instead of blogging more about business advice, I wound up blogging more and more about products and services for business owners. In theory, this was absolutely fine — I took on projects with companies that had good reputations and relevance to my industry, and I was writing honest, thoughtful posts full of my own opinions.

The problem was that my readers were used to my business advice as my primary content, and that was why they came to my blog over and over again. As I started to post less of the content that my readers wanted most, traffic started to dip.

This isn't an uncommon problem, and the way many bloggers have fixed it is to create a second blog just for reviews and product features. This solution is great for readers, but unfortunately, isn't as attractive to advertisers. They know that your regular readers won't pay as much attention to a review blog, which functions much like a television channel that shows commercials 24 hours a day, 7 days a week.

Yet there really are many product-and-review blogs that are well done and are very successful. These blogs have a few things in common that make them work well:

- ✔ **They are extremely picky about the products they choose to write about:** Great product blogs don't review every product they receive. They instead choose high-quality, relevant products that they know will appeal to their readers. They probably turn down more products than they actually write about.

- ✔ **They write engaging content:** Reviews can be informational and trustworthy, but they can also be boring to read. Great reviews are written in an engaging way that makes them enjoyable to read. It's kind of like the difference between an average commercial and the Super Bowl commercials: If you're going to be a great review blogger, you want all your blog posts to be as entertaining as a Super Bowl ad.

- ✔ **They put their readers' interests first:** Good product blogs take the feedback of their readers and use it to ensure that they're delivering the content their readers want. That means sometimes turning down some tempting opportunities when there's only something in it for you and not for your audience.

- ✔ **They follow best practices:** I'm referring to all blogging best practices, not just those that apply to review bloggers. Top-drawer bloggers have a strong brand, a professional appearance, quality writing, relevant advertisers, consistent content, and everything else I've talked about in this book.

Failing to Focus Your Efforts

I like to call this Shiny Object Syndrome. You're building a great blog, getting things done — and then, out of the blue, you have a *really* great idea. And suddenly you're devoting a good chunk of your time to develop the new idea instead of building the ideas you've already started. What ends up happening is that you have a lot of absolutely amazing projects started, but none of them finished.

This is a mistake I've made in the past on more than one occasion — and I may make it again someday. A really great idea is hard to resist, especially when you know you have what it takes to pull it off. Sometimes the idea is so good that you would be a fool to not pursue it. But it can be very difficult to know the difference between a *distraction* and a *new direction*.

I've gotten better about keeping my entrepreneurial Shiny Object Syndrome in check by doing the following things:

- **Sit on it:** A great idea today is still going to be a great idea next week. I try to impose a mandatory waiting period on myself so that I can sit with the idea for a while and really think about how taking on a new project will impact my existing projects.

- **Evaluate how the idea fits in with your current projects:** Sometimes a great idea can build on the foundation you've already built. I take such ideas most seriously — and evaluate all the ways they can help my existing business. Sometimes an idea is good enough to put into action but may just need to wait for better timing. Other times, you can see its value immediately and how it helps you grow in many ways. Yet other times, the idea doesn't really fit at all with your current projects, and would end up dividing your attention and sending your energy in two different directions. Unless I'm willing to give up what I am currently working on, those are the ideas I try to avoid.

- **Get a Shiny Object Syndrome buddy:** I have a group of friends I talk to on a regular basis — and we give each other advice and support for each other's businesses. We all tend to have varying degrees of distractibility. We have a pact between us that we start no new projects without bringing the idea to the group first. We are the first to point out the weaknesses in each other's plans and we hold each other accountable to our goals — even when we aren't happy to hear about it.

Putting All Your Eggs in One Basket

This will be a familiar theme from elsewhere in the book. There's a reason for that: Unfortunately, there are too many ways to make the mistake of putting all your eggs in one basket, and I've learned many of them the hard way. Losing one big advertiser can cut your revenue down to zero. Relying too much, say, on Google for your traffic can be devastating if Google happens to decide to change its ranking algorithm. Relying on one really great gimmick can make your blog start to seem unoriginal as more people start using the same gimmick. Selling only one kind of product or service leaves you vulnerable to changing trends and economic environments.

Far too many things can affect your blog in unforeseeable ways. For example, Illinois recently passed a new state tax law that would require Internet businesses to collect taxes on purchases that originate with an Illinois-based affiliate marketer. Because this sort of tracking is a logistical nightmare for many e-commerce sites, they went away: Instead of complying with the new tax collection rules, they ended their relationships with all their Illinois-based affiliates. Overnight, a good percentage of my income disappeared. Thankfully, affiliate marketing is only a part of how I make money from my sites, so I'm not out of business. But now I only have my advertising revenue to fall back on. So I need to find new ways to monetize my sites in case something unforeseen happens to any of my advertising partners.

It takes a lot of work to find ways to diversify your income, develop a plan of action, and put new systems in place. But doing so will make your blog a source of income that you can truly rely on, rather than a gravy train that dries up with no notice. Here are some more ways you can protect yourself from future changes in the blogging industry:

- ✔ **Work with multiple advertisers or ad networks if at all possible:** You should also sell your own advertising if your ad networks allow it.

- ✔ **Develop multiple sources of site traffic:** Strive to have 33 percent come from search engines, 33 percent come from other sites, and 33 percent come from bookmarks or entries directly typed in. Google may be a huge traffic driver to your blog, but it changes the way it ranks sites hundreds of times every year. You never know when one of those changes could knock you down to page 3 after you've spent a while on page 1.

- ✔ **Develop a mailing list:** Not only can newsletters be another source of traffic for your sites, but they can also be a very effective way to increase sales. People who are willing to give you their e-mail addresses are your most loyal fans and are most interested in what you have to offer. I show you how to do this in Chapter 8.

- ✔ **Develop diverse products and services to sell:** If you're a consultant, develop e-products or small introductory service packages for low-end purchases. If you sell crafts on Etsy, you can also sell your own templates, patterns, and unused supplies.

- ✔ **Sell in multiple online marketplaces:** Even if you have your own shopping cart on your blog, you can also sell on eBay, Etsy, or other online marketplaces. That way, if one of your stores somehow loses traffic, you've already established stores in other locations to rely upon.

Neglecting the Blogging Basics

I have to admit that after blogging for a few years, I began to let myself skip some basic blogging tasks such as responding to comments, commenting on other blogs, building new relationships with other bloggers, and staying on top of site maintenance. When I started Woo! Jr., I forced myself to do these things all over again, because I knew it would help give my blog the kick-start it needed to get off the ground.

I was humbled and surprised to see how well these practices worked — and realized that just because these tasks are basic blogging skills, they're not just for beginner blogs. They are *basic* because they are what built our industry — and because they continue to be extremely effective marketing tactics. Here are some of the things I foolishly thought I was too successful to have to do anymore; be sure you keep up with them:

- **Respond to comments:** It may not be realistic to respond to every comment (especially when you're established and have multiple blogs you maintain), but when a conversation starts on your blog, you should be a part of it. I also make sure I answer direct questions, because if one reader has asked it, there are surely other readers who are wondering the same thing.

- **Comment on other blogs:** Commenting on others' blogs keeps people aware of your site and can still send traffic back to your blog. Additionally, all bloggers love comments, and many times comments lead to conversations, friendships, links, and future partnerships.

- **Thanking people for links:** When Sparkplugging had more than 12 writers, a considerable number of links came in on a regular basis from other blogs. It became difficult to keep up with them; I wasn't able to thank people individually for them. If there's one thing I would go back and do differently, I would make time to say, "Thank you." A link is extremely valuable and isn't given lightly.

- **Linking out to other blogs:** I can get lazy about linking to other people, but I kick myself every time I allow that to happen. It's absolutely true that the more you link to others, the more they link to you.

- **Blog maintenance:** After you've been blogging for a while, you'll find that your categories may get cluttered, you'll have too many tags that are only used once, old links get broken, or links you've created can point to pages on other sites that are very different from where they first were intended to appear (sometimes in the worst possible way!). Not only do these things create a bad user experience, but if left undone, they can lead search engines to drop your site rank or drop you out of the index altogether.

Acting Too Entitled

Of all the mistakes you can make as a blogger, acting too entitled draws the most ire. I don't like it if I'm left off a Top Moms list, or if a colleague with less experience than I have is on a social media cruise, or if my favorite brand just hired that *same mom everyone else hires* for yet another sweet sponsorship gig. If you think you deserved the recognition or opportunity more than that other person, fine — but if you gossip about it, or (worse) try to undermine another blogger's success, it's an unfortunate line to cross. It's quite possible that you do indeed deserve the thing you wanted, but unfortunately, you can't be on everyone's radar during every moment of the day. And ultimately, acting as if you should be the center of attention undermines your own credibility far more than it does to anyone else.

I have several friends who have worked on behalf of brands to do blogger-outreach programs. Their experiences were uncomfortably eye-opening: They discovered a high percentage of moms demanding free products or requesting extremely expensive items to review. As I explain in Chapter 10, you have to be able to offer companies something of value in return for what they give you. Being a mom blogger isn't enough to justify getting free products. If you want to be treated like a professional blogger, you need to have built a following, have sharp social media marketing skills, and know both the written and unwritten rules of professional blogging.

The bloggers who have caught the entitlement bug have also earned the unfortunate title *prima donna.* Thankfully, they're the exception and not the norm in the mom-blogging community. Most of the mom bloggers are warm, generous, and grateful for the opportunities that blogging brings to them. Regrettably, these women — the professional and talented majority — are not the ones whom the outside world imagines as the mom-blogging community. A few prima donnas have planted the "mommy-blogger" stereotype of women acting like spoiled children. The easiest way to know if a request is appropriate is to simply ask if it is appropriate. And the best way to counteract this stereotype is to simply always maintain your professionalism (even when sometimes it means biting your tongue until it bleeds).

As mom blogging grows as an industry, we continue to prove this negative stereotype as wrong, unwarranted, and outdated. But when even a handful of people act this way, it reflects on the community as a whole. Professional mom bloggers must continue to disprove this detrimental image in order for all of us to succeed, because if more people go the prima donna route, opportunities to work with brands and advertisers will eventually disappear.

Failing to Plan for Success

If I had any clue whatsoever that starting a little hobby blog five years ago would turn into the writing and publishing career I have today, I would have been *so* much more careful about the decisions I made in those first few months. Interestingly, *most* bloggers didn't start out thinking they were going to make a living at it. They were usually just starting a blog to have fun, realized they were good at it, and then suddenly found themselves in a business they hadn't anticipated starting in the first place.

I can't encourage you more strongly to take your blog seriously and treat it as a business from Day One, especially if you have even the slightest hope of turning it into a source of income. If you want your blog to be successful, you have to treat it as if it's *already* successful. That means planning for long-term growth from the beginning, so you don't box yourself into a corner later. Here are some missteps that bloggers have taken early on — speaking from my own or my friends' experiences — that we wish we hadn't. Make sure you don't make these same mistakes:

- ✔ **Started a blog on Google's Blogger and used the default URL of** `http://`*blogname*`.blogspot.com` **instead of buying your own domain name.** If you do the simple thing and leave it at that, much of the work you do is left behind if you ever need to upgrade to a more functional and scalable self-hosted WordPress blog. You can't automatically redirect readers from an old page to a new page, and in some ways, it's like starting over from scratch. Moving from Blogger to WordPress is a big endeavor; you'll probably need some help with the technical aspects, and the whole process will be much easier and more effective if you control your own domain name. I talk about this in Chapter 2.

  The extra hassle can be avoided if you start on WordPress from the beginning. It may be a little more work to get up and running, but the flexibility, functionality, and scalability you get with a WordPress blog is absolutely worth the upfront time investment.

- ✔ **Wrote many profanity-laden blog posts sprinkled with a lot of TMI.** Okay, if your audience really wants that sort of thing, it's absolutely fine to do whatever builds a personal brand you can leverage into other opportunities — as long as you don't expect to attract advertising. This kind of content scares away advertisers in droves, because companies are fearful of associating their brands with controversy. Controversy leads to angry customers, and angry customers boycott companies. You'll limit your opportunities if you want to work with brands at some point in your blogging career. I'm not advocating changing your personality or who you are — I'm just suggesting there may be other ways to show your true self without scaring away future opportunities.

- ✔ **Failed to focus on a niche.** Specializing in a specific field is extremely important to almost every aspect of the future professional opportunities that can come your way. Your media opportunities, advertising opportunities, and branding opportunities will be extremely limited if your content is too general. You don't get on the *Today Show* by being the mom who talks about anything and everything. Broadcasters look for moms who can speak on topics that fit into specific segments, such as online bullying, Super Bowl party planning, or being a mom entrepreneur.

- ✔ **Failed to define your personal brand.** If you don't take branding seriously, you can't control the image you're projecting to your colleagues. (I discuss personal branding in detail in Chapter 6.) Worse, you run the risk of letting others define your brand for you. The longer you ignore branding, the harder it is to take it back and define it yourself.

I talk a lot more about planning for success in Chapter 15, including explaining why you want to build a business that's *scalable,* meaning you can grow business revenue (to a larger scale) without having to double or triple the hours you work every week. I also talk about planning for the future end of your blog, and why it's important to plan now for the day you may want to walk away from your blog while ensuring that you don't end up empty-handed.

Not Taking the Time to Learn the Ropes

The general population has the perception that blogging must be really easy, cushy work — and that all you have to do is set up shop, and the freebies will start rolling in. For example, a blogger with just a few months under her belt put together an experiment in the hopes of building her brand-relationship experience. She decided to put up her own money and solicit written positive reviews for a car company from other mom bloggers. She hoped the experience would open doors to paying opportunities in the future. Unfortunately, this woman knew very little about what she was getting herself into. Her e-mails to other bloggers were unprofessional and presented very unrealistic and inappropriate expectations of participants for a rather meager $10 gift card. Even though she wasn't officially representing the company, she made it seem as if she was, and nobody would have expected a blogger with so little experience to act on her own accord in this manner. The unfortunate outcome of this situation was that the large car company got blamed for being unprofessional and inappropriate in a highly visible way. Its official representative on Twitter had to refute the claim that it was involved, and suddenly it had a very bad PR experience on its hands that it didn't create. Even worse, the story grew so quickly that large websites such as TheConsumerist initially ran the story as if the car manufacturer had tried to "bribe mommy bloggers to bury bad press."

Had the woman in question really learned what it takes to run a professional blogger-outreach campaign, she would have been well aware that her requests were in violation of the FTC guidelines regarding social media marketing campaigns. She would also have known that acting as a representative for a company would bring a significant amount of legal liability upon herself. And she would certainly have known that her request was exceedingly inappropriate, especially as a violation of the Word of Mouth Marketing Association's code of ethics.

The other unfortunate outcome of this situation was that the blogger who initiated all this brouhaha had a lifelong dream to run her own business. But in less than 24 hours, she decided to pull down her website and get out of an industry she knew far too little about. She posted an immediate apology and admitted she hadn't taken the time to learn about the laws and the ethics code that govern our industry. And since she had no marketing experience, she had no way of knowing she was in over her head until it was too late and the damage was done.

Because there have been no follow-up stories regarding the incident, I can't say what finally happened to the woman who instigated the episode. At worst, it's likely that the car company would have a strong legal case against her; at best, it got a very large bill from its PR firm for the month.

You wouldn't try to design a building without going to architectural school, or represent someone in court without taking the bar exam first. Okay, blogging and social media are not rocket science, but they do have real effects — and it's important to understand our industry thoroughly before you participate at a professional level.

Here are some of the blogging minefields that you really need to find your way through; be sure you understand before you jump in headfirst:

- ✔ **Know the FTC disclosure guidelines** and ensure that you have a process in place to disclose *in the manner they require* (putting up a disclosure page isn't enough). I talk about this in Chapter 9.

- ✔ **Know the laws governing sweepstakes and contests in your jurisdiction.** Just as important: Make sure you comply with those laws, especially the ones regarding winner selection, notification, and tax liabilities. I also talk about this in Chapter 9.

- ✔ **Know the CAN-Spam requirements** for running legal e-mail marketing campaigns. I talk about this in Chapter 8.

- ✔ **Know the tax implications of accepting free products, services, and travel expenses.** These things need to be declared as income. This is covered in Chapter 9.

- ✔ **Know that if you buy or sell text-link advertising, you could get banned from Google.** In Chapters 9 and 13, I talk about how to sell text links safely so you can avoid this problem.

Chapter 18

Ten Successful Mom Bloggers

*E*ver since there were more than a handful of mom bloggers, there have been Top Mom Blogger lists written. The writers of these lists are usually not moms themselves — or even bloggers, ironically enough. Lists are great to be included on; it's kind of like a badge of honor. But in reality, these lists — and most other similar lists — aren't always representative of who is really out there kicking it out of the park. The lists tend to become self-perpetuating, as newer versions always seem to reference old existing lists, and new, fresh talent doesn't get recognized. For every Top Mom Blogger list I have ever seen, I can name just as many (or more) women who could have been included but weren't.

So, when it came time to write my own Top Mom Blogger list for this chapter, I was very wary of repeating the same old names. Certainly there are some recognizable women in this chapter, but their Internet fame had very little to do with why I chose to include them here. Instead, I chose ten successful mom bloggers who all had distinctly different business models, so that you can see in action all the information I've shared with you in this book. It's one thing to read about business strategies, but when you put all this information in context, it's tremendously helpful as a way to understand exactly how the strategies in this book work in the real world.

I also vetted this list extensively to ensure that every single person in this chapter is making a sizable income from blogging. And by *sizable,* I mean these women's earnings range from what they'd earn in a stable, well-paying part-time job to the high six-figures or more. (This chapter could easily have been titled "Show Me the Money!") So, in short, these bloggers are not only visibly successful, but each one also has a solid business and can put her money where her mouth is.

I want to point out that although their businesses are quite drastically different from each other, all these women have some telling characteristics in common:

- ✔ Nearly all of them started blogging for fun, and only later turned it into a business.
- ✔ All of them were extremely passionate about the topics of their blogs.

✔ All of them built businesses around their natural strengths and past experiences.

✔ All of them put their readers' interests before profits.

✔ All of them took *a year to several years* to earn a stable income from their blogs.

✔ All of them offer strikingly similar advice to new bloggers.

✔ None of them are resting on their laurels. They all know that our industry changes fast, and these women continue to work their tails off to maintain and grow their businesses.

Without further ado, I give you my own list of ten mom-blogging rock stars. Some of these women are dear friends. Some I wish I knew better. And others I just met as I worked to find perfect examples of certain blogging business models in action. All of them are *amazing,* and I'm extremely honored that they took the time to answer my questions to be a part of my book.

Heather Armstrong

www.dooce.com

On Twitter as @dooce

Recently Lisa Belkin of the New York Times Motherlode blog (http://parenting.blogs.nytimes.com) named Heather Armstrong the Queen of the Mommy Bloggers. Few, if any, moms have achieved the kind of success Heather has with Dooce (see Figure 18-1). Her blog was the first to take a personal journal and turn it into a profitable mom-blogging business. But being first isn't why she's so successful; Heather is an extremely talented and engaging writer, a savvy businesswoman, a personal-branding virtuosa, and one who knows how to stir up controversy to her advantage. When I interviewed her for this book, I figured she had taken an unusual route to success. But I was rather surprised to find that Heather's success very much defies most common-sense business advice — including some of my own in this very book.

Heather's full story can be found at http://dooce.com/about, but to restate it briefly, she started blogging to simply talk about life as a single woman living in Los Angeles. A year later, she was fired from her job for talking about her co-workers on her blog. Soon thereafter, Heather got married, moved closer to her Mormon family in Salt Lake City, and had her first child, Leta. Heather's life rapidly spun out of control as she crumbled under the effects of postpartum depression, and she checked herself into a psych ward. Her blog chronicled the entire journey, including her eventual recovery from the depression to her life today.

Heather's blog has always been a lightning rod for controversy, especially because of her openness about being a former member of the Mormon church, and her willingness to be so honest and vulnerable about her struggles with mental illness. I think it is this raw honesty that draws so many visitors, including both fans and haters. Personally, I don't think I could deal with the amount of criticism she has received over the years.

It's worthy of note: Should you decide to write about extremely personal issues and controversial beliefs on your own blog, you should be prepared to grow a very thick skin.

Even though Heather's husband quit his job to work on Dooce in 2005, she feels that her blog has become something far more important than just a family business. Her ability to raise awareness about postpartum depression and other mental health issues has made a huge impact on the lives of thousands of her readers. Some of them have struggled with the same problems, and her blog has given them hope they can survive the pain they are currently in. Others have loved ones with mental health issues, and have written her to say that until they read her blog, they thought their spouses or family members were making things up. Heather's writing has shown them what their loved ones are going through — in many cases, for the first time ever.

Heather rose to popularity so quickly that she has never had to pursue advertisers, brand campaigns, or other work opportunities. This is very much the exception and not the norm in the blogging world, but it does indicate that success breeds more success. She credits several factors for her success — uppermost is the ten years of hard work she has spent writing consistently — along with a good bit of luck. She also knows that having the luxury of a business partner (her husband) has been critical to her ability to focus on her strengths without having to worry about the business end of things.

Heather's three tips for blogging success are:

✔ Understand how much work blogging is — there is a big misconception about how "easy" it is to blog.

✔ The Internet is permanent and universal. Don't think that blogging anonymously or saying hurtful things won't come back to haunt you; they will.

✔ Find websites with communities you like — and participate in those communities. Doing so will get your name out there. It shows that you care about what you're saying.

Started blogging: February 2001

Blog provided stable income in: October 2005

Income estimate: High six-figures to possibly over a million dollars in annual revenue.

How Heather makes money: Advertising on her blog, two books (one of which was a *New York Times* bestseller), public speaking engagements, and brand partnerships such as social media marketing for HGTV and a spokesperson deal with Verizon.

For more information on how this kind of blog works, read Chapters 6, 10, 12, and 16.

Shellie Goyal

www.craftgossip.com

On Twitter as @craftgossip

Shellie Goyal and her mother started publishing online all the way back in 1999 when they started Craftbits.com (www.craftbits.com), a craft project website. The site grew to the point of providing a small-but-stable income; encouraged by their success, they decided to start the CraftGossip blog network (shown in Figure 18-2) at the beginning of 2007. CraftGossip now has 19 blogs on different craft and DIY project topics, and is maintained by 19 blog editors. It's now one of the most widely read craft blogs — and one of only a handful of blog networks started and owned by moms.

CraftGossip earns enough income to pay all 19 of their editors a percentage (in the editor's favor) of the advertising revenue each blog earns. The old site Craftbits.com is so well established that it continually out-earns the newer blog network, even though its founders have less time to dedicate to updating its content. They also have a mailing list with over 100,000 newsletter subscribers. This newsletter serves to send traffic continually to their site, plus it's another way to sell advertising space.

Shellie's three tips for blogging success are:

✔ Write about something that you are passionate about, but it doesn't have to be something that you know a lot about. For example, Julie Powell from *Julie & Julia* wrote about her attempts at completing Julia Child's *French Cooking* book — and in spite of all her mishaps, she kept at it. She was passionate about what she was doing, even though she didn't know much at all about cooking (at first, anyway).

Figure 18-2: Shellie Goyal's CraftGossip blog network.

✔ Get a decent design. Before visitors even read a word of your blog, they will judge it by how it looks. It doesn't have to be expensive; there are a lot of free themes available, or you can hire someone to create a design for very little money. Try crowd-sourced design services such as `http://99designs.com`.

✔ Give something away for free. A giveaway is a great way to get people to your blog, and you will find a lot of these people will *stick.* You don't have to spend an arm and a leg.

Started blogging: First website established in 1999; her CraftGossip blog network was established in January 2007.

Blog provided stable income in: February 2010

Income estimate: Between the two sites, Shellie earns enough that both she and her husband can comfortably live and work from home.

How Shellie makes money: Shellie's sites get enough traffic to enable her to work with several different advertising networks; her site sells its own advertising as well.

For more information on how this kind of blog works, read Chapters 3, 12, 13, 15, and 16.

Jennifer James

www.mombloggersclub.com

On Twitter as @mombloggersclub

Jennifer James started blogging in 2004 as a way to connect with other women. She had two little ones in diapers and needed an outlet to express herself. In 2007, she decided to start Mom Bloggers Club (shown in Figure 18-3), because at the time there was no place for moms who blog to network and connect with one another. Brands reacted — and almost immediately approached her to buy advertising and to create campaigns. She initially turned them down, resisting the intrusion of advertising into her community. She also admits she didn't really know how to work with brands at the time.

She finally realized it was foolish to continue to turn away revenue that could build a very healthy business, especially because the requests continued to fall in her lap. She taught herself how to work with brands, set pricing, and most importantly figured out how to share the income with her community members. She is now known as one of the pioneer bloggers in the area of connecting brands and bloggers.

Mom Bloggers Club now has over 13,000 members who participate in brand campaigns such as sponsored posts and well-paid ambassador programs, and who also have access to banner advertising through the Mom Bloggers Club ad network. Jennifer's business is so well established now that she hires regular independent contractors for project management and writing work. She also helps thousands of bloggers earn extra income from their own blogs and social media interactions.

Jennifer's three tips for blogging success are:

✔ Make sure you have the right intention for starting a blog. If it's just to make money, you've already lost. There has to be true passion behind your blog.

✔ Never underestimate the power of a well-designed blog. It will take you very far.

✔ Attend at least one blogging conference a year. Sometimes it takes money to make money. You will meet and network with people who may have great opportunities for you.

Started blogging: 2004, Mom Bloggers Club founded in 2007.

Blog provided stable income in: 2008

Income estimate: Jennifer earns the equivalent of the salary from a really well-paid full-time job.

How Jennifer makes money: Consulting with clients who want to work with mom bloggers, advertising revenue, and creating social media campaigns for the members of Mom Bloggers Club.

For more information on how this kind of blog works, read Chapters 7, 8, 9, and 13.

Michelle Lamar

www.michellelamar.com

On Twitter as @michellelamar

Michelle Lamar started her White Trash Mom blog in 2005, just to understand how blogging worked. Initially, she blogged anonymously, but as she started becoming more successful, she decided to put her real name on her writing. The blog was intended to be sarcastic and funny, and she never intended that it become anything more than a humor blog. Two features on Guy Kawasaki's prominent How to Change the World blog (http://blog.guykawasaki.com) and in the *Washington Post* changed all that: Michelle was soon contacted by several book agents who wanted to help find her a book deal. She published *The White Trash Mom Handbook: Embrace Your Inner Trailerpark, Forget Perfection, Resist Assimilation into the PTA, Stay Sane, and Keep Your Sense of Humor* in August of 2008.

Michelle soon found that not everyone got the *joke* of her writing style and White Trash Mom persona. Her 15 years of prior marketing and business experience were getting lost in a personal brand that misrepresented what she was truly capable of. She decided to start a separate blog at www.michellelamar.com in order to establish her personal brand as a separate entity from her blog's brand (which you can see in Figure 18-4).

As a part of her book's promotional tour, she was traveling around the country and aggressively seeking additional freelance writing and marketing work. Her blog and book weren't earning the kind of income she wanted or needed. On that tour, she met one of her future employers who hired Michelle almost immediately for several projects. Soon she was offered the full-time position of Vice President of Media with a small marketing firm. Now, Michelle is an Account Manager for Spiral 16 social media monitoring software. Her blogging experience has landed her not one, but two lucrative full-time jobs.

Figure 18-4:
Michelle
Lamar's
blog at
Michelle
Lamar.com.

Michelle continued to find that her White Trash Mom persona was undermining her credibility, so she closed down the blog by the end of 2009. Yet it was her experience as a blogger and a social media mom that led to her getting hired in the first place. She has maintained the contacts she established while blogging, and relies heavily on the credibility and trust she earned as a mom blogger. By all measurements of success, her White Trash Mom blog enabled her to build her expert résumé and find a perfect work-at-home career.

Michelle's three tips for blogging success are:

✔ You might not get rich blogging. But if you do it because you love it and you are passionate about it, good things will happen.

✔ Get involved in your blogging community. The community of online moms offers you a chance to meet some amazing women whom you will form lifelong friendships with.

✔ Focus on your niche. Bloggers gain credibility by becoming a resource for readers who trust them to provide information on their topics of interest.

Started blogging: Early 2005

Blog provided stable income in: Her blog never earned stable income, but her resulting jobs did.

Income estimate: Michelle's position earns her a well-paid full-time salary with benefits.

How Michelle makes money: Her blog served as a steppingstone into her new career, and her current job is her sole source of income.

For more information on how you can use a blog to find a job, read Chapters 4, 7, 8, and 15.

Gina Luker

www.theshabbychiccottage.net

On Twitter as @shabchiccottage
On Etsy at www.etsy.com/shop/theshabbychiccottage

Starting in 2007, Gina Luker dabbled in blogging — but after some life changes, she decided to become more focused as a writer. Taking a college professor's advice — *write about what you know* — she started The Shabby Chic Cottage (shown in Figure 18-5) in early 2009. She started it as a digital scrapbook to keep up with the changes of remodeling her childhood home. Within a few months, she realized that not only was she attracting regular readers, they were commenting frequently. After only three months, she received an e-mail asking to purchase advertising on her blog. When her blog was six months old, at the prodding of her readers, Gina opened her self-named Etsy store. And within a year of starting her blog, she was earning enough from advertisers and her Etsy sales to quit her day job.

Gina's absolute passion for crafting and remodeling comes through in every blog post and project she creates. As a part of my interview with her, she offered extremely wise advice for anyone who wants to sell her own products through her blog:

> "If a blogger wants to open a shop, they both have to be closely integrated with each other. From banners to photography style, down to the way the descriptions are written, you should be consistent everywhere. Branding is a *huge* part of making a successful transition from a blog to a shop — one that feels more like an extension of your blog than a completely separate site. Not only will it help brand identity, but your readers are much more at ease buying from a store where they feel as if they have a relationship with you. It's similar to buying from a friend — you have already built the trust with your readers; just convert it to merchandise sales."

Figure 18-5:
Gina
Luker's The
Shabby Chic
Cottage
blog.

Gina is one of my favorite examples in this chapter, because she's doing *everything* right with her business. She's passionate, created a thriving community, built a strong brand, provides excellent customer service, and isn't afraid to go after the sale of her products. She is also one of the few Etsy sellers to utilize e-mail marketing to her past customers, which makes a big difference in her revenue. Okay, here's the familiar eggs-and-baskets theme, but notice how she has smartly diversified her income sources — not too many eggs in any one basket. It's almost like she read this book before I wrote it!

Gina's three tips for blogging success are:

✔ Become involved. You don't just move to a neighborhood and magically have a circle of friends — you have to get out and meet people. Blogging is like that. You create your space (your blog), and then share it with others. If you never leave your own site, you'll be there all alone.

✔ Stay true to who you are. Each person has a unique perspective on life, so what she sees is fresh and new to her. Talk about your passions — whether it is parrots, hot sauce, even bad '70s fashion. There is a blog, and an audience, for everything under the sun.

> ✔ Don't let a blog take over your life. It can and will — if you let it. You'll be up at 3:00 a.m. just leaving "one more comment." You won't have anything to write about if you don't take time to live. Set a blogging timer (ten minutes, one hour, whatever you choose to devote), and stick to that. When your time is up, do whatever it is you are passionate about — then you'll never run out of things to say.

Started blogging: Personal blog established in 2007, her professional blog in April 2009.

Blog provided stable income in: April 2010

Income estimate: Gina doubled her previous full-time income as a journalist in her second year of blogging professionally.

How Gina makes money: She sells advertising on her blog, sells her crafts in her Etsy store, has written an e-book, and also sells home decorating e-books written by others through affiliate marketing. She's also started speaking at conferences to help others learn about what she has done.

For more information on how this kind of blog works, read Chapters 6, 8, 13, and 14.

Audrey McClelland

www.momgenerations.com

On Twitter as @audreymcclellan

Audrey McClelland started her first blog back in late 2006 with her mom and sister, calling it The Pinks and Blues Girls. They started out as a product-review blog but quickly found they wanted to write about topics they were more passionate about. They rebranded the site as Mom Generations (shown in Figure 18-6) to reflect Audrey's interests as a fashion-loving mom, her sister Jane Couto's interests as an aunt and as a dog lover, and mother Sharon Couto's interests as a grandmother and (extremely active) empty nester.

In 2008, Audrey started her ambitious 365 Days of Fashion Advice for Moms project and quickly drew an avid audience. Brands and advertisers started noticing as well. By the end of 2009, Audrey was asked by Tide to be the mom-fashion correspondent on the red carpet for the 2010 People's Choice Awards. The next day, she participated in a celebrity fashion talk panel with Tim Gunn and Gretta Monahan.

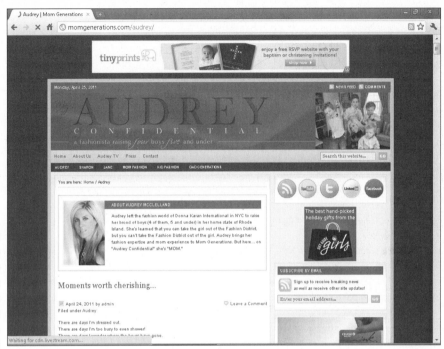

Figure 18-6:
Audrey
McClelland's
Mom
Genrerations
blog.

Audrey has gone on to work with brands like Suave, T.J.Maxx, Lifetime Television, and HP. She has been on the Rachel Ray show and posed for images as a part of The Estee Lauder Company's breast cancer awareness campaign. She is one of the most in-demand mom bloggers that brands want to work with, thanks to her professionalism and ability to bring in results. She has also chosen her blogging topics of beauty and fashion wisely — in these niches, there are many opportunities for brands to work with bloggers.

Audrey's three tips for blogging success are:

✔ Find your niche. You need to have something to blog about day in and day out. You want to love what you write about, so truly, find something that will entertain and sustain you. That way blogging never gets old.

✔ Find some blogging friends. Everything changed for me when I found my "girls" online. Working on the Internet can be lonely sometimes. It's important to find virtual officemates. They keep you going. You can bounce ideas off them and know that they're there for you if you need them.

✔ One of the biggest things that new bloggers fail to do is blog *enough*. Make sure you're posting four to five times a week. If you don't have new content continually, people will stop coming back. It's like tuning into the same TV show every week: If they're not going to put up a new episode, you won't tune in. It's the same in the blogging world.

Started blogging: Late 2006, but changed her site name to the current MomGenerations.com in March 2007.

Blog provided stable income in: January 2009

Income estimate: Audrey is the sole provider for her household, making over six figures.

How Audrey makes money: Integrated, custom social media campaigns on her blog, as well as advertising, writing, and many spokesperson positions with large brands. Audrey has also partnered with another mom to create a new series of live fashion and beauty events called Getting Gorgeous. She is also writing her first book with co-author Colleen Padilla.

For more information on how this kind of blog works, read Chapters 6, 7, 13, 15, and 16.

Carrie Rocha

www.pocketyourdollars.com

On Twitter as @CarrieRocha

In 2006, Carrie Rocha and her husband made a commitment to each other that they would live debt free. Because increasing their income wasn't feasible at the time, they focused their efforts on reducing their expenses. The inspiration for her blog came in the midst of the Great Recession, as she saw people in her community losing their homes and jobs while she and her husband had just paid off $50,000 in debt. She literally felt compelled to share what she had learned about saving money to help other families spend less in their daily lives. Pocket Your Dollars was launched in March of 2009. You can see her site in Figure 18-7.

Less than a year later, Carrie's blog was featured on Minneapolis's top-rated evening news. Within the next 24 hours, Carrie's blog earned over $1,000. It was a critical turning point for her as she realized her blog could truly support her family. As the sole breadwinner, this financial success was critical to her continued pursuit of blogging as a career.

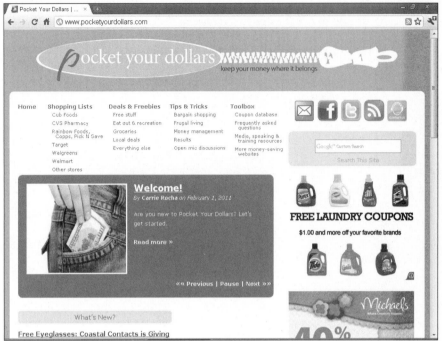

Figure 18-7:
Carrie
Rocha's
Pocket Your
Dollars blog.

A blessing in disguise came along in January 2010, and Carrie was laid off from her job as the COO of a non-profit organization. Pocket Your Dollars has been the sole financial support of her family since then. Today the blog offers coupons, money-saving resources, and frugal living tips. She is writing her first book on personal finance, which is coming out in 2012. Carrie is also a regular contributor now to many Minneapolis radio and TV stations, and she even gets recognized as "That Deal Lady from TV" when she is out and about.

Carrie's three tips for blogging success are:

✔ Pick a deep niche. (Carrie is a woman after my own heart!)

✔ Remember that there will never be just one blog in your niche — ever. That's okay. Blogs are like churches; there is one on every corner. You are responsible to take care of those who come to yours, not to worry about the ones who go elsewhere.

✔ Just start. Avoid paralysis by analysis.

Started blogging: March 2009

Blog provided stable income in: January 2010

Income estimate: In 2011, Carrie expects to make double or more than what she did in her former COO position.

How Carrie makes money: Pocket Your Dollars is primarily monetized through ad networks and affiliate marketing. She does not sell any of her own advertising. Carrie also gets paid as a professional speaker and is working on her first book based on her blog.

For more information on how this kind of blog works, read Chapters 12, 14, and 16.

Beth Rosen

www.4keysmedia.com

On Twitter as @bethrosen

Beth Rosen is a unique case study in this section because she has taken the power of blogging and social media offline to create her business. Beth was an extremely early adopter of technology, starting her first website in 1996. Additionally, at the time, she was hosting a local radio show for area moms. These two forms of communication merged in her career around 2000 when she became one of the first podcasters to broadcast online. Soon thereafter, Beth added videoblogging to her business.

Because Beth is very active in her local community, area businesses began asking for her help as they began to learn how to use social media marketing. She quickly grew a steady flow of work as she worked with these offline clients to promote their businesses online.

Beth has never made a cent directly off of her blogs. Instead, blogging, podcasting, and videoblogging opened doors for her to develop strategic brand partnerships. Her business has grown from working with local companies to now working with national brands. Today she has added event marketing to her repertoire, in which she hosts VIP parties with top mom bloggers for top brands. She is also a cohost on the Chicagonista Live online talk show (http://chicagonistalive.com) with fellow moms and bloggers MJ Tam, Duong Sheahan, and broadcast journalist Nancy Loo from WGN-TV. You can see their site in Figure 18-8.

Figure 18-8:
Beth Rosen
is a cohost
on the
Chicagonista
Live talk
show.

Beth's three tips for blogging success are:

- ✔ Jump in right away to learn about Facebook and Twitter once your blog is set up. Social media will open up a lot of opportunities for you. You are probably already a powerhouse of knowledge, and being active in social media will amplify that.

- ✔ Use your social media and blogging experience to find local consulting opportunities. Most local businesses are still very new to social media marketing and would be happy to hire someone in their own community to help. Many times, these potential clients will already know you, making it even easier to find work.

- ✔ Seek out offline opportunities. Not only is there less competition for your skills, but many times you can produce better results for clients when you combine your online savvy with your offline relationships.

Started blogging: 1996

Blog provided stable income in: The early 2000s.

Income estimate: Beth earns a lucrative full-time income from her consulting and has plenty of freedom to turn down work she isn't interested in.

How Beth makes money: Consulting with clients who want to work with mom bloggers, planning and hosting live events, and occasionally creating video content for her clients.

For more information on how this kind of blogging and social media marketing business works, read Chapters 6, 7, 8 and 13.

Renee Ross

www.cutiebootycakes.com

On Twitter as @cutiebootycakes

Renee started her Cutie Booty Cakes blog (shown in Figure 18-9) to market her business, which was creating cakes made out of diapers for baby showers or other events. She's another one of those great examples that blogging success frequently doesn't happen the way she thought it would. It wasn't longer than a month before Renee stopped blogging about her diaper cakes and started building a platform for herself as a blogger. She spent a significant amount of time networking with other bloggers, and within three months was invited to participate in a Disney World mom bloggers' press junket. This was a significant turning point for her business, and she continued to build up her social media influence and brand experiences to find new spokesperson opportunities.

She also began using her blog as a way to share her personal weight-loss journey, eventually losing over 50 pounds. She ran her first half-marathon in October 2010, raising over $5,000 for the Leukemia and Lymphoma Society.

Renee's hard work has paid off in other ways as well. She has been hired by brands such as Walmart and Hanes and appeared in national television commercials for EA SPORTS Active in late 2010. She has also been featured prominently in *Parents* magazine and *Southern Living* magazine. She continues to promote herself and her personal brand by speaking frequently at conferences and events and is in the process of finding several more spokesperson opportunities.

Figure 18-9:
Renee
Ross's Cutie
Booty Cakes
blog.

Renee's three tips for blogging success are:

✔ Write about the thing(s) that you are passionate about. Her passion has evolved over the years, but she remained true to her voice and has been very transparent.

✔ Success does not happen overnight. You can be the best writer in your niche and not have readers. Your success depends on your willingness to go the extra mile.

✔ Learn everything you can from successful bloggers who are doing what you want to do. Watch how they navigate the Internet, read ProBlogger.net (`www.problogger.net`), and attend conferences to meet bloggers and learn from them.

Started blogging: July 2008

Blog provided stable income in: April 2009

Income estimate: High-level part-time income

How Renee makes money: Primarily from writing and videoblogging for brands, and spokesperson positions. She also earns some revenue from advertising on her blog.

For more information on how this kind of blog works, read Chapters 7, 10, and 13.

Silicon Valley Moms

www.technorati.com/women
Formerly www.svmoms.com

In March of 2006, Jill Asher, Beth Blecherman, and Tekla Nee started the Silicon Valley Moms blog (shown in Figure 18-10) as a way to connect local moms together through quality content and shared experiences. Later that year, they began talking with some moms in Chicago who wished they had a similar local blogging opportunity. The SV Moms realized that an opportunity had just presented itself — and they decided to expand nationally, forming the Silicon Valley Moms Group. They honestly didn't know where they were headed, just that their idea was working.

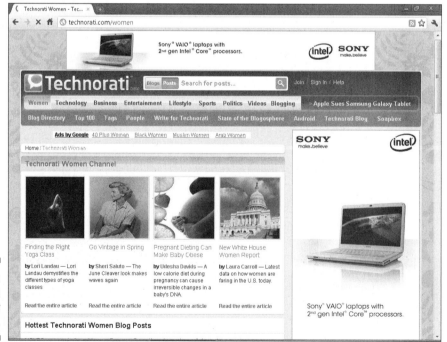

Figure 18-10:
The Silicon Valley Moms blog.

By mid-2008, they had seven blogs established and landed their first brand campaign: a large-scale road trip sponsored by Chevy, in which many of their writers traveled the country to get to the BlogHer conference. Over the course of the two years, they expanded to 13 blogs for moms in New York, D.C., Los Angeles, Canada, and several other cities, plus an additional 50-Something Moms Blog. They built the business by selling their own advertising and by doing more live events in the local areas where their bloggers lived. At their peak, over 350 moms were writing for them.

By mid-2010, the Silicon Valley Moms Group started to lose steam, and rumors started spreading that the sites would close down. But in November of that same year, Jill, Beth, and Tekla announced that they had sold their blog network to Technorati Media, the blog directory that had also purchased BlogCritics.org for a rumored $1 million. Jill has gone on to work directly for Technorati, Beth is now Chief Technologist for CoolMomTech.com, and Tekla is Senior Editor for IEEE Spectrum, a technology, engineering, and science news magazine.

Co-founder Beth Blecherman's three tips for blogging success are:

- ✔ Determine the niche that you have background in and are passionate about before you start your blog.

- ✔ Make sure that niche comes through in your blog branding and across social networks to help with outreach.

- ✔ Bloggers who want to make their sites into businesses should create a business plan and implement business procedures such as marketing materials, accounting, legal, and so on. You can also always upgrade your site from a hobby to a business, but you will also need to upgrade by creating a business structure as well. No matter what, understand the FTC blogger guidelines and always disclose your working relationships with brands and advertisers.

Started blogging: March 2006

Income estimate: Financials are unavailable due to the confidentiality involved in the sale of their blog. Suffice it to say the income was impressive enough to include it in this chapter!

How the Silicon Valley Moms Group made money: Jill, Beth, and Tekla sold advertising on their blogs, and also acquired sponsors for local events held in their blog network member communities.

For more information on how this kind of blog works, read Chapters 6, 10, 13, 15, and 16.

Index